Advance Praise

"Salner's powerful poetry, richly drawing on his own experiences, is distinguished by a mastery of the nitty gritty details of the jobs of working men and women. Now he brings his considerable abilities to his first novel, *A Place to Hide*. A tale of life on the lam with a deeply human dimension, *A Place to Hide* is a memorable read."

— William Heath, author of *The Children Bob Moses Led*

"[Salner] knows the dust and steam of physical labor. The characters find themselves psychically naked on achingly bright, open, empty roadsides, then buried alive in dank undergrounds of mines, prisons, tunnels. It is a world by turns tender and indifferent, one Steinbeck might've written."

— Adam Brooke Davis, author, Professor of English, Truman State University

"[*A Place to Hide*] evolves into a powerful examination of cultural encounters.... Add mystery, intrigue, and enemies into the mix for a powerful story filled with compelling action, psychological depth, and tension....Historical fiction readers, as well as those who appreciate solid psychological depth, will find this a compelling narrative indeed."

— D. Donovan, Senior Reviewer, *Midwest Book Review*

A Place to Hide

A Place to Hide

a novel

David Salner

Apprentice
House Press
Loyola University Maryland

The author photo is by Barbara Greenway.

First Edition

Hardcover ISBN: 978-1-62720-344-9
Paperback ISBN: 978-1-62720-345-6
Ebook ISBN: 978-1-62720-346-3

Printed in the United States of America

Acquisitions & Editing: Lauren Battista
Design: Katie McDonnell
Promotion Plan: Natalie Labib
Managing Editor: Danielle Como

Published by Apprentice House Press

Apprentice House Press
Loyola University Maryland
4501 N. Charles Street
Baltimore, MD 21210
410.617.5265
www.ApprenticeHouse.com
info@ApprenticeHouse.com

To Barbara, for more than I can put into words.
Also to Lily, Paul, Karen, Kevin for friendship and support
To the memory of two friends, Robert Greenway and
George Johnson

—

Prologue

An engine idled roughly in the darkness, almost under his window—he'd heard it last night too.

He shut the window. The hotel room would get stifling, but that throaty rumble had gotten on his nerves. Butte was a noisy city, the grinding of smelters and mills, the midnight rhythm of hoist pulleys and gears, a nonstop clamor the residents of this town had gotten used to long ago. He wasn't a resident, but Frank Little had been a miner himself, and he'd lived his whole life in a hubbub. Now he craved silence.

He was a wreck. He frowned at the cast on his right ankle. Maybe that damn fracture would teach him to take things easy. He lay back and remembered the half-finished letter to Ma on the dresser. The outlines of furniture were barely visible in the shadows. Beside the dresser was the chiffonier where his one suit hung.

A nice room like this could spoil a fellow. In a cheap hotel for miners, they'd given him the best room, Room 10, downstairs near the entrance. He was a famous visitor. Infamous in some quarters. If you were a Mexican miner you loved Frank Little because he defended you against shotgun-toting lawmen; if you were a young miner, your lungs already full of rock dust—you knew he'd wage war on heaven or hell for you. Hard rock miners had to have

1

guts; to be a union organizer for these men he had to be able to step into a deadly firestorm and show no fear. They were desperate to get something out of life, get something for all the hard knocks they took. And he was desperate to help them get it. The miners knew he was a pure man of the struggle. He was everything the miners thought a man should be. Except for one thing. He was crazy.

He was crazy to come here at all. In 1917, Butte was a dangerous city. The newspapers had termed it the richest hill on earth, the heart of the world's copper industry, and this sleek orange metal was in high demand. Highly profitable to the copper barons, precious to governments at war, deadly for the men who put the rocks in the box. Deadly, especially for the 164 men burned to death three weeks earlier, when a live cable thicker than a man's leg ignited and acted as a wick touching off oily timbers and equipment throughout the mile-deep caverns. A wick also for the miners' rage. A desperate strike broke out, which he'd come here to lead. And since getting here he hadn't stopped raising hell.

He was not a reflective fellow. Where injustice was present, action was the remedy, not reflection. He'd learned the value of action, first as a miner himself, then as an organizer. He'd won a few strikes, led miners and harvest hands in free speech fights across the West, been beaten and jailed a dozen times at least, come out of it busted up but head high.

Now, however, doubts were beginning to gnaw at him. He was familiar with the rough power of the mine owners. Nothing new there. But he felt another force, a fury that sprang to life in Europe and was rearranging all the equations. He was face to face with the Great War. In June, America had entered the slaughter. A patriotic fervor was sweeping the country. Young fellows donned khaki uniforms and posed with their sweethearts before stepping into the jaws of death. And in the mines, mills, and fields, men and women were being called on to work harder, to sacrifice for the war drive. Only a troublemaker, an enemy of the brave soldiers fighting for democracy, an ally of the Hun, would stand in the way.

He was in the crosshairs, along with these hard-rock people. They were fed up, their children hungry, with no future, while someone else got rich. Was this strike a good idea? Maybe not. But he could feel their indignation, feel the same youthful anger he'd known as a kid when he first entered the mines. It wasn't the physical pain of mining, bad as that was, but the insult of knowing those who got rich never went underground, never knew what it was like to stoop and broil in mile-deep tunnels near the fire that raged at the center of the earth. That outrage was something he could not contain.

The justice of the miners' cause was writ large in his mind, and justice required action. But action meant consequences, which was what he didn't want to think about. So why now? Why second guess himself now, when it was clear as a bell what had to be done?

He pressed his fists to his chest, held them like a prize fighter, squeezed fists together until his arms cramped. A tremor passed from one fist to the other, the vibrations crossing his chest, shaking him to the core. Was Frank

Little afraid? Some of the men had turned their back on the strike. Maybe that was it. Or maybe it was something else, like that auto outside. Even with the window closed, he could still hear the engine stumbling as it idled.

But "maybe" wasn't the way he lived his life. He was a fighter and couldn't back down. That's why the miners had written that three-word telegram to the international office of the Industrial Workers of the World: SEND FRANK LITTLE.

He turned away from the window to study the sliver of light beneath the door. The speech he'd given to the strikers that day had gone well, but he was dissatisfied. They were up against the Company and the Great War, and they were holding their own.

And he was tired. He needed to relax and will himself to sleep. He tossed the bedding aside and stretched out in his shorts.

After a good night's sleep everything would be all right. At first the pain from his ankle bothered him, but soon he felt himself drifting, entering one of those dreamy, pre-sleep moods where memory prods imagination. It was taking him back to his boyhood in Oklahoma, a happy time despite the want. A cavalcade of images passed through his mind. He picked out neighbors from the rush of faces swirling around him, those who'd helped Ma raise him. They were poor farmers, settlers grateful for Ma's generosity. They were his friends, proud of the work he did and the fights he'd won. He thought about Ma and James, his little brother. Ever since Pa had abandoned them, Frank had been a father to James. James had worshipped him, had followed him into the mines and from town to town throughout the lawless West.

He imagined that all these neighbors were listening to one of his speeches in a large theater. They laughed at his jokes, for no one could lampoon the rich better than him. When he was done, they rose and gave him a thunderous ovation. But when the auditorium began to empty, Ma and James weren't there. All the people from his childhood were standing there, but the two most important had been erased from the scene.

He awoke with this thought and felt—it seemed for the first time in his life—that he was totally alone. He was lying in a hotel room, almost naked, and that car was still outside. It had been there yesterday as well, right under his window. It dawned on him what that meant. They were coming for him and he was alone.

Fear was sweeping the world, distorting the souls of men and women. Panic and disorder reigned; and in this fervor just causes had been swept aside, and those who railed against injustice had become the special targets of the madness. He'd made himself a target for the violence and hatred of the times. Why hadn't he seen this before? Out of the terror the Great War had spawned, right now, men were coming for him.

But what about his little brother? I've never had much time to fret about James, who was a good fellow, he knew that for sure, but he was a follower. "I've taken him for granted," Frank realized. "Alone, would he be able to cope? I hope to Christ someone will be there to look out for him."

But his thoughts were cut short by the sound of wood shattering. The light from the hallway blinded him as four men burst through the door and into the room.

Part I: The Code of the Road

July 21, 1923

1.

The driver hunched over the wheel, a skinny man, a sliver of moon in the darkness. The labor of the gears gave way to a steady engine rattle. Then his voice quavered and echoed, the reedy notes filling the cab.

I want to be happy
But I won't be happy
Till I make you happy, too

A good voice, a little flat but tender. He took his eyes off the road and grinned at his passenger, James, the big man, just waking up—

Till I make you happppyyy, tooooo

"We gotta' get you washed up. The dirt you're wearing is thick enough to grow crops."

James hadn't been thinking about his appearance. His last bath was awhile back. Since then he'd had his knees in a beet field all morning, weeding in the mud, and he'd spent the afternoon sweating in a barn. The chaff from his work spiraled in the air, hovered around him as he restacked bales and swept up. Stuck to his skin, caught in his lungs. He was used to physical labor. He'd worked in worse for most of his life. But it was still dirt.

Together they'd unloaded a new tractor from the back of the Mack, and the driver had stuck around. Stuck around, and after they were done, put a hand under the tarp and pulled out a prohibition beer, held it there, sleeve loose around skinny wrist. "A grown man should be able to drink a beer after hard work."

The driver had offered a beer, and they must've had three, shoulder to shoulder, leaning against the Mack, laughing about what men who've just worked hard laugh about. They were in plain view but didn't see Arnoldson.

How could Arnoldson not be out there? With the slitty eyes of a parole boss, always watching.

It was nothing for the driver to down a few, but for James, each sip was an experience. The smell of the hops filled the yard. His first in six years. Before prison most people thought of him as a steady-Eddy kind of guy. Unless something came over him and he wasn't. Which had happened a couple of times and he didn't know why. Now, he felt like a kid again, drinking liquor his older brother brought back from who knows where. He was thirsty and sick of laughing at his own bad joke about how parole was the cruelest part of his sentence.

But now he was coming to, bouncing on a thin seat cushion. How many miles, how many hours later? With each passing minute he was putting more distance between himself and Arnoldson. Feeling good, a little washed-out, just short of a hangover. Empty of worries, at least the old ones. At least for now. He'd never been much of a drinker before, but who knows, maybe he'd take it up in his new life. The driver's jacket was folded neatly on the seat between them, Stetson on top. Maybe he'd have his own things again, a nice hat, dress boots, things to care for as much as to wear. He was on the road enjoying the night air and the darkness. Didn't that prove he'd made a get-away?

Or that he was still drunk.

The long downgrade meant they were on the eastern slope, headed out of state. He felt like a man who's jumped off a building and just realized what he'd done. Too late to go back. The truck is going fast, the wind on his cheeks, but is he falling or flying? About to hit the hard earth after a ten-story drop—or breaking free of Arnoldson, free and clear at last? He turned away. He had to hide his face because it was wide-eyed, with a realization plastered all over it: he was a fugitive.

Could he come to grips with this transformation? He wasn't sure if he'd chosen it. He'd never had much practice at choosing. Sometimes he'd see, days later, that a decision had been made for him. Going along with it was the extent of his choosing.

He stared through the square front window as the lights of the truck prowled the black macadam, flickering over the hand-lettered signs marking the towns—

Miles City

Baker

By now, Arnoldson would have discovered that his star ex-con had jumped parole. They might have to travel far to outdistance that fury.

11

The door slamming echoed in the stillness of the night. He woke up alone in the cab. Should he worry about where the driver had gone? That and a lot of other things. He hopped down to the lot, knees buckling at first. After every-thing he'd been through—and wondering about what lay ahead—aches and pains were the least of his trouble. But at that moment an aching back was important, and it was good having that to worry about. He arched his spine, pressing his fists to the hollow above the hips. The column of bones stretched out. A creaking sound in the dark between trucks.

"Pretty smooth ride with these pneumatic tires," the driver had said. "My first truck had solid rubber—a couple hours of that and your kidneys felt like punching bags." Worry-warts pointed to the danger of blowouts, but anyone who drove long distance loved the air-filled tires.

And they *were* smooth—for a couple of hours.

The vibrations drained through his boots down into the packed gravel. These new trucks could cruise at 40, and they'd been going that fast, at least. The road at night was good, but the stillness of wherever they were was bet-ter. The air just before dawn held a trace of mist, cool as mint in the nostrils. He sensed the other trucks but his view was blocked by the canvas cargo roof of the next one over. He opened the buttons of his fly and peed into the gravel. That always felt good, to be alone for a moment and free to do that. At this stage in his life he was a man for sim-ple pleasures. If others wanted to argue about the Yankees or Red Sox; or who was better, Beethoven or Mozart; or even what was the best way to mix up scrambled eggs, with milk or without—he was glad they knew enough to argue, or thought they did. He wasn't simple, he just preferred to listen.

Then he walked around to the back to see what kind of load they'd picked up while he was dozing. Three stacks of hides or something just as ugly lashed tight with baling wire.

He hoisted himself back into the cab. He was pretty agile for a big guy. One month out of prison and he was in the best shape of his life. Soon the driver stepped in and slammed the door.

"The road is ready, my friend—what about you?" Then, nodding toward the load of hides behind them— "Stinks, doesn't it. That's why I like to keep my foot on the pedal and the wind in my hair."

The driver held something against his shirt, hidden in the hunch of skin and bones. Then he extended his hand, fingers curved around a sandwich made with two fat slices of bread.

"That's a nice turquoise ring," James told him as he reached for the sandwich. "I used to see a lot of turquoise in the mines." Turquoise was embedded in the rock they blasted in Arizona. That's where he first mined copper, in Morenci, which was a boomtown back then. The air in those mines was cool after the desert heat, unless the shaft was deep enough for you to feel the earth's core. You'd tie a bandana around your brow and in a few minutes it would be soaked. You'd brush the sweat from your eyes with a filthy sleeve making them sting from the acid in the ore. Even today he could feel it. Then, in the middle of an endless shift, you'd look down and see the bluish green stone winking at you. Hallelujah! You weren't supposed to take anything, but they all did. A little bag of turquoise was stashed in his room. Then he got laid off and he and his brother ended up in Montana, minus the stash.

"Prettiest stone there is."

"No offense," the driver replied, "but you shouldn't be talking about any copper mines. It won't do you a bit of good."

He shook his head, not understanding. What gave this man the right to tell him what he shouldn't talk about? He was going to get angry. He didn't often get angry, although he often thought he *should* because something men were supposed to fight over had been said to him. But in the silence that followed he began to see that what this man said about the mines might be true. Because the driver knew about June 8, 1917. Of course, everyone in the West knew about the fire and the strike, and even today, six years later, you couldn't find a waitress, a trainman, or a bindle-stiff goat herder who hadn't heard of the Speculator Mine Fire and what came after.

Maybe that's what he was running from, not just Arnoldson and prison but from that heat. All the miners who witnessed it were dangerous. They'd been through hell, so that made them devils, each and every one. How could they not be, after what they knew? About the concrete that men clawed at before they died. The company had worried that miners might use secondary tunnels to avoid work, so it ordered these passageways sealed with bulkheads. Teach the shirkers. Dozens of men died in the fire when they clawed their fingers to the bone against the rough concrete, clawing like animals as they gagged in thick smoke.

He knew it was true about the fingers because he'd helped bring up the bodies. The dying of those men entered into everyone who carried them, the moments of clawing. Doomed from the start, useless in any practical way, what good were their efforts at rescue? Not much. Unless it was that they carried within themselves not only the failure, but the attempt.

How could the survivors, how could they not have revenge on their minds? For their sons, their fathers, their friends. How could they forget about the bulkheads?

Frank had been a leader of the strike that broke out in response. An angry strike, doomed to failure, the miners blacklisted.

Over time, the surviving miners would prove—or pretend—they held no grudge. Bygones be bygones. They could go back to work in the mines. He alone had reason for a grudge that would never be relinquished. He'd found Frank's body at the end of a rope. Vigilantes had left him, a shadow twisting in a soft dawn breeze. That's one murder the sheriff never prosecuted. Of all the miners in Butte, of all those angry and grief-stricken men, his cause for anger was the greatest.

For days after finding Frank's body, he'd walked in a cloud of grief. He'd joined with other angry men and made threats, wandered up and down Wyoming Street, wailing threats and curses, never harming a fly. But apparently his threats against the authorities were sufficient grounds for a life sentence. Then early parole and apparently this driver had offered to help him escape. Which, because of the beers, he couldn't remember. Was he still dreaming? Would he wake up in a new life or back in jail? He pressed palm to forehead to keep his head from spinning. Now that he was a fugitive, he had to think about things in a new way. How to hide. To speak and laugh and never reveal himself.

"Good sandwich." he told the driver, although he hadn't yet taken a bite. "Thank you." He let out a sigh and the long breath said thank you again.

**

On Highway 12, truckers can shower for a quarter. "Two bits for all the hot water you've got," the driver sang out to the attendant. "My helper unloaded hides at a tannery. Changed oil, grease, a cable, a tire—you name it, Bill changed it. The air in the cab is getting pretty ripe."

He hadn't done anything but sleep, not even help with the hides, and Bill wasn't his name. But it was a good one. Maybe it was just the name he needed.

A shower makes you feel like a new man, a clean shirt also, which was another gift from the driver. He had a large suitcase full of clothes in the back of his truck because he lived on the road and was a good dresser. They were both tall, James and the driver, with long arms, but the shirt was tight across his chest.

"How'd you know my name was Bill, Bill Waite?" He was happy now, at being clean and because he had a new name. He extended a hand toward the driver. A little late, but does an introduction have to be first thing?

"Amos Kincaid. I thought I recognized you. Weren't we classmates at the same school?"

"If you went to the School of Hard Knocks—"

"None other. A finishing school. I don't know about you, but it damn near finished me. I grew up in Denver. My father worked for the railroad, laying track, when he wasn't laying out drunk or laying into me with a fat fist." The driver, Amos, took a bony hand off the steering wheel and clenched it for emphasis. "I learned a lot from Dad." His face fell back into the wide grin that was always plastered there. "Every boy needs an example like that, to teach you chapter and verse in the book of how not to act. He spent time in jail stealing company property, stealing from the neighbor's store, stealing from in-laws. He'd steal anything that wasn't nailed down. I learned to never steal when you might get caught at it. That's a lesson I'm still working on. He had enemies and got beat up a lot, so I learned never get in a fight you can't win. I've got that lesson down, more or less. That's why I hardly ever fight. Hell, I'd fight all the time if I thought I could win. He used to beat up on me when I was little." Amos's eyes lit up, like he was recounting happy times. "When I got big enough to whomp him back, he screamed bloody murder and loaded his twelve-guage. 'Get the hell out of town if you know what's good for you.' That was his only good advice. I hit the road, picked fruit, dug ditches, worked in a warehouse where the boss saw what a fool I was. 'Son, you should be a truck driver.'"

"You ever go back to Denver to see your mother?"

"Now that my dad's dead, I go back every chance I get. I'm a momma's boy. I love the hell out of that old lady."

As he watched Amos shift gears, he tried to remember how to drive. He'd never had much practice, but he could if he had to. Like most boys growing up, no money in his family for a car. But somehow all men learn, or at least they won't admit to not knowing. As a miner he might've saved for an auto but got thrown in jail. Clutch in, pull the lever into neutral, clutch in again, rev up, hope it doesn't grind too loud when you shove it into the next gear. He watched Amos changing gears to slow down. Eyes deep-set but twinkling, lips spreading in a smile like his life's a breeze even though it isn't.

The school of hard knocks teaches tenderness to some men. Amos's voice filled the cab with it.

Drifting and dreaming
While shadows fall

That song was a surprise, and the way the voice fluctuated, a quivering, reedy sound, almost like a musical instrument. Not really singing. Music had changed while he was in jail.

They slowed at the edge of a town. Just ahead, the morning sun spread a ribbon of yellow at the horizon, all the small trees and hills standing out against it, everything they were heading towards. The sun lit the low clouds with a border of pink flecks and long orange strands. The summer morning was a thin whisper, thinner than a song. They sped through countryside he didn't know and would never

see again. He didn't have to know Highway Twelve—he'd
be on another highway soon enough.

Love's own sweet story
told with your eyes,
drifting and dreaming,
sweet paradise.

**

They stopped and ate and he went back outside, feeling
good in the loneliness of the place. Feeling good sometimes
has a worry, a trouble inside it. There was a great emptiness
around him because he was free and for other reasons. A
round sign towered over the landscape.

GASOLINE

MOTOR OIL

TEXACO

Three pumps with thick black hoses. The gas-station
man was filling a truck and had already pumped gas into
three others parked just down the roadside. The morning
sun leaped off steel hoods and windshields, off the varnished paneling of pine slats.

Amos had clothed him and knew how to sing. The
other two trucks belonged to his friends, the men he'd just
had breakfast with. The small talk in the restaurant was
good. He couldn't remember the last time he'd heard the
small talk of free men. He introduced himself as Bill, and
that felt good too. He couldn't keep up with the chatter

19

and jokes and didn't even try. He leaned back in his chair. Then he thought these men might want to say a few things without him there. He liked it when folks were considerate about things like that and tried to do the same.

He went outside to breathe.

Cars and trucks drove by with a roar of engines pinched down to a squeal as they passed and disappeared down the lonely highway. Silence again. Bill was alone. He said his name over and liked how easy it slid from his tongue. Funny how you could be called James your whole life and take a new name and, in a few hours, get used to it. Especially if you had to.

He hadn't been alone like this for a long time. An auto drove up in the lonesomeness. The car door opened and a heavyset man pulled himself out holding on to the door. It seemed to take a long time for him to let himself down from the running board. Then he stared around like he owned this piece of land and spat into the gray dust made when equipment drives over gravel, crunching it to powder day and night. He walked toward the restaurant. When he got close the fat man nodded at him, but without friendship.

He started to rehearse a story about himself, a story for this man in case he was nosy. He'd invented stories as a kid, to avoid punishment. As a grown man he didn't often invent stories. Sometimes he'd deny some wrongdoing because he had a good straight face, eyes that gazed ahead without blinking; mouth that seldom smiled or frowned. When men make up a lie, they think of details from another man's life: jobs, children, divorce. Things he might have to use. Of course, any guy can invent a story. But can he live it for the rest of his life, however long that might be?

The heavyset man walked past him and into the restaurant. He brushed close and left a sharp smell in the air, like he'd just had a shave or a drink. Or both.

Bill paced on the gravel and dust by the side of the road. There were a few houses, about a quarter mile east, and a small town in the distance. He knew that kind of town, knew there was a river nearby because he could see the line of trees and brush, dark green from soaking up the river's moisture. The mind sees things and connects the dots. The magic of a place like this was that he could connect them all the way back to his childhood. After crossing the tracks you'd come to a level spot in the bank where you could sit down, right there, and fish for bass, big catfish if you could get the damn line out far enough into the channel. Most of the houses had fences and milk cows. This looked like a town where the people never had to sell out. But poor people weren't always like billboards so you could see them from the road. Walk a few blocks and you'd find them.

Maybe the man who'd just gone into the restaurant was someone to worry about. You could tell the meanness in a person by his eyes. To a degree. But hadn't he been fooled by people with kind eyes? He no longer wanted to stand there by himself and began walking down the road toward Amos's truck.

That's when one of the other drivers came out, walking fast, smiling into the sun, a big man taking long strides. He put a hand on Bill's shoulder, guiding him toward one of the trucks.

"We had a talk in there and decided you should ride with me."

Bill pulled back because he hadn't thanked Amos for the clean clothes and breakfast, but the hand on his shoulder tightened.

"I'll explain it to you, but we'd best get on the road, *now*."

He squeezed his belly in under the wheel, glanced at the mirror, accelerated hard as the truck lurched from the gravel to the paved road. They drove through the little town, over a range of hills until the land leveled out as far as the eye could see. They were driving straight into the sun.

"Was it about the man who just walked into the restaurant?"

"Yes. And Amos has some problems up in St. Paul. You wouldn't think such a good kid could get into so much trouble."

He was sorry about Amos's trouble and that he hadn't thanked him and that all lives seemed so crowded by fear.

"Nothing he can't handle, but better for you not to be in his truck. Better for both of you. Better for us to put some dust between you and that place."

He waited, he always waited for people to finish what they were saying. Finally, this new driver went on, "Don't worry, Kiddo, we have a code. It's called the Code of the Road. The truck driver looked out at this great country of ours, God's country, half uncivilized, full of bad guys and wild Indians, and he saw that a code was needed because the roads were lawless and new. And this was where the truck driver spent his life. You can't work in a place without rules, day after day, in a wild, back-stabbing place. Not all truck drivers are good, but a good one follows the Code. We help each other and we help other folks. We give rides. We don't ask questions."

This driver's name was Branson. He had two wives. His big round face was careworn. He was surely balding under the straw hat he never took off. Stress takes a toll. But when he started into a story his eyes lit up like a little boy's. "I have so many bills, I'll be driving until the day I die, and past that—if the steering wheel isn't too hot to handle in the place where I'm going.

"Me and my first wife had a bad case of puppy love. We had the itch. I'd go over to her house and we'd find a hedge or a stone wall to hide behind and we'd go at it. Looking back, it's a wonder her folks didn't see us. Or maybe they did. Those two kids, at it again. I send her money so she has no cause to complain. I'm the one that came out of it singing the blues. I hardly ever see my first son, Emanuel. My wife said it had to be spelled with an 'E' or people would think it was Jewish. Jewish is fine with me, I said. What name in the Bible isn't Jewish?

"Anyway, she had her way. It seemed a shame to give a little fellow such a serious name then never see him."

The teenage couple lingered in Bill's mind. Going at it, rolling in the grass. Maybe Branson was a skinny kid back then, but Bill saw him as big man, not able to hide, shoulders and butt sticking out from behind a stone wall or a spindly tree.

Branson was funny but not so tender as Amos. He talked nonstop about the towns they drove through, about life on the road.

"Always look for a place with trucks in front of it when you need lodging. That's a place that don't charge an arm and a leg and don't ask questions, and if they do you won't have to answer them."

Branson's talk was easy, in the way Amos's singing had been. A driver had to fill the cab with who he was. This cab was filled with the talk of a man who saw things and remembered them. "I grew up in North Dakota and thought I knew enough about being poor to write the book. We lost our farm and had to work for my uncle and a couple of other tight-fisted, hard-nosed bastards. It was my way or the highway, they told me. The highway sounds like the place for me, I hollered over my shoulder. I was already married by then. I'd grown up surrounded by farmers and thought I was the only poor boy in the world. Once I got out on the road, I saw my troubles didn't amount to a hill of beans.

"My first week out, I had to make a pick-up in St. Paul at an old steel shop off Rondo Avenue. I could tell it was a poor neighborhood. I was a little afraid I'd run into a tough Irish gang. That's what frightens truckers, Irish gangs. I keep my own shillelagh under the seat. You see, Bill, I got some Irish in me, too. It's a good oak walking stick only I never go walking. I'd rather fight than let someone steal what I worked hard for. Although not always. If it's a couple guys bigger than me—I'm not so stupid I think I'm the only big guy in the world—I tell'em, here it is brothers, and welcome to it.

"Anyway, I backed into the dock and pulled the brake and went around to help load up, but the warehouse guy was standing on the dock, dusting his hands. How he'd loaded seven boxes of faucet castings that quick I'll never know.

"I stared at those hands, because the skin was black on top and the color of mine underneath. I'd never stood within a hundred yards of a black man.

" 'You can leave now, boss, you got your load,' the colored man said. He didn't seem friendly, which surprised me. A white man will act friendly even when he's about to stab you in the back. I had to see a lot more of the world before I understood the way that man acted. Hunger and the whip. They leave their mark. But I'm not telling you anything new."

How much did Branson know about Bill? Had the truck drivers talked about him while he was outside the restaurant? It didn't matter, because Branson started talking again, his words filling the cab. Listening to people talk is like hearing a stream, a flow of things. What if Bill had grown up in the city and not in Oklahoma by the banks of a creek that flowed into the Cimarron River? What if he'd never heard a stream? He'd hear words, but how would he understand the flow of what people were telling him?

Every so often, Branson took his eyes off the road and winked at him, like Amos had done. The wide face broke into a grin that seemed to hang there a long time. Too long, when there was a road to be watched, a road coming toward them at a high rate of speed.

"I once gave an outlaw a ride. He was drunk at the time, a baby-faced kid. I don't usually pick up drunks but this kid had a face you couldn't turn down. Later, I learned that he'd just batted his eyes at a bank teller in Grand Forks and told her to put all her money in a burlap sack. The newspaper quoted her saying he gave her a twenty and said, take it, doll, this one's for you."

Not long after, Branson read in a newspaper that the guy had also shot a deputy.

"He offered me a lot more than twenty. 'I better not,' I told him. 'If I passed a c-note and got caught, which is sure to happen with my luck, I might start to blab to the cops under torture. Every man has a breaking point. If I don't take your money, we're friends for life. I'll always be the same straight-shooting guy who gave you a ride.' That outlaw gave me a serious look like he understood and then passed out."

How many times had Branson told this story? Maybe a little different each time. It didn't matter, each time he told it, it was true.

"You're a good kid, Bill." With this statement Bill couldn't completely agree. Not wholeheartedly, anyway, but he let it slide. "You haven't said five words but I trust you. It's a gift. I shoot my trap for five hours and you don't know me from Adam. You don't say a word and I'd trust you with my life.

"Now grab the seat of your pants while I change the subject. They say country people are more trustworthy because of the barns and the little brick churches and the old-fashioned ways. I'm a country boy, and I can tell you are, too. We country boys are trustworthy—if you know how to read us. But the same is true of city folks. Both are trustworthy, but you'd better learn their ways."

He underscored this remark with a thoughtful silence. A person who doesn't talk much tells you a lot when he finally opens up. A person who talks all the time tells you something with a silence.

Then Branson laughed and reached across the seat and squeezed Bill's shoulder. "We don't know one-tenth of what we think we know. The smartest man in the world doesn't have as much brains as a head of cabbage."

Branson liked Bill because he was a good listener and laughed at the stories. Not all of them were happy but most were funny, maybe true. He liked Branson but knew this ride wouldn't last forever. The farm towns gradually got larger, filling in more and more of the countryside; corn and wheat gave way to gravel lots, which gave way to macadam. Farm houses gave way to stone buildings and factories large as a cattle range.

**

It was dark again when they stopped near Chicago at the gas pumps by another restaurant. No dust, only black tar and cars the same color surging by, disappearing with a metal whoosh. Tall stone buildings and brick apartment houses rising like cliffs from the street. The night had a different feel to it. In a small town, the night is lonely. The darkness of a city is noisy and crowded.

As he jumped down from the truck, the traffic streamed

by, lights playing over him. Where could he hide?

But Branson was there, a hand on his shoulder, guiding him into the restaurant. The screen door slammed behind them and air blew from the big fan behind the counter, warm, heavy with grease. They walked through a cloud of sounds, of people talking and dishes clattering, to a big table where three men were hunched over plates. A little yellow from the eggs was still there.

Even before the men looked up, Branson's voice boomed out, "Professors talk about the wonderful sand hill cranes of Nebraska, those gawky birds traveling thousands of miles with a flap of their wings, knowing how to come back to the same place every year. Every year, on the money. People who live in Nebraska say you can mark the date on your calendar and wait for those travelers to show in the sky. The perfect timing is one of the wonders of the natural world. But what about the dumb trucker? Isn't our sense of direction and timing just as remarkable? Somehow the four of us are roosting here in this greasy spoon outside Chicago, a simultaneous landing, two weeks after I last saw you fellows."

He opened his napkin with a flourish and spread it over his round belly. "Only you birds didn't wait, you went ahead and ordered breakfast without us."

"I'd rather have breakfast with the cranes," one of the others responded, a short burly man with a red face. "At least they wouldn't run off and leave me to cover the tab."

Then Branson squeezed his shoulder. "Bill, meet Speedy. But don't let his nickname fool you. You won't be young any more, by the time this slowpoke lets you off in New York City."

Part II: New York City

July 25, 1923

1.

Dreams may have value. Surely they do, for people put great stock in them. But for a man like Bill what counted was something else, the art of knowing who to trust.

Speedy, the misnamed truck driver, had just dropped him off. Trusting him and the other truckers seemed to have worked out. But the three-day ride left him punchy. He wandered outside the Battery Depot into the afternoon light, which broke over him, hard, like a glass pane, a brightness shattering. The light shrieked down from a ring of buildings with distant rooftops. It fell from a great height on this man who'd seen enough in his life to always expect the worst. Looking up into that light made him dizzy. He had to steady himself.

The street struck him hard as well. The sidewalk exploded on all sides. A fierce crowd of businessmen hurried in a whirlwind around him; shoppers—including smart-looking women—peered at him with disdain; two newsboys bawled clashing headlines; a hot food vendor gestured with skinny hands, chanted a rigmarole he couldn't decipher; two ragged men sat a few yards away, backs against a stone wall. The light reflecting off polished shoes flashed over their drooping faces.

Would he, one day soon, be slumping against a building like that, like a sack whose contents had long ago emptied out? Close by, a knot of people clustered around a chubby man pumping out syllables, a swift rattle, a rhythm of hard city words skipping like stones in the hot light of day: "Yes, boys, jobs! Make your wife happy! Make your girlfriend happy! Make them both happy! Don't waste a second. The Canal Street Tunnel pays top dollar for honest men, good men—top dollar. And you're a good man, aren't you? Ok, then, seize the chance, seize the day, the main chance, the bull by the horns, seize it, man, SEIZEIT. We have openings, go to work this afternoon, get paid this Friday! SEIZITMAN! The best payday you ever saw! SEIZEITMANSEIZEIT!"

It was now Wednesday.

"Of course there's openings," muttered one of the bystanders. "Anyone who reads the morning papers knows that. Another sandhog drowned last night."

This bystanding man was well-dressed. Bill wanted to heed his warning, to smile knowingly and walk away. Couldn't he walk away? He was a free man. He'd just jumped parole, had journeyed across half a mighty continent to find himself in a madhouse city, in a world that was strange but surely crowded with opportunities. He could follow the lead of the smart man, toss a cane in the air, catch it, and walk away. He had good reason to shun risky workplaces. Before prison, as a copper miner, he'd known the full weight of a shift of dangers. He knew that fear was a millstone, how a millstone could grind.

Should a man who'd dared to become a fugitive from the law now settle for another bottom-rung job that was spurned by this one smart fellow and surely many others?

32

But into this expanse of reckless freedom came an uneasy knowing. A flutter at the heart that told Bill he was not, could not ever hope to be, this bystanding fellow. Should not dare to think of himself as a man with the freedom to examine life's rich alternatives. He wasn't much of a chooser. He didn't have a cane to toss in the air.

The bystanding fellow offered fine advice, but it didn't apply to Bill. He felt in his pocket and was seized by a moment of panic. Where were the few bills Speedy had given him? With relief he felt the corner of the top bill.

"It's a loan. Pay me back next time I come to town." Speedy didn't expect to see those bills again, let alone the sorry fugitive he'd just dropped off at the depot. What Speedy got from the deal was a handshake. In 1923, ambition was a prized and valued trait. Society honored it. Bill was fortunate that to Speedy doing a good deed to another poor fellow was the sum of his ambition.

These few bills were not a loan, but they weren't enough for a month's rent, either. For luxuries like that he would need a job that promised quick cash. Besides, working with other desperate fellows under a river might provide just the hideout he needed.

A half-dozen men trailed behind the barker, the seizit man, as he walked to the end of the block where the shoppers melted away. For a chubby man, he was nimble and fast, like a balloon rolling swiftly down the sidewalk. He turned right and stepped smartly a few more blocks. Bill followed close, nervous about getting lost in this immense hubbub. As they galloped through swift-moving crowds, Bill felt a jab to the shoulder. It made him start with the thought that someone was trying to get his attention, maybe a tough-guy wanting him to turn, to present a better target for a punch in the face. Bill might have been passive, but he'd learned to defend himself. Because of his size he'd avoided some attacks, been the target of others, of big guys who fought for the hell of it. So, he'd often defended himself, sometimes with fair results, sometimes not.

Today, especially, he had to be on his guard. He was in a cold-hearted city, surrounded by unknown people. He swung around, a rough look on his face. Staring back at him were two brown eyes, a little frightened by the sudden response.

"This should be quite a job we're headed for," said the brown-eyed man, eager to show he wasn't a threat. He was slender, about the same height as Bill, with the rounded shoulders of someone used to bending over to catch the words of shorter people. Something about the sound of the voice, the effortlessness of it, told Bill that the man loved to talk. Quiet fellows have an instinct for that. They can tell from the very first words if someone is a talker. And usually they're glad if they are, because it takes the pressure off.

"Hard to imagine a highway under the Hudson." The man wiped at a drop of sweat about to roll from the bridge of his nose. "I remain skeptical, but there are men who think Clifford Holland, the chief engineer, is one of the great geniuses of the age."

Bill had been asleep in Speedy's truck when they crossed over the Hudson. He knew that Manhattan was an island and guessed that the river separating it from the mainland must be one of the grandest in the world. But he'd never heard of Clifford Holland.

By this time the seizit man had led them to the edge of the business district, where an industrial site opened up. It contained a rail yard and siding for heavy equipment. This world of cranes and cables, of iron rails and stacked heavy timbers, was familiar to him. For years before prison, day in and day out, he'd trudged through such sites, and at night he'd slept within earshot of them, sometimes jamming cotton in his ears. He didn't love heavy labor, but it was familiar, and better than prison.

Two sets of narrow-gauge tracks slanted down a grading and into round tubes punched into the earth. Like portals to a drift mine. Or, since he'd never seen a mine in the middle of a giant city, the gates to somewhere else—like hell, except that was the place in Montana he'd left behind.

Their leader proceeded to a solid stone building in a corner of the lot and pulled on the wide door. He held it open for them, which meant this parade of men had to squeeze around him before finding themselves in a hallway with an underground feel, pleasant after the heat of the pavement. At another door they entered a large room where a man with a half-slung tie was speaking, another fellow who'd not missed too many meals. When he saw the seizit man in the doorway he gave a nod, like he'd just glanced into a mirror and recognized himself. He continued his spiel, because that's what he did, day in day out. He was another talker but not like the fellow who'd jabbed his arm.

"And at the end of the shift you will go through the Decompression Area." He repeated those words in singsong,

"The Decompression Area. And why is the Decompression Area so important? Because you'll be working in compressed air far underwater and could get the bends if you come out too fast."

At these words, chairs slid back over countless tiny eight-sided black and white tiles. Men stood up.

"I thought these was *ground-level* jobs," one of them called out.

"These jobs are under the river, which is why they pay so good. Look around this city. You see any work for unskilled men that pays like this?"

Fear had entered the room. It was dusk-colored and seeped through shaded windows. It told these men to heed no assurances, for if they were foolish enough to remain, the night ahead would be full of danger. They were frightened. They could afford to be frightened.

Muttering about the bends, some tossing insults behind them, they pulled on the heavy door and left when it sighed open. The door closed slowly, which allowed for a view of several women walking in the corridor. Bill had not seen many women, not for six years of prison and a month of parole. They were framed in the doorway just long enough for him to notice that they were pretty, very neat and professional. But they didn't smile. They knitted their brows. They hugged papers to their breasts.

The man with the half-slung tie shook his head in disgust. "Any more timid souls who want to run off to Momma?"

How did this man know where Bill wanted to run? If only she was still on this earth and not under it. This is the way most grown men feel. They understand that of all the people you will ever know, your mother alone will truly love you.

He held his ground, however, along with one other man. They turned toward each other, their faces no more than a yard apart, connected by nothing but air and a shared glance.

He was the talker with brown eyes who'd walked beside him and told him about Holland, the chief engineer. A closer look revealed a trim moustache and an intelligent face. Hard to imagine that face beneath a river, buried under a sheen of sweat and dirt. A good profile, an eagle's nose. Around the eyes, wrinkles like spokes. Otherwise the skin was smooth copper, only a little tarnished.

Bill's own skin was a little more etched and bitten, a strapping body in a hide pockmarked by time.

The talker turned toward him with a what-the-hell shrug and nonchalant curl of the lip.

Bill respected the effort, but the gesture didn't succeed. The eyes revealed something besides what-the-hell. Something that could be seen in the eyes of men entering the mines for the first time—or arriving for their first night in prison. As a miner or a prisoner, you learn not to show your fear. But you never get used to a life based on terror. Fugitives, too, he was learning. In fact, terror is everywhere. We walk around in air that is heavy with it.

Once upon a time a man much older than Bill had looked into his face and laughed. He was a wall with an open door, and the man's eyes walked right through him.

"This baby is afraid," he'd said. "Go back to Momma. A mine's no place for a frightened boy."

Since then, Bill had learned to mask his fear. And to never laugh at the fear of another. Of course, after he'd grown passed six feet by several inches of broad-shouldered height, such a remark would not have occurred to most bullies.

The company man they'd been listening to signaled for them to follow him and scurried ahead. Halfway down the long hallway he pulled the steel handle of a frosted-glass door and ushered the two of them into a room where nearly a dozen men were already standing in line. They held their trousers in one hand, their shoes in the other. The room was quiet except for a gruff voice from the front of the line.

"Cough."

The doctor had gray hair, a moustache pasted on the upper lip and trimmed off at the corners. He was checking pulse, blood pressure, and other things. He asked questions but seemed bored with the answers. He swayed, half asleep on his feet. No miner would live long who paid so little attention to his work. A prisoner who was not alert might not live long either.

"When was your last bowel movement?"

"Yesterday," Bill answered, although this was not the case. He'd been on the road.

A chance to succeed—or fail by telling the truth.

He'd had one previous doctor's exam in his life, on his first day at Montana State Prison. He'd truthfully answered all the questions about his health, which had always been good before that.

"Can you work with more than twenty psi bearing down on you?" He knew what this meant from hearing it explained several times to the men who went before him in line. He knew that fourteen psi was the normal pressure of air at sea level and that the added pressure held the water at bay, kept it from bursting through the loose mud of the riverbed. At bay, or so they said.

"You will feel like you are carrying a hundred extra pounds on your frame and frequently hear a loud washing in your ears."

"That's ok, Doc, I'm strong as a bull." And this was true. He'd gone underground at fifteen and worked six years in the mines until his arrest. He wasn't the only one arrested but he was the one who got the long sentence. A lawyer told him he'd be better off to confess and own his crime. He'd lied often enough, as often as most men. He would lie to get this job. But he wouldn't own a crime he didn't commit. Not that one.

"One last question: are you afraid of enclosed spaces, of water and the sound of water all around you, do you fear drowning, the certainty of death as the dirty water of the Hudson rises up to your nostrils and over your head?"

"What I'm afraid of, Doc, is not getting paid this Friday."

To the same question, the man with the frightened brown eyes had answered: "My wife and little girl have developed the habit of eating and are troublesome to live with unless I can feed them on a pretty regular basis."

When the doctor grinned back at him, Bill could see the two men had the same close shave and neat moustache.

39

He could tell they were educated men. But the man he'd shared a glance with had eyes that were gentle as well as frightened. Gentle, above an eagle's nose. The doctor's eyes were hard glass.

**

Then the sound of steel kissing rubber. The doors seated and sealed, and a wiry man with a huge head turned toward them. "I'm Orlando." A smile ignited his round face. It told each and all that he was pleased with himself and expected that others would be. "I run the locks. My job is to make sure you men have a good shift. Orlando is your friend, maybe your best friend. Ask anybody who works at Mr. Holland's Tunnel."

The dozen men in the narrow room mumbled their greetings. Orlando turned a handle, and air began hissing into the room. "I read numbers and operate this here valve. I call it the headache valve. Fortunately for you fellows, I know what I'm doing."

Bill concentrated on his breathing as the air whistled. He was conscious of the weight of the air, the burden of it on his shoulders, the feeling that his lungs were balloons, that he had to breathe in with care or they'd burst. The pressure on every inch of his skin increased moment by moment, compressing him into the shape of someone smaller, with barely the strength to lift his limbs. Who was this weakling? Surely not the man who'd entered New York an hour ago, that tall, strong fellow.

It was laughable, to be concerned about something as automatic as breathing. But it was important work, and he was afraid that if he didn't take heed of it, he might foul it up. Soon there was a collective sigh as the men in the tight chamber relaxed, getting the hang of it. Then Orlando glanced at one of the many gauges on the wall and walked to the other end of the room. He turned around, eyes bright. "You fellows are now sandhogs—go at it!"

He lifted a lever and the seal broke with a pop, and the steel panel slid open. He waved them through the portal, like a butler showing a party of VIPs to the room where they'd been invited to dine. This pomp was a nice touch but didn't boost their confidence. They stepped over the rubber gasket and into a world of arc lights and shadows and muted sounds. A metal clanging came from somewhere but it was indistinct, like someone beating armor at the bottom of the sea.

To enter this strange world required a brave leap. While still a boy, he'd been forced to enter the underground world of blasting and roof falls, then graduated to prison, even more terrifying. After working in the mines and living behind bars, why wouldn't parole to a farm have been a piece of cake? Bill's view was that parole is a great institution for those who like to grovel. He'd always thought he could grovel as well as the next man, and certainly a lot better than his brother. Frank had never mastered the arts of the stooping shoulder and the fawning smile. Bluster and moral rectitude would be sufficient, or so he thought. More than once Bill had pulled Frank away from a fight he couldn't win, and for a skinny fellow Frank was a good fighter. It was his fury. It helped him win some fights—and get into others he couldn't.

Bill could grovel, as long as there was an end in sight. Which there wasn't in his parole to Arnoldson.

An unknown world awaited these newly christened sandhogs. As they hung back Bill took the lead, the only one who thought the unknown might be a good thing, at least better than what he was used to. He went down the stairs like he knew what he was doing. At the bottom, without warning, his knees buckled and his stomach churned. He found himself in an immense room, which began to spin. Everything was a swirl of mud and rust-colored puddles; rail tracks and carts and other things made of iron were swirling around him, until he steadied himself, stood still, feet planted wide apart in the muck. The heavy air had kicked him in the guts, but he straightened and saw ahead a concrete bulkhead where tools were stacked. These were his tools. He rejoiced at the sight of them.

Once in his working life, and only once, he'd been asked by a foreman: "What are you waiting for, an engraved invitation?"

He'd never seen an engraved invitation. What would it look like?

He seized two good shovels and handed one to the talker whose brown eyes he'd looked into. Reaching toward him his new partner grasped the wood handle. Through this strange medium of heavy air, this talker uttered a string of sounds that were blurred and distorted and included two syllables that sounded like *naahgghuuh* and may have been "thank you."

Bill was struck by something humorous as the mud rained down on them. In this setting, dignity was difficult to imagine. Yet his new partner was making an attempt, despite the mud, and Bill respected that.

Work cannot be performed without a partner, someone who might listen to complaints and would expect you to listen in turn. This is the iron law of work. Bill had learned this law in the mines and was certain it applied here. And this brown-eyed, eagle-nosed fellow was the only man on the planet at that moment that he shared any connection with, slight as it was. Together they began filling a cart from the dirt piled by the bulkhead. It was loamy and damp and had a brackish stink, which was unpleasantly multiplied by the high-pressure atmosphere.

They worked slowly. Their limbs toiled in the slow wash of the sea.

When the cart was full, they pushed it down the tracks to the other end of their giant work chamber, to a door where a man waved, shaping the words, "Hurry, push, push!" His lips shaped other words as well. It was heavy with sodden earth and the weight of the air but once they got the cart started it moved easily down the rails. They left it in the good care of this hurry-up man and turned back toward their bulkhead, where another man had positioned a new cart just in time to catch rocks and mud deluging down the chute. That cart was quickly topped off, but the cascade continued, and muck oozed over the floor. Then shovel and push, shovel and push, they tried to keep up.

That brown ooze was sickening if you thought about it. They weren't that foolish.

The chute they worked under originated on a platform high overhead. Men worked up there, the noises of their work barely audible through a rumble that was constant and vague. He knew by an instinct learned in the mines that the men on this platform were toiling at the face of the tunnel, that place where progress occurred, where the work inched forward. Clean-up was all important in such a messy excavation. There were four doors behind them: two above for people, including the one operated by Orlando; two below for carts, one of them operated by the hurry-up fellow. On scaffolding high overhead two men with black skin toiled. Bill had known a few black men, but there were not many in the mines, a few in prison. These two struggled with an enormous wrench, tightening the fist-sized nuts on a ring that swept the inner circumference of the tunnel. The men appeared small beside the wrench, which they maneuvered with difficulty. Bill might have imagined that he could handle this tool more easily, but he wasn't that foolish.

As the hours passed, he was aware of how little they accomplished. They couldn't keep up with the spill. The shovel was heavy, even without a load. When you thrust it into the muck it stuck there, glued fast to the jealous earth. You had to take small bites, to nibble at the work. Bill's partner was having even more trouble. The thought crossed Bill's mind that he should let someone know that he was the one who'd done most of the work. But that thought was followed quickly by another: Shame on you, shame on you even to think it.

Prison had taught him to look out for himself first and foremost. But that wasn't who he was, at least not who he wanted to be. Now, he had to seek for something better, more in line with an old self, a self that would never betray a partner. He had to look out for this man who was having so much difficulty, even if it meant getting reprimanded or dismissed. But when the foreman came by, he signaled them with a thumbs-up. Then he held his hands in the air and broke an invisible branch and they followed him upstairs and through the overhead locks into the narrow room for lunch.

**

As Orlando reduced the air pressure, a powerful hunger took root in his body. The lining of his stomach burned with it. He hadn't eaten since breakfast at first-light on the road. He was not an authority on hunger but knew a little, how it produces a special acid that burns in the mind as well as the body. In the mines, he'd worked all day without food, more than once; in prison, he'd lived for a week on water and a little bread, on three separate visits to the hole, all in his first year. After that, he'd learned how to avoid that place, a lesson that some men better than he had never mastered. But this present hunger had come on suddenly, with the lifting of the air. It burned through him, cell by cell, gnawing downward from belly to bowels.

The other men had prepared for their shift, with cheese, smoked fish, or hot dogs from a street vendor, perhaps now cold, but at least something solid. They opened oil-paper wrappers, paused over the smell of their treasures. They took their time, eyes scanning the sweet fat coating the meat; the rough, briny skin of pickles or the sheen of olives, both kinds, green and dark; or the glistening broth on a mealy potato speckled with parsley; a soft slice of black bread with a sliver of onion; the dry texture of a chunk of crumbly, blue-veined cheese. Even the smell of the cabbage created a yearning in him, especially the crumbs of bacon it was boiled with. These men were in no hurry to eat, which prolonged the agony. They had no worries about their next meal and could afford to dawdle and savor this tantalizing moment. They did not wolf their food. Out of politeness they exchanged news with their workmates before plunging into the delight of the meal.

"It's not so bad under water. I couldn't afford the high rent on the money from my old job. If I can stick it out here, my family won't end up on the curb with the garbage."

"Eighth Avenue ain't the worst place to live, but it's getting high-priced, like you say …"

"Everything's high. Yesterday I took a dollar to the store for milk, bread, and a couple eggs. A dollar I took— and no change."

"At least you had a dollar. Last time I held George Washington, I squeezed him tight."

The need for conversation was a sharp hunger as well. He slumped on a bench in the low-ceilinged room, which was so narrow he had to pull in his knees or bump the fellow on the opposite bench. Not recognizing Bill's discomfort, this man grinned toward him, gesturing as he spoke, a fat sandwich in his hand. Gesturing but not offering. If one of these chatty men noticed that he wasn't eating he'd tell him, he seldom ate this late at night, for it was already past nine. That's the line he rehearsed, so he'd have it if needed. He wanted to be part of the confab but realized— glancing around at the crew—they had something in common: they were New Yorkers. They had news of streets and neighborhoods to share. He knew nothing of New York and could not talk about where he was from, either. What could he tell them? That for six years he'd lived without news, behind yard-thick walls? How could he make small talk and not betray himself? They wouldn't know why he'd jumped parole, wouldn't believe that he had to. They would know only that he was worse than the bums they'd passed on the street on their way to work. Bums were in every town under heaven. Bill knew about bums but did not know the why of them, the many whys that explained them.

He was worse off than a bum. He was an outsider. In that there was danger. It wasn't the truckers' job to prepare him for this situation, but he wished they had.

All around him were men who shared connections. If he met their stares, his eyes would be furtive, nervous, so he stared at his hands. When he got tired of that he leaned back on the bench and pretended to doze. If they asked his address or where he was from he'd have to be gruff, dismissive. In his new life he'd be a loner. It was a high-paying job, yes; it was a type of safety and freedom, no doubt; but was it such a happy prospect to have no connection to the life around him, none except loneliness?

At that moment, he felt a jab at his shoulder and turned toward it. "My wife packed three sandwiches." It was his new partner, with the eagle nose. "She knows damn well I could never eat more than two. You better take one so it won't go to waste. You know what they say, every time you waste a sandwich, another Chinaman starves."

Bill shrugged so as not to appear overeager, and put out a hand for the sandwich.

47

"My name's Virgil, Virgil Pushkin Shulman. My mother called me Virgil, but my wife says I'm Pushy."

"Bill ... Waite." How easy it was to use that invented name. "My name is Bill Waite. Thanks, Virgil."

Everyone called him Pushy, and he had accepted this, agreed to a lifetime of fun at his expense. He had dignity but could laugh at himself. An unusual combination. But he'd call this man Virgil. He'd never forget.

Virgil's eyes were examining him. Bill looked away because it could not be a good thing to let another man look at him like that, to give him the chance to look deeply into his eyes and learn certain things.

Virgil Pushkin Shulman was Jewish. Bill guessed that without ever having known a Jew. He'd known *of them* in Butte, none before that, none growing up in Oklahoma. His teacher, an old German who'd served with distinction in the Union Army, had taught him that the Jews *didn't* kill Jesus, the Romans did. Bill didn't care if they did. The sandwich that Virgil gave him was pastrami.

"Before I left for work, my little girl told me to be careful. Can you believe that—a four-year-old, already knowing so much? We give her a good home, the best we can, but she sees things we don't want her to see. The Lower East Side is not a great place for a child to grow up, especially where we live, Fourth Street east of First Avenue. Do you know that area, Bill?" Fortunately, he didn't wait for an answer before adding, "If this job works out, we might be able to afford someplace uptown, or at least Brooklyn."

Uptown? Unlike Bill, Virgil had a dream. And he had an easy way of tackling the silence between men. He could talk in a steady, entertaining way. At that moment, this was the most marvelous talent imaginable.

"But I would have mixed feelings if it came to that. The Lower East Side is the only home I've ever known. My friends are there. In fact, everyone I know is friendly, even the sharks. They joke with you then cut your throat. What would I do living someplace where the joke wasn't included?" Bill almost laughed at this. He saw the humor in things—jokes, pranks, an old lady wielding an umbrella chasing a big man down the street—but almost nothing made him laugh out loud. Some faces don't permit a laugh to escape even though it takes place inside. For the last six years, he hadn't had much use for laughter.

"And there's something grand about the place," Virgil continued. "About all of us crammed together speaking a dozen languages. Among Jews alone many languages are spoken—and sometimes understood.

"Perhaps no one else shares this thought, but I am convinced that someday historians will write a special chapter for us, telling how when humanity was ready for the Twentieth Century, we entered it through the Lower East Side. We looked around, seeing war and influenza on the horizon, and some of us wanted to go back to the Nineteenth. But that's another story . . ."

Bill grasped this thought but couldn't formulate a comment because his head was already spinning from the scene changes. From growing up in Oklahoma; then hard-rock mining all over the West; then the thing with Frank he didn't want to think about, a brutal thing that screamed at him and filled him with terror whenever he thought of it;

49

then prison and parole and a quick trip across country to New York. He'd left Montana, where the sun set on great vistas of blood-colored rock, and was now burrowing under a river with a partner who was telling him they were part of the grand march from the Nineteenth to the Twentieth.

But it didn't matter, since Orlando was standing before them, a grin blazing across his face. "Ok, gents, all good things must come to an end."

The whistling of the air began again, which made conversation impossible. But Virgil was still talking, telling another story. It was hard to follow because it began with his wife and little girl and extended back in time to something that had happened to his mother when she was a child in Russia. Something about a "pogrom." Bill had read extensively in the prison library without encountering this word. Then the friendly voice faded out as the steel door popped open and they stepped over the rubber gasket and returned to their labors and the great washing in their ears.

Back at their bulkhead he had to overcome some stiffness in his limbs but soon established a comfortable rhythm. Virgil tried to keep up. The first half is the hard part of a shift, especially the first shift of a new job. Especially the first shift under a river. Whether or not they accomplished much Bill couldn't say, but the second half flew by.

**

At two a.m. they sat in the locks again for what seemed like forever while Orlando let the air pressure drain away. His face was pale after so many hours. Orlando managed a smile, but it was no longer bright. Then he walked to the other end of the room, pressed down on a lever, and the steel door unkissed. He saluted, and with a final fading flourish waved the crew into the washroom. Their bodies were happy to be light again. One of the men jumped about like an excited spaniel among all the joyful hollerings. The men took off the coveralls they'd been given before their shift. Bill rinsed off the worst of the grime and the mud caked into the little wrinkles around his eye sockets, watched grit swirl in the basin.

His plan had been to find a park bench or train station to sleep in for a few hours and at sun-up to find a room. Out west he'd employed these hobo arts more than once. He wouldn't confess to this homeless status. A little foolish pride still left from the long-ago days when he could afford it. But if he followed Virgil, sooner or later they'd come to a suitable place to catch a few winks.

What greeted him outside was the loneliness of the city. The concrete and stone at night, the frozen rivers of tar. He didn't know where his new partner was leading him, but he was learning that Virgil could walk as fast as he could talk. Bill figured that Virgil might not want to be followed, but where else could he go?

The night air breathing over damp skin revived him. He could tell from the signs that they were still on Canal Street, passing silent shops and warehouses, walking for what seemed a long time. Then they turned left, which must have been north, up a wide street marked Second Avenue. Virgil turned and acknowledged him with a broad grin. "I guess I'm not the only sandhog headed for the Lower East Side."

The street lamps glowed white, each one a cluster of silver moths spreading their wings against the darkness, buzzing to let everyone know they were alive. They were now in a district of apartment buildings. The fronts towered overhead. But not everyone slept. From the torn shades in a few windows, whorls of yellow leaked out, thumbprints of light on the inky stillness.

From time to time Virgil made pleasant small talk to which Bill nodded. A gesture lost in the darkness.

Bill couldn't help meditating on the crowded quarters they passed through. He was impressed by the vastness of it, but it wasn't entirely new. Butte was pretty much one large mining town slum. He was familiar with this nighttime impression of silence and knew that it was a deception. All around them, the city teemed with secrets, with souls muttering and clashing, embracing. The great expanse of it was new, but the drama taking place was not. Behind these lifeless stone walls, history worked tirelessly, at war with sleep. Families had been jammed together, shared their few beds. Shared lives that may have been small to those who looked from a distance but up close were huge with misfortune, surging with hope.

The business establishments that occupied the ground floors were locked, their lights out. Iron railings fronted them, block after block. Occasionally they passed night spots half-buried down a short flight of steps. People emerged from them, smoked and laughed. Doors opened, music and voices leaped out.

"Speakeasy," Virgil said.

In 1917, when they'd thrown him in jail, many families in Butte still lived in shacks. Although some lived in tenements a few stories high, none lived stacked like this, story above story. Not a few neighborhoods in Butte lacked plumbing whereas all the buildings in New York had indoor pipes, water faucets and flush closets, or so he'd heard. But did these advantages mean a better life? The walls told him that in these buildings people sweated in the summer heat. Young couples caressed in the corner of a family room, afraid to whisper or breathe. He was doing his best to absorb this new silence stretching river to river across an island of towering stone that concealed people fighting and embracing and hushing babies.

Virgil stopped at the corner of Second Avenue and Fourth Street and tilted his head into the blaze of a streetlamp. Two furrows ran across his brow. The city was holding its breath as he weighed his words.

"You don't have any place to stay tonight, do you, Bill?"

The buildings looked down on a man who had no place to stay.

"I thought I'd stay with friends . . ."

"You can stop at my apartment. If Rosie bought a quart of beer, we'll have a chat. If she didn't, we'll have a chat anyway."

"You're sure it's ok? I'm not dressed very good."

"You're dressed the same as me. If we were rich men in fine clothes, we might have no one to talk to."

Virgil led him across a broad intersection to the opposite corner, where he paused in the blaze of another streetlamp. "You'll meet my wife Rosie."

2.

They walked down Fourth Street sidestepping piles of rubbish, scooped-out rinds. The smell of rotten fruit plus the heavy odor of foul meat hung in the warm night. Unpleasant, but who hasn't smelled worse and never said a word about it?

Street lamps lit scorched facades. Everything was hemmed-in, shadows of tall buildings walled by more shadows, giving this street the feel of the exercise yard of a prison. The facades were seven stories high. Bill counted them, like a prisoner gauging the difficulty of escape. Each had a black-iron fire escape, a fretwork rising into a starless night. The imprisoning walls caused a moment of fright. He'd never get used to the cramped life of this place, he thought to himself.

There was more going on here, on Fourth Street, than on Second Avenue. A surprising amount considering it was after two a.m. As he got used to the surroundings Bill could see figures lounging under streetlamps, moving in a slow nighttime rhythm. On one stoop, four men played cards; on another, two studied chess moves. They faced each other, holding the black and white figures on a board balanced level on touching knees. Just beyond that, at another entrance, two women lounged on the steps and a man in rolled-up sleeves stood above them, smoking.

"Whorehouse," Virgil hissed out of the side of his mouth. That was a topic Bill knew something about. No copper miner would lack at least a passing acquaintance with such places. Alluring lights, plushness going to seed, hard eyes of the women. This whorehouse was not a house at all but stairs and a summer night and, somewhere above, an apartment where a Victrola played soft music.

At the middle of the block Virgil snapped his fingers and sprang like a boy up a flight of steps. Bill followed through a propped door into a tiled vestibule ablaze with the light from a hanging bulb. After the decay of the street, this hallway seemed bright, antiseptically clean. At the end was a staircase glistening like marble. Bill could see now that the stone visible everywhere in this city wasn't always soot-gray. Here, it was white and full of soft blue striations. Maybe it was limestone or just superbly mixed cement. The stones rang. Their boots echoed off each bright step. At the fourth-floor landing they paused for a breath.

"The atmosphere is lighter this high up," Virgil panted. "Hard to catch your breath when you're used to our river-heavy brand."

After mounting two more flights they approached a door on which was nailed a tarnished tin sign, 6B. This number would become very familiar, but at that moment Bill hardly had a chance to glimpse it before the door was opened violently from the inside. A woman stood in the doorway, shaking her black hair, full of rage. She was a pretty woman, but that wasn't Bill's initial impression, which was sheer terror.

"You're alive." She glared from the shadows of the apartment. "Tomorrow, if you go to work in that place under the water, I'll be true to my word. This door will be locked against you."

On seeing Bill, her black eyes narrowed suspiciously, but she held her ground.

"Rosie, I'd like you to meet Bill. He's worked at more dangerous jobs and swears he can keep me alive. I'm in good hands." Virgil's voice may have quavered before regaining his articulate mettle.

Bill couldn't remember having this conversation about his other jobs, but from the way Virgil grinned and gestured, he knew enough to come to his aid with reassuring words, or try to, before she cut him off.

"I don't know who this Bill is, but he will have his hands full, because my husband is a real *shlimazl*." Shlimazl sounded like a made-up word, although the meaning wasn't hard to guess.

"This job is one of the safest I've worked on, and Virgil is a great partner. He gave me one of your delicious sandwiches."

When Bill offered his hand, she studied it for a moment, like she was going to spit in her own hand first as people out west sometimes did. But she seized it with surprising strength, imparting a rapid pressure to the meat between forefinger and thumb. Through dry callouses, the warm blood of the two hands met.

"And if some day my husband doesn't come home safe, I'll know who to kill with my bare hands."

So a pledge had been struck: to keep an awkward man safe. Flinging himself down six flights of steps entered Bill's mind, but Virgil held up his hand in an effort at reassurance. "Don't worry, Rosie is only this fierce on first making an acquaintance. She likes to establish who's boss. I'm sure you have no doubt who that is."

Before Bill could respond she seized his arm and pulled him into the apartment. "For a strong man, this work might come easy," she said, squeezing his bicep. "But my Virgil has never done such work."

"He's a good worker, Mrs. Shulman."

"I'm Rosie. Now sit in our armchair."

He did as he was told and stared around the small room, small for a kitchen, even smaller when doubling as a sitting room. The plaster walls gave an impression of height because of the ornamental cornices. Lovely interiors, a trace of old-world charm incongruous in a tenement. Walls and ceiling were a brilliant white, lit by a single bulb hanging by a gnarled cord from the middle of the kitchen ceiling. This room was connected to a dark front room, where a breeze lifted gauzy curtains. The fringe at the bottom floated and fell on the warm night air. Under the night's soft breath a little girls slept. Sylvie was her name, about whom Virgil had spoken so proudly while they'd had lunch. The first thing Virgil would do on entering the apartment was to go into the darkness of that room and kiss the sleeping girl's forehead. A kiss, even a soft one, is loud when you know it's coming.

The breeze and the darkness of the other room put Bill in a peaceful mood. A narrow window in the kitchen opened to an airshaft. The easy chair was in the cross-breeze. The air came to him filtered by the length of the apartment, delicious, cooling.

Virgil reached into a cabinet with warped veneer doors and a heavy steel latch. One more lock in a night of latches and air-tight seals. A cork popped. The beer was cold.

"The safety procedures are elaborate." Virgil began. Then he outlined the process they'd gone through that day beginning with the physicals. "I passed with flying colors. I am ideally suited for this work. We spend our shift in a balloon of safety. Our job is more like working in an office than underground."

"That's true, Rosie," Bill chimed in, right on cue. He suspected that his voice lacked conviction, for he was tired, had traveled nearly 2,000 miles and spent a shift under a river. In this new life, lies would be frequent. But he'd told enough for one day. He wanted only to relax and enjoy the kindness of the beer. Rosie, however, was not done.

"Where did you learn to do such work?"

She was setting a trap for him with her probing. "I worked in Pennsylvania," he stammered, knowing there were mines in that state. Right away, he regretted this answer because he didn't have one blessed bit of knowledge about Pennsylvania or the type of mines it contained. He knew how to tell a lie, to a degree, but only to other liars. Bosses, jailers, cops. Honest people are hard to lie to. He imagined the guilty look on his face as he waited for her to continue the cross-examination.

"The husband of a friend worked in anthracite mines, not far from New York City. Is that where you worked, Bill?"

"No, Rosie," Virgil broke in. "Bill is from the western part of the state, Greene County." His voice was authoritative. Even Bill believed that's where he was from.

"But the two of us have already answered enough questions for one day. They wanted to know the strangest personal details when they hired us. Of what concern to a giant company is the functioning of my bowels?"

This last remark subdued her curiosity, at least for now. The way he'd jumped in amazed Bill. If Rosie were watching, she'd have seen his mouth drop open. Very deftly, Virgil had started something, the process of fabricating a safe and plausible identity. Bill was from *Green* County, named for the color. What a pretty name! He was later to learn the spelling was *Greene*. It was far enough away that he wouldn't encounter anyone in New York who knew the place. Was it a real place? No doubt the countryside was green, with steep hills and a dark river. He'd grown up there, on his parent's small farm. After a shift in the mines—they would have been coal mines, hard and dirty work, for sure—he'd toss out a line and stare across the river, across the rail tracks and into a steep hillside full of trees that almost blotted out the sun. Did they have prohibition beer? Would he have been able to afford it? Amazing the questions that occur once you start to invent.

Rosie didn't believe a word. But Virgil was carrying the conversation, smoothing over questions, putting a humorous coloration on the day's events beginning with the chubby barker, "who was so out of shape, he wiped off his face and panted after a two-block walk, beaming at us like he thought a throng of honest working men should be proud of him.

"I wonder how much they paid him to tell us about a job he'd never done," Virgil offered. "He had the gift of gab but wouldn't know a day's work if it sat down beside him and ordered a pastrami sandwich and a cold beer." Rosie smiled although she'd no doubt heard such a turn of phrase before. Emotions passed over her face, a loving smile, a suspicious glare.

Bill studied Rosie as she laughed, as she took a breath and exhaled slowly, the soft air from her lungs entering the stillness of apartment 6B. It was probably then, as she relaxed, that he noticed how pretty she was, with hair like the forested hills of Greene County, rolling, dark with shadows. She turned toward her husband when he told a joke, with a mischievous grin. She was used to his sense of humor, including the predictable jokes, and delighted in groaning at it. All the while, her brown eyes studied her husband and his new friend. She warmed to their talk of a new job, a new world opening up. But she was being generous with them. Bill didn't know much about poor women except that they were suspicious. Suspicion is one of the threads that holds life together. Tug at it too hard, and the entire fabric comes undone.

**

That night—early morning, actually—he fell into a sleep full of images of the Wide West. He woke from this restlessness and drifted into a deep sleep in which he dreamed of himself as a fifteen-year old, leaving home in

61

Oklahoma, searching for work in the West with his brother. He dreamed of that laboring boy who'd grown into a man and disappeared. On the other side of the earth, more than 2,000 miles away, a man climbed from a chasm in time and entered a city teeming with rapid talk where millions of lives would shield him from pursuit, from Arnoldson's fury.

Would that Oklahoma boy even recognize the man he was about to become?

Dressed in the skin of a new life, he awoke to his first morning in New York City.

**

The heaviness in his muscles told him of the long night spent under a river. He had a job, a hard job, and he'd enjoyed a cold beer afterward. And he had a friend. And Rosie, could he count her as a friend also? He was in their apartment, rolling over on a small bed, opening his eyes. There, glued so close their noses almost touched, were the eyes of a little girl.

"Sylvie, stop staring," Rosie's quick, commanding whisper hissed out.

Do children really have the features of their parents? Even a skinny child has a pudginess about the face that no adult has, a turned-up nose when the mother's is narrow—and children never have the prominent chins of their parents. But this child had the sharp, laughing eyes of her mother.

Bill had slept in yesterday's clothes on top of the covers. He apologized.

"You're a great deal of trouble, Bill Waite," Rosie responded with a grin. "Personally, I don't see what Pushy sees in you. Keeping him alive for a night—if that's what you did—well, that's something. I'm not sure what, but it *is* something."

The little girl grinned ear to ear, shaking like a puppy with excitement over a new playmate. Not knowing how else to respond, he rubbed the top of her head.

She took his hand in two of hers and kissed it.

"Now, even the little girl wants to keep you," said Rosie. "Lucky stray."

She shook her head in a theatrical mime of disgust then burst out in a commanding voice. "Everybody up, we have a busy morning. Bill, drink some coffee and look lively."

Bill stared searchingly about the room. "In the hallway," Rosie responded to the unspoken question. Out there he found a small closet with a commode. He came back into the apartment and washed his hands in the kitchen sink.

"Take a gulp and let me introduce you to an important person."

At the door— practically under his nose—stood a tiny woman with a wrinkled face and rounded shoulders. His first impression was that she was fragile. First impressions of old women are almost always false.

"Mrs. Hollowczek is the Building Super of 145 Fourth Street. They don't honor her with the title because a Super is supposed to be a man. But she's the Super."

Mrs. Hollowczek beamed at Rosie but her face was all business when she turned toward Bill. "Basement room—is yours if you want."

He trudged the seven flights down to examine the room, down the white stone stairways, bright and clean. But below the ground floor was a cavern of shadows and dust. A slip of light from the airshaft entered through a high half-window, dimly revealing a concrete floor covered with flaking brown paint, a janitor's sink in the hallway, and another closet for a toilet. The closet had no door but was private enough, since it was obvious that no one ever came down there, and the building employed no janitor to get in the way.

With the help of her tenants, Mrs. Hollowczek kept the building clean—except for the basement. The trash on the floors had been there a long time. But it wouldn't take much to clean it up. He was trying to convince himself that he liked it. But that effort wasn't necessary, since he didn't have much choice. She hadn't offered him a key because there was no lock and no door. That might present a safety issue if his whereabouts were known. But who would know to look here for James Little alias Bill Waite? Door jambs without a door might be an open invitation to burglary, if he had any belongings.

Back upstairs he had to catch his breath. Even a man used to a strenuous life puffs after seven flights.

"It's just what I need. But I can't pay until Friday."

Rosie was not impressed by his enthusiasm, and Mrs. Hollowczek seemed skeptical as well. "Will be cold in winter," she grunted. "I try to find better place for you then."

From these words it could be gleaned that the hard life that had lined her face hadn't snuffed all compassion. It was under the surface and not available to all comers.

"It's a start. No doubt you'll move up in the world," Virgil laughed with a trace of self-consciousness, which stemmed from an awareness that no one else would laugh. Or would try not to laugh. Sometimes the effort not to laugh might make people break out in laughter. People who loved him.

But Sylvie could always be counted on to bark out a little girl's laughter. Maybe a day would come when she also would roll her eyes.

Bill borrowed broom, mop, and bucket, which he filled with scalding water, over and over. Out west he'd never known such hot water. It erupted from the faucet and steamed in the basement sink. With each pass he made over the floor, more scum dissolved. He emptied the bucket and watched the gum and grit gurgle down the drain. Traces from who knows what inhabitants, human or otherwise. How many years had these remnants been drying there before he put a wet mop to them? He rung out the gray fibers and swept the dry mop back and forth until only a few damp spots shone on the floor. The morning was hot and close. Even in this cool, underground shelter he'd worked up a sweat. The shirt stuck to his back. He stank but had no clean clothes to change into and no money to buy any. That was not the only worry, but it was the one on his mind just then.

He would still have plenty of strength for afternoon shift. Funny, he thought, how this same weary feeling in his muscles was enjoyable today, whereas on Arnoldson's farm he'd felt taxed, a sad beast. And the more he'd obeyed Arnoldson's orders the greater the burden. He was a laboring beast, picking weeds, repairing fences, or tending to milk cows—he had the hogs to watch out for as well, but they're never much trouble.

"I'm not a hard man to please," Arnoldson had told him. "And if I approve of you, certain privileges apply." Arnoldson had approved of his work, and this gave him the thought that he was changing Bill "for the better." But that was the thing Bill could never accept. There is no such thing as honest work under the scruples of someone who wants to change you. Wants to erase what *you consider you:* He sensed that, to Arnoldson, any spark of anger would constitute the ultimate provocation. Jacob Arnoldson surveyed all of creation and noted that it was pliable and could be made obedient to his will. Obedient, or else.

Bill paused, a fist wrapped around the mop handle, to recall another incident. He was in the barn cleaning manure from the stalls, shoveling it into a barrel he'd placed on the wagon. The wheels rested on the packed earth, wood rims deep in filthy straw. He had to scoop up the mess and hoist it overhead into the barrel. With each heavy shovelful the hard frame bounced and the vibration was conveyed through the whole wagon to the tongue and the harness of the old mare. Arnoldson hadn't named her, so Bill just called her "Horse." When it was full, he'd tap Horse on the croup and together they'd spread the load in a section of field that needed fertilizing. Horse often made spur-of-the-moment additions to this undertaking. Not the most exciting way to spend an afternoon, but not the worst Bill had ever known. He'd just swung another scoop of it up and heard the soft *thump* as it landed in the barrel, almost full now, when a voice broke into the rhythm of the work, the peaceful tedium of it.

"See how he works." How long had Arnoldson been watching him? He and two other men had stolen into the adjacent stall and were staring over the planks, eyes glued to him like he was a rare specimen.

"These men have heard about you. They wondered why I treat you so good. So I thought I'd bring them out here so they could watch you work for a spell." Arnoldson's treatment of him wasn't "so good." He didn't whip Bill like he did Horse, which might have been what he meant. He bowed his head and continued to work, since apparently it was a great pleasure for these men to see someone fill a manure barrel.

As the three men turned to leave, Bill overheard Arnoldson's voice fading out: "See how even-tempered he is? You could watch him all day long and he'd never get riled."

Something about that incident awaited an explanation.

**

A knock shook him from this reverie. Rosie, rapping at the door jamb, dark eyes glistening in the half-light. She smiled. Apparently, her attitude toward him was softening. She clutched several boxes to her blouse, to the soft rise and fall of her breathing.

The blouse was a fine thing with a neckband of shimmering beadwork. An ornate, old-world touch, like the fine cornices in the apartments.

"I bring gifts." Her hands were warm as she unloaded the boxes into his, a brief touch reminding him that apart from shaking her hand the night before he hadn't felt a woman's skin in many years.

She drew his attention back to the boxes. "These are weapons for the all-out and endless war you will be waging against the enemy of the poor. Jews and Gentiles alike, we are all afflicted."

Bill smiled, showing that he appreciated the roundaboutness. Conversation with her might require some guesswork. Was this the way all people in New York spoke?

"Look out!" One crossed within an inch of your boot. You should have crushed him and rubbed his slimy guts all over your clean floor. Now he'll live to make love all night and sire five billion ugly and unsanitary children. You have lost your first battle. But don't worry, man, you'll have many more!"

He did not tell her that he'd already lost more than enough battles. Maybe she already knew.

She showed him how to mix the contents of the boxes into a paste and dab it around the edges of the room. "Dynamite won't kill roaches but boric acid will—often will—sometimes will," she laughed, more like a playful little sister than the skeptic he'd met the night before.

As a miner he'd become adept at mixing black powder and blasting the ribs of the earth. Now he was mixing white paste in a dented bucket.

"Put some up there." She pointed to a shallow horizontal alcove above the door. She must have examined the room on an earlier occasion, because this hollow in the wall was not clearly visible, especially to someone coming into the room through the doorway below it. It didn't exist and then, where she pointed, it did. He'd mopped the floor several times and never noticed, but apparently Rosie didn't miss much.

"Make sure to cover your perimeters, unless you want armies in combat formation all over your bedding. Take these clean clothes. Pushy is not built exactly like you, but at least they'll mostly cover your bones. And wash up. Mrs. H and I could smell you seven floors up."

She left him to this battle plan. Earlier, Virgil had given him a sheet and quilt, which would at least soften the floor. Bill was clean and refreshed by the time Virgil's knuckle bones tapped on the jamb at 2:30 in the afternoon.

As they trudged west down Fourth Street toward Second Avenue, the afternoon sun revealed the wonders of the Lower East Side. He gazed upward through what appeared to be billowing sails, sheets and other washed laundry hung up to dry on lines ingeniously rigged between buildings, spanning the busy street.

He noticed the two identical packages Virgil was carrying, both wrapped in oil paper and twine.

"Rosie has prepared a kosher lunch for you. After our first paycheck we can buy meals on the way to work."

"Will we be able to find kosher food?"

"Why would we want to," Virgil asked. "There's a saying, if it tastes good, it must not be kosher."

A weighty meal, Bill thought, as he hefted the package Virgil had handed him. And probably a good meal, no matter what his partner said. The prospects of a night's work were brightened by a meal. And a friend. They turned at Second Avenue and walked briskly south down a sidewalk busy with shoppers. Old women toiled with small carts full of goods, blouses wet under their arms. Fruit and vegetable stands crowded the sidewalks. The green and red colors of the produce were arranged in little pyramids on the tops of upended barrels. Awnings protected the goods from the sun. Heavyset men with arms folded above their aprons had an eye out for thieves. To a quick glance, the fruit looked quite good. Where did it come from? Where did they have the gardens to feed a city like this?

The basement speakeasies were in the shadows, behind stoops and railings. These cellars beckoned, cool on a sticky afternoon. And the beer would taste good. All around them, men in business suits sweated as they moved in and out of offices, some of which had signs with peculiar characters consisting of wavy lines.

"That's Yiddish for *bank.*" Virgil stopped for a moment, like a tour guide before a point of interest. "You'll see and hear that language around here. Hebrew is different but looks similar. You'll encounter that language in Jewish schools. I grew up hearing Yiddish, so I understand it. But I never studied Hebrew, although many poor little souls can't pass beyond childhood without having to learn it. 'Why, Virgil Pushkin,' my father used to ask. 'You'll live a long time, God willing, and when you die will it matter to you if you can't read the Hebrew letters on your stone.'

"Those words mean sewing factory." Virgil pointed to a narrow building that didn't look like a factory. A smaller sign below it read *Cohen Bros, Men's Shirts.* "I used to work there. I'm a pattern maker by trade, but they cut way back on new patterns. The old days of custom work and good craftsmanship are a thing of the past. The Lower East Side alone is losing hundreds of sewing jobs a year."

"For me, I don't care so much." They'd stopped for a moment by the entrance to a building that looked like any other tenement. "I could live on a pickle for lunch and a raw onion for dinner and for entertainment a good belch would suffice. But I want a little better for Sylvie."

Virgil waved a greeting to three young women who'd just come out of the shop and were standing on the steps. A patch of afternoon sun caught one as she peeled a work smock up over her head. The blouse under it rose up, exposing a slender midsection. Bill stared. She giggled when she met his eyes, slowly pulling the blouse down. She tucked the smock under her arm and waved gaily at the two men.

This sewing factory was not like any factory he'd seen. It was located in an apartment building like the one Virgil and Rosie—and now he—lived in. How could the floors take the pounding of factory machines? Wouldn't the vibrations break mortar loose and crack plaster? What about the danger from fire? These questions didn't seem to concern his quick-striding friend. Or so he thought then.

"One day I worked around the corner from home, in a busy neighborhood, in a shop full of Jewish women. The next afternoon I'm under the Hudson River, breaking my

71

back with Irish and Italian laborers, and with those black fellows, wherever they're from."

**

As the shifts passed, Bill was growing used to Orlando's round smile, was buying into the way he fussed with latches and valves. He no longer felt he was being cast into a tomb when the steel door sealed behind him. Familiarity breeds acceptance. This is the rule for hazardous jobs, so long as one lives long enough for it to apply. But the grinning gatekeeper had gradually convinced Bill, after much initial skepticism, that he was a reliable guardian. He had a big ego. That was obvious. Shouldn't someone who holds so many lives in his hands take himself pretty seriously?

Like veterans, he and Virgil descended the stairs each shift, understanding the work a little better, learning the peculiar surroundings and beginning to recognize the faces of more and more coworkers. Although as soon as they got used to someone, he might be replaced by another and quickly by another, the turnover was that great. In time they got to know several of the men who worked on the platform above them, very senior men: surveyors, blasters and their helpers; and Bill had introduced himself to Lorenzo, one of the black men who worked on the scaffolding at the other end. Close up Lorenzo was short enough. High overhead, with one of the oversized wrenches he hoisted, he was a tiny and slow-moving toy.

The area they worked in was more than double the size of the tunnel that would one day convey vehicles under the river. The final architecture was not explained to them, but they gathered that a shell within a shell was involved, with a space in between for electrical cables, and a walkway for maintenance or emergencies. What shaped the tunnel from the primordial mush of the riverbed was a giant circular steel shield that was pressed forward inch by inch like a giant cookie cutter, only powered by pneumatic pumps instead of a housewife's firm hand. As this pressure was exerted on the face of the tunnel works, mush squirted out in great sausage shapes and was carried away by conveyors or fell on the floor to be shoveled in carts. But some of the tunnel face could only be removed by brute force, since boulders and beds of rock were often encountered. Men hacked away and set charges as they would in a mine.

Once, a skull was found in the muck. Was it the remains of the ancient Dutch or the even more ancient native people, pressed by the centuries, deeper and deeper into the riverbed? A rumor gained circulation that a crime gang was paying sandhogs to hide the bodies of its victims. A columnist for *The Daily News* pounced on this rumor and reported it as fact:

SANDHOGS DOUBLE AS CRIME GANG UNDERTAKERS

Laborers are finding that Boss Holland's engineering boondoggle provides a convenient final resting place for victims of organized crime. These fellows—sturdy and grunting—may lack education but they have the brains to recognize a lucrative payoff when they see it. According to reliable sources, the laborers are loath to shed any sweat on tunnel work because they consider they're funereal sideline

as a more remunerative priority. At shift
change they leave the tunnel in felt hats
and Brooks Brothers suits. A list of sandhog laborers reveals that fully 75 percent
sport Italian last names.

Virgil found this column and read it out to them at
lunch, causing more amusement than indignation.

To hold off the multimillion-ton river, air-pressure
puffed up their work chamber. But too much pressure would
result in blowouts that shot up through the river bottom.
The water spouts were visible from the shore, some powerful enough to disrupt ship travel. A cave-in might occur
from too little or too much pressure and would mean they
had to climb to an upper level, above a steel safety curtain,
and hope the water stopped there. As the work progressed,
great steel ribs were bolted into place to secure the works.
This fastening was done by the iron men like Lorenzo who
turned giant wrenches atop high scaffolding.

Crews had also started from New Jersey, toiling at the
face of a great tube that was the mirror image of the one
Bill and Virgil worked in. Shift after shift, day and night,
they worked toward each other from portals that began a
mile and a half apart. Would this rough labor follow the
precise sketches on the engineers' drawing boards? Would
the two faces meet and kiss? As newspaper readers held
their breath, sandhogs slogged and clambered in heavy air.
When the kiss occurred, they'd be out of a job.

**

By the third week, he and Virgil were already the senior members of the crew. Young, strong men worked a day or a week under the river and left for a job with worse pay. Either they got a touch of bends or they couldn't take the strenuous work, the filth, the heavy air. They'd rather be iron workers, toiling above the city, watching miniature autos creeping so far below that the horn honks could not be heard. Or meatpackers shivering in a locker. One job they would have jumped on was street cleaner, someone who cleaned up after horses. But that job had been pretty much phased out. A handful of delivery and haulage work was still done in the old way, but gasoline engines had replaced most of the horses.

Bill's main concern was for Virgil, whose body had never been toughened by hard physical labor. And this work was hard, even for Bill. But his partner was determined, straining to hoist each shovelful, always near exhaustion, toiling through pain and injury.

In truth, Bill was a worrier, a trait which he seldom betrayed. He had a flat poker face, rarely the hint of a smile at the corners of his mouth. Calm is what it expressed, contrary to what was going on inside him. And in his life there had been much to worry about. No longer quite so concerned with Arnoldson's pursuit, he could devote much of his worrying to the welfare of his new friend.

He remembered what Rosie had said and didn't doubt that she would be capable of killing him with her bare hands. He'd steal a glance at him in the act of plunging a shovel into a drift of brown muck. Somehow Virgil always knew when Bill was looking his way and would glance up with that "what-the-hell" attempt at a grin.

The work was hard but the shifts seemed to fly by. On the first Monday of their third week, they climbed down to their level, below the platform at the face, a little less frightened by the shadows dancing against the mud and rock walls. The topic of a sandhog's health and safety seldom came up when people talked about the tunnel. What people discussed was Mr. Holland, the brilliant engineer. Without doubt, he had a vision. And he fought for it with all the strength in his prematurely decrepit body. He and the other guiding lights stressed the most advanced engineering. Blueprints and paperwork would guarantee safety. Learned men had formulated a complex underwater environment. It was the wonder of the entire world. If sandhogs felt terror it was because they were not sufficiently educated, not sufficiently trusting in the science.

Sandhogs were an afterthought. And if no one else worried about their safety, why should they? Unless you had a partner, someone for whom you felt responsibility. That buddy provided you with an excuse to fret, to make extra sure, on his account, that the pressure was not being reduced too quickly or to concern yourself that the blasting was being done by men who knew their trade. It wasn't for yourself that you worried but for your partner. This was a mutual thing, a caring that had saved many lives. Good engineering is necessary. But the only truly failsafe equipment is the human heart.

It was for Virgil's sake that Bill was so observant. He'd learned to be watchful in the mines, and in the tunnel he was known as a stickler for safety.

**

Virgil and Bill headed for their conveyor and the sausage of muck flowing onto it. Their work gleamed under the arc lights, long and swirling and sloppy with river water. Subterranean slime—but to them of great value. Job security takes many forms and is jealously treasured. Giant pastries and pastas of mud swirled around them. Another night, another shift in this panorama of nightmarish, brown ugliness. They prepared themselves to wage war against the great weight of the night, to ply shovels, to pit muscles against mud and heavy air and mighty inertia.

It was Virgil who noticed first that a new fellow had gotten no further than the second level and was sitting on the first step below the safety curtain. A shabby little fellow, head in hands. Virgil walked back to him and touched his shoulder, but this little act of concern didn't seem to help. The figure turned away and started back up the stairs, on all fours, like a toddler. He climbed to the top, by the door to the locks, and leaned on a red mushroom of plastic with all his weight. This was the panic button, and it sounded within Orlando's air lock. The fellow leaned on it again and again, while Orlando was within, hurrying to align the atmospheres.

Bill stood next to Virgil, staring at the boy-like figure. He could not have been seventeen, looked younger. Obviously not cut out for this work. No matter how well it paid. No matter how hungry his family was. What could the rest of the crew do? The fellow had rejected Virgil's kindness. He had made his decision. The crew began returning to work. Bill was resigned, like everyone else, until he looked more closely at the boy and imagined the defeat and shame he would feel. He saw himself at fifteen, first entering the mines. He'd been terrified not only at the dangerous new world but to be among rugged men accustomed to danger, who'd proven themselves many times over in the battle against fear. Back then, hadn't his brother and a few others helped him? Bill climbed the stairs and put his hand under the boy's chin and turned his face up. The boy didn't resist. The weight of his head rested in Bill's hand like the skull of a dead creature. Then their eyes met.

"We're all frightened down here," is what Bill whispered, although the exact words may have been lost amid the reverberating terrors of the night. But the lad understood enough of the message to gain heart. Bill braced the poor skinny boy in his arms and coaxed him down the stairs.

At the bottom, he presented him with a shovel. This work was weird, but after a while it was just work. They began to shovel, while Virgil moved to another work area. High overhead, Orlando peered out of the locks, looking for someone to rescue. Seeing no one there, the door sealed shut and the round face with the wide smile was gone.

Bill fell into the rhythm of another shift, one eye always on the new fellow, whose name was Michael. A new friend was a good thing. And so was a good deed. Out of the great swirl of recent events, the 2,000-mile trek into an unexpected life, Bill had come to doubt that he had any character at all. He didn't think of himself as either praise- or blame- worthy. Certainly not deserving of praise. That was true especially since he was starting this new life with a clean slate. But now, with a good deed under his belt he could be reassured. If he would have left the boy on the steps, it would have been reassuring also, but of something else.

And no doubt Michael was a good friend to have. He lived quite a bit west of the Lower East Side, almost as far as Eighth Avenue. Not such a bad area. But Michael and his aunt shared a tiny apartment. Did that mean his parents were dead? Bill had been learning that while the Jews and the Irish mixed it up quite a bit, and generally got along, they held fast to certain ideas about each other. These ideas didn't get in the way of friendships, but when an unkind act was required, a hurtful idea is a handy weapon for your arsenal. About the Irish it was the idea that they were all corrupt and politically connected: cop on the beat, union boss, city politician. They might appear poor on the outside but by virtue of Tammany connections they had a ladder to success; for Jews, financial ruthlessness was their ladder to success. Italians also figured in, for they had a ladder as well, and it was the scariest one of all: the language they shared with the Sicilian crime families.

To look at Michael, however, was to disprove this lad- der theory. Somewhere in his family tree was a political connection, but he himself was a poor lamb not much able to benefit himself let alone his friends.

3.

The August heat pressed down on the city, heavy sheets of humid air stapled in place by skyscrapers, nailed fast by stone and concrete. He returned after midnight to a cool basement room. He'd scavenged cushions and more bedding from trash left on the curb. And other treasures, including a soiled plate and mug he'd washed four times and washed again. The bedding was dusty and worn but didn't seem infested with bedbugs. Not at first glance, but this was the Lower East Side. He lay on the floor, dreaming on piled quilts that someone else had once dreamed on. Why should the fact that they were well-used have bothered him? He was no better than any man, woman, or child. No better than the previous owner.

He'd gotten used to the idea that at work a wide river flowed above his head. Barges and even large ships plied these waters and sounded lonely horns in the darkness. Although he'd become more confident in the operation of the locks and the bubble of pressurized air they spent their shifts in, confidence is relative. He didn't dwell on the doubts. He had work to do. You can't worry about the way of the world.

Now, he had two men to look out for: Virgil, the *klutz*—the term Rosie frequently employed to describe her husband; and Michael, the Irish boy they'd rescued from the top of the stairs.

"You're a great man for this work," the boy stated, as they ate lunch together the following day. Bill was glad for another ally and friend but didn't need the admiration. Buried in it was an inquiry—how had you gained this experience?

Virgil was always there to guide the conversation: "He worked in the coal mines of western Pennsylvania and knows enough about this kind of work to write a book. But he's modest and will never speak of it, so let him be."

Michael concluded that Bill Waite was a quiet and private fellow. But not at all stupid. Since he ate the same food as Mr. Shulman, he might be Jewish. But didn't he have the wide face and high cheekbones of one of those Bohunks who lived around Pittsburgh?

Michael cleared his throat, like he'd been wanting to say something for a long time and finally got up the nerve. "Mr. Shulman, do you have a Jewish name—I mean, how come some Jews have names that don't sound Jewish, like Wolfe and others have names like Goldberg...."

"Michael, are all Irish boys named Sean Kelly and the girls Meghan? I'm not so sure we'd be better off if you could tell a fellow's family background instantly from the name. There's a joke about Jewish names that illustrates my point." At the word joke Michael flashed a grin. Virgil had fallen for the bait.

"Have you heard the one about Ben Goldberg?" With these words a hush came over the lunchroom. "He was sitting in a bar beside a blond-haired English fellow. Goldberg introduced himself, and the English fellow started to do the same but only got as far as his first name, Alexander, when this Ben Goldberg hit him in the nose. 'Ouch!' Alexander said, 'what was that for?' 'That was because of all the suffering under the Russian czar,' Goldberg replied. 'But my family is English and has nothing to do with Czar Alexander.' So, the Jewish fellow apologized and introduced himself and they returned to their beers, until the English fellow squares off and slugs Goldberg even harder. 'That was for the Titanic,' he says. 'But I had nothing to do with that! The Titanic hit an iceberg," Goldberg moaned, rubbing his nose. To which Alexander responds, 'Iceberg, Goldberg, what's the difference.' "

A low groan broke out from the rest of the crew.

"You see," Virgil continued, unfazed, "names can mislead us into foolish and harmful actions."

"I get the point, and I agree with it," said Petey, an Italian fellow sitting at the other end of the room. "And not all Italians are named Tony or Sal. But, Virgil, if one of us hits you in the nose it won't be because you have a Jewish last name—it will be because of jokes like that."

**

What no sandhog got used to was the great weight he worked under and the exhaustion before sleep. Each muscle distended. Arms and legs liquefied. This was not a bad feeling for Bill, not entirely, this total exhaustion. It distracted him from the image that sometimes haunted him, a shadowy figure with huge shoulders, trailing him through the darkness of Fourth Street after his shift, appearing for a moment under a streetlight, ducking down a basement stairway. As a parole boss, Arnoldson inspired fear, but there was something else about the man that made Bill cringe, and he didn't know exactly what it was.

Bill had first encountered Arnoldson on a day that began auspiciously enough, if a day in prison can be described as auspicious.

"Brush your hair, and don't dawdle," the guard had said. He was a little daft but friendlier than the rest of the guards. He stood in the doorway, fists on hips, grinning like a monkey.

Bill's hair was black and coarse and didn't need brushing.

They walked past a row of cells identical to his own. Peering from each was a man who lived in shadows, a curious man. He knew some of these men, shared a forbidden word over meals, but many he didn't know. By the time they entered A-200, the corridor that connected his cellblock to the offices at the front of the prison, he was smiling, thinking the news couldn't be bad. For a man serving a life sentence the only bad news was the hole, and he was not being thrown in the hole. After six years and several visits to it, he knew how to avoid that place.

He was a savvy prisoner, which is what all prisoners think. They paused outside the warden's office. The guard gave him a gentle push across the threshold. Once inside the room, his eyes adjusted to the light, a few rays on the broad back of Warden Middleton. The warden had one hip on the desk and was talking to another man. Middleton knew Bill was there but didn't turn toward him. The striking thing about the other man was the shoulders. They overshadowed the warden. That and the hands extending from his shirt like large claws, red and tough. But there was something else in the man, maybe in the eyes, that made even Middleton afraid of him. The warden kept rubbing his chin and nodding at everything the huge man said.

Bill wasn't supposed to listen to them and tried not to. Then they stopped talking and began studying him. Head bowed, hands clasped behind back, breathing. Around men like that, sometimes even breathing was considered an offense. The warden was an office man, but this other man was hard and sun-darkened. Bill avoided their eyes because he didn't want them to see into his own, see the hope that had risen there. Didn't want them to know he was at their mercy. He'd always been at the warden's mercy, but more so now, as he stood at attention waiting to hear their news. He looked down on the shiny desk, at the circle of light from the lamp with the leather shade. The tray on the left was empty, the one on the right held several papers awaiting pickup. The rest of the desk was clear of everything except a green blotter. The warden had no real business, except the lives of 400 men.

The air held a fragrance. Lemon oil, a good, sharp smell, a remnant of toil. Every morning a convict rubbed the wood with a chamois cloth. The air had been whetted like a blade.

"This here's my friend Jacob Arnoldson." The warden had fat cheeks, even plumper now as he grinned with his news. "You'll work on his farm. He's your new boss. Do as he says and you have nothing to fear."

Bill stood there, dumbfounded, for what seemed a century.

"Sir, may I ask a question?" The warden nodded. "Am I released on parole?"

"Maybe," Middleton answered, still with the grin.

He got no contract with binding language awaiting his signature and the date. No asterisk after the word free with a note about what that little word meant, as determined by the state of Montana. Warden Middleton didn't shake hands and wish him luck, so the daft guard couldn't. Neither did this man Arnoldson shake hands. The rough hands would've clamped down like a vice.

Middleton's attitude on that day alerted Bill to watch his step around this man. What else did he learn about Arnoldson? That total obedience was required. Obedience was something Bill could do. At least for a little while.

**

His past had been a parade ground, flat as a pancake, where he was visible to all, his every move available for inspection and comment. That was because of his brother, Frank Little, the famous labor agitator and martyr. Most of the radical miners, and there were quite a few of them, idolized Frank for his boldness and his scorn for authority. But 1917 wasn't a great year for that bold style. Newspapers from coast to coast had covered the debacle of the strike and the lynching, often with words to the effect that the agitator got what he deserved. Uncompromising when the labor movement surged forward, Frank had no idea what to do when the tide turned, when war hysteria was sweeping the country and copper was a precious military resource, a patriotic commodity. It takes some discernment to lead a fight when the flag is in the air and the red, white, and blue is snapping in the breeze all up and down Main Street. Discernment was not Frank's strong suit.

The brother of Frank had himself become a target. A man who had no desire to be a leader. Which didn't stop the Montana authorities from wanting him to pay the price for a notorious last name. But James Little no longer existed, and Bill Waite could relax, relax in his basement, well-hidden, one life among millions. The dreams he had in the cool basement weren't all bad, insofar as they could be remembered on waking. Fear and sorrow were still present but no longer his only companions.

**

He'd worried that Rosie didn't believe a word of the Greene County story, which was confirmed one day, when she caught him off guard as he was coming upstairs with his head down. "I need to talk with you, Bill Waite. Not here. Let us go down to your subterranean lair for a private word."

As they descended, his heartrate quickened, for he was a man who enjoyed routine pleasantries but tried to avoid anything as challenging as a "private word." He wasn't a bad liar—most men who have to fight for a living in a hostile world learn the fine art of putting the best foot forward, by taking wide or narrow detours around that patch of real estate known as the truth. He was good at pulling a straight face or uttering a simple denial accompanied by a headshake. To the question, "Have you ever been arrested?" he could give just as convincing an answer as, "Have you ever bathed with Hindus in the Ganges?"

Virgil had invented the Greene County story after somehow guessing at Bill's fugitive status. Elaborating on the initial suggestion, Bill had come up with additional details, filling out his identity as needed. That process of fabrication had a safe and gradual feel to it. But against the ram of a smart woman's discernment his new identity was bound to crumble like flimsy plaster and lath to a wrecking ball's pounding.

When they arrived at the anteroom with the janitor's sink, she wheeled around and faced him, hands on hips. "Pushy says you're a fugitive from injustice. Is that why you're on the run?"

"I—" he stammered. He knew that was why, but he hesitated to claim so much importance for himself.

"If he trusts someone, that's generally good enough for me. But our open door includes my little girl, so I need to know the truth about this fugitive man who has come into our lives."

"Rosie, I *am* on the run . . . "

Something about his flustered appearance must have made an impression on her, for her voice took on a more coaxing tone. "I know that already, Bill. Why else would you have shown up at my door at two a.m. in filthy work clothes? So, take a deep breath, start at the beginning."

"I left Oklahoma in 1911, to work in the mines out west with my brother . . . " With some difficulty he told her about finding Frank's body. When he got to his imprisonment, he was speaking more easily but stumbled over the month he spent on parole. He had trouble accounting for his extreme aversion to Arnoldson and why a mere human would be so disturbing to him.

After he finished, she laughed. "You'll do, Mr. *Waite*," She pronounced his last name with a smile, as if it was their joke. This was the last time she referred to his new identity with any irony.

Which was fine with him. He wanted to keep that other life in a compartment. He didn't want to talk about it, even with friends. He didn't want to be reminded of how he'd held Frank in his arms, felt the stillness of that live-wire man. It was better to bottle up some memories, like recalling Frank standing before crowds large and small, speaking with a hard-edged timbre about the reality of life in the mines. Those truths were simple, but not that many dared to speak them publicly. Then the well-known agitator stepped down from the stage and gave his little brother an affectionate embrace . . .

Bill Waite had escaped but sometimes, especially when alone, a wave of panic seized him. Virgil was a great comfort because he understood without being told and because he spoke of things Bill needed to hear. Understood Bill's fears and put them in the sweep of history. Bill was no longer a weak and vulnerable man but a proud figure standing on an important stage. Bill didn't believe everything his friend told him, but the words were a much-needed kindness. Though Bill might never lose his worries, he was making headway. At least he might one day find in himself the calm that his fellow sandhogs thought they saw in him. But regardless of placid exterior, everyone has the same mess of feelings inside them. They laugh and love, when they're lucky. But most of all, they worry.

**

In his basement sanctuary Bill tried to construct a new life. He wasn't sure what it would be, but it had to be new. He buried himself in what was new, and there was plenty of that in New York City. Forget the old and replace it with something you'd never imagined: a wide avenue jammed with shiny automobiles and not one horse and buggy; bridges attached to pylons of braided wire, fat as an elephant's leg, rising into the morning mist; no outhouses, but spigots of running water, hot water whenever you liked. Yet, curiously enough, filth everywhere. Antlike men in white hats swarming around the hulls of giant ships while a crane lowered heavy crates to the dock, landing them an inch from their feet. Sidewalks that shook when underground trains hurtled by. And the manners of the people! A swagger in the men—and the women too—that outdid even the Irish of Butte.

He gradually began to understand the talk, or at least not be shocked by it, but knew better than to try it out himself. *Ain't she an air-tight baby. Mind your own beeswax. Ain't you a big timer. Get a load of the gams on that billboard. Who's the goose in the glad rags? Everything's jake if you've got the jack. Don't mess with a Mick's mazuma. Don't come between a kike and his kale. That grandfather clock spent all night lapping the giggle water. I was ossified, ab-so-lute-ly ossified. Go chase yourself, ya damn grubber. Ish kabibble to that.*

90

They didn't call it the New World for nothing. But it was new to many who lived here and not just recent arrivals. In New York City, there were plenty of saps just off the boat and even a few rubes like him, small-town people, who looked around, dazed, like they'd just fallen off the back of a speeding truck. All of them were outsiders trying to pass as insiders, thousands and thousands, and more each day. They had so much to learn, so much to forget. Memories of the old world, of someplace special, whether it was Corsica or County Claire. Or Montana or Oklahoma. His own quest to forget was accompanied by occasional feelings of disloyalty toward Ma. Was he a traitor toward those he had loved because he walled himself off from his past, from his last image of Frank and the great mystery, the terrible power that had left him dangling from a railroad trestle?

4.

In Butte, he'd go for a sauna on Saturdays, a custom introduced by the many Finnish miners, the only time they'd get truly clean. Which was more than miners who didn't follow this practice could say. But now he could shower at work and had a tap with scalding water in his basement hallway. He'd pad out of the basement room holding a razor. If anyone happened to look below the bottom stairs, they'd see a man well over six feet tall, dressed only in a towel, bending over the janitor's sink. But no one looked. Bill's ramshackle warren had no doors but was private enough. And though still unsightly the sink was now clean. The basin had brown and yellow stains no matter how often he brushed and rubbed at it.

He dreamed of buying a galvanized tub with his second paycheck. He'd keep it clean, dry it, then turn it upside down and use it for a table or desk. Or he could put ice in it and cheese and several pieces of fruit. After his shift, if he was still hungry and he and Virgil hadn't picked up something at an all-night stand on Houston Street, he could toss out the ice, turn the galvanized tub over for a table, and enjoy slices of apple and the cheese he loved, maybe a few olives on the side. A galvanized tub was a useful piece of equipment, he argued to himself. Whether it was or it wasn't, he had a few dollars, and they were burning a hole in his pocket.

He enjoyed the small acts of rebuilding. His new life would be built from tiny things. Possessions, distractions, a tiny cabinet where he could keep a bottle of spirits and a glass, bits and pieces that could be valued separate and apart from everything else, that glowed with their own inner value and beauty, detached from the chain of memory, from the years trailing dangerously behind him. Somewhere in the darkness was a train freighted with danger. If he listened he could hear the cars rattling and clacking in the night. But the pursuit of needful possessions was a mighty distraction. And what possession was more necessary than a galvanized tub?

**

They headed out for a day of shopping, Virgil leading the way down First Avenue. "Every product in all damnation," he commented. "And a few are hot to the touch." His meaning was clear. If anyone had lost a pearl-handled revolver or diamond-studded tiara and found either of them in a stall on Hester Street, he or she should say nothing but go home and invest in better locks.

They walked down First Avenue to Houston, where Michael met them, then continued south on Allen Street. Michael looked even younger outside the tunnel. Maybe he'd taken up shaving, although the need for it wasn't apparent. He wore a wool working man's hat, the bill pulled forward but not enough to cover rebel strands of light brown hair. The hat was a little large. He'd probably been told by his aunt to buy large so it would last no matter how much he grew or how badly he needed a haircut. He must have had freckles as a child because you could almost see them, on a day like this, when a little morning breeze rubbed his cheeks. The three friends shook hands. Since the boy called each of them mister, they forced themselves to address him as Mister Kerrigan, and not to smile about it.

They could hear the hubbub of the market before they could see it. A babble that swirled and lapped toward them. The owners of those voices had no awareness or the slightest care as to how they sounded. And a voice that doesn't care what it sounds like is always lovelier than the other kind. A crowd is uninhibited; it whispers and hollers and swears it will be understood even when the words are nothing but a mishmash of syllables in many languages. Maybe Bill was the only one who thought about each and every word and weighed it until the need to utter it had, in many cases, disappeared. Not this crowd. He loved every minute of it.

A close look at his face, usually hard, expressionless, showed that the eyes were dancing like those of an innocent child. Pummeled by bad fortune, worried and wearied by a hard life, this man was entranced by the new life flowering around him.

As they turned the corner and pushed into the throng an image of cloth sailing in the wind leaped into his mind, of yards of fabric flapping from the end of a bolt, of loose shirt sleeves and billowing pants and long flowing skirts; on all sides, awnings rippled in the warm breeze; and overhead, clotheslines full of clean sheets and pristine unearthly underwear fluttered before his eyes, on taut ropes that creaked and cooed in their pulleys.

They'd entered a great swirl of clothes and bedding. On filthy streets, the cleanliness of newly made goods prevailed. Pigeons shuffled indignantly away from the insults of Sunday footwear. Arguers jammed the street and filled it with hoarse voices in a multitude of languages. Some were in their best clothes, having come directly to these stalls from one of the many Catholic churches nearby. Others were there to haggle, which was hard work, so they dressed in work clothes with sleeves rolled up.

The late morning sky was unusually clear, and the crowds and the first-floor shop windows were just beginning to be touched by the sun. In the packed block, the air was becoming close and sticky. The three friends couldn't walk side by side, so they let Virgil take the lead as they wound around a jumble of carts and makeshift stalls that blocked the sidewalk and spilled into the street. Shopkeepers puffed themselves up as they pointed at articles of clothing. This is the stuff, they bragged, smacking a hand on a stack of cotton shifts or wool pants. Bill needed a change of clothes, at least one, and a hat. Under the iron gaze of a woman, certainly the vendor, he fingered a shirt but didn't like the $1.50 price.

Michael assumed a respectful manner as he stepped forward. "Ma'am, you know your business, but the price is a little dear." Then he started to pull Bill away, whispering loud enough for her, "The shop my aunt works at sells those shirts for a dollar each."

"Those are good shirts," the woman cried in an injured voice. "Nobody here has good shirts for such a price. I can't afford to sell for less."

"It's not that we don't have a few dollars in our pockets," Virgil chimed in. "But our dollars aren't made of elastic. Two dollars for two shirts." He was at the other arm, also making a show of tugging at Bill.

"Don't run off, gents. Losing a sale is like losing a friend. Two dollars for the both of them. I won't make a penny, but at least I'll come out of it with three new friends."

He did his own haggling on a pair of trousers, which he got for $2, and it felt good to get a prize like that so cheap. Could it be that all these thousands of people felt as good, all working at the same game with its complex, unspoken rules, a game the generations had been playing at for years? He didn't try to speak as rapidly—it was enough to speak clearly and without hesitation. And meet their eyes. He had nothing to fear from them, for he was a sandhog who made good money, and he had two friends to back him up, not to mention Rosie and little Sylvie, and coworkers who trusted him. Although not all were with him now, he felt them in his corner. Not to mention, he had a basement room to himself. No, it wasn't a nice room, but many single men in this part of the city didn't have that much. But mainly, he was a sandhog. People had a certain regard for this occupation, which was often in the news. Most didn't want it for themselves, but they admired someone who could do that kind of work. More important to the shopkeepers: sandhogs made good money.

The three of them were being watched. Anyone who pulled out a five-dollar bill would be noticed. That little boy who trailed after them was waiting to see if they spilled some change, or left a pocket unguarded. Michael could puff himself up, scrappy though still scrawny. Bill and Virgil were over six feet, taller than most men on Hester Street, and Bill had wide shoulders, which stood out among these men. As if from the narrow streets of the Lower East Side a breed of men with narrow shoulders had evolved. Or maybe it was the poor food. Bill didn't look either Jewish or Italian. But there were Greek and Magyar-looking fellows here as well. Scandinavians and Irish lads taller than he was. The truth was that nationalities on the Lower East Side didn't come in neat packages and labeled brands. No one would suspect that he was a former hard-rock miner convicted of conspiracy to commit murder in the State of Montana, parole jumper, wanted fugitive.

Here, he was a success, spending Sunday with two successful friends. Young women smiled, lashes closing above rouged cheeks. Some of the younger women wore sleeveless frocks that fell only to their knees. Kneedusters, fellas called them. When a woman caught his eye, he tipped his hat, the derby Virgil had given him.

He'd grown used to the way his face felt among these crowds. Life on the Lower East Side had brought out a hint of a smile, a glimpse of pearly white bicuspids, only slightly snaggled. No one was perfect. Besides, didn't the flawed teeth accentuate the new friendliness of the face?

Quiet and respectful, Bill could fit into any crowd. And to have money in his pocket, that helped. He was happy to be distracted by such thoughts, rummaging among goods that seemed treasures. Until as he turned away from a cart full of denim work clothes and looked back across the street to the other sidewalk, he happened to see, in a shop window, the reflection of a man about ten feet behind him, gazing in his direction. There was something out of place about him. Not just the trim, professional cut to his clothes. It took Bill a moment to realize what it was. He wasn't shopping.

This professional looking man had picked up a delicate lady's blouse and pretended to examine it. But even in the reflection, Bill could see the eyes were on him and no one else. He was concentrating, the moustache pressed into a thin line. A remote worry had emerged from the shadows at the edge of his thoughts. Was this man a detective sent by Arnoldson? Bill wanted nothing more than to get out of this man's sight, to dive back into the crowd. But he couldn't move. The possibility of pursuit had frozen him to the spot.

Bill's unease had heightened to the point that a wave of nausea swept over him. Virgil seized his arm and steadied him, as the crowd continued to search for bargains, to harangue and plead with each other, oblivious to Bill's presence. "You aren't in danger—that man you were staring at is the buyer for an exclusive Park Avenue shop. I encountered him when I worked at Cohen Bros. He's a ferocious bargainer, but no threat to you."

By this time Michael had joined them. To allay the boy's concern, Virgil repeated the explanation he'd just given Bill and continued in the same vein, "When that man prospers, many become miserable. Seeing him sneak around this place is like watching a big *gonif* among the little *gonifs*. I don't bear him any special ill will, but I hope he goes home with *bupkes.*"

"So maybe it's time for us to leave," Michael offered.

"Nonsense," Virgil responded. "We need to get you a stylish hat. Sandhogs should cut a certain image in the world. I think a Panama would make just the right statement. Mr. Kerrigan, allow me to escort you to a haberdashery stall where you'll find good products at a reasonable price."

Michael was very pleased to have Virgil make a selection for him and stuffed his old tweed cap in his pocket. Then, at Bill's suggestion, Virgil picked up a set of embroidered handkerchiefs for Sylvie. Soon, they'd had enough of shopping and began to push through the crowd. Michael looked perfect in his new hat, tipping it elegantly on every occasion. It helped to transform him from a scrawny lad to a young gentleman.

On the east side of Hester, when they were almost out of the market area, Bill noticed a shop with a spread of tools and household items, including a galvanized tub for $3.

5.

Anthony, a boy of at most thirteen, hurried over to clear dishes left from the last customer, then seated Bill at the usual table, near the counter, face to the door. It wasn't really because he had the same instinct as outlaws in the Old West, to want to see danger as it approached. But to see what was happening out in the street, beyond the wide windows of D'Alessandro's restaurant. He may not have appeared interested, as he slouched before his place setting, but he followed intently the life on the sidewalk. He saw the same families over and over and felt he knew them, including their children. It was important for him to follow what was happening with a couple whose argument he'd witnessed last week. Or would the same pretty woman be out shopping today?

"Bill, are they treating you okay in that tunnel?" Anthony asked. He looked hardly strong enough to lift even the small weight of these plates let alone a heavy tray of dishes, and to keep at it all day. No doubt some hulking men had applied for work in this busy delicatessen and not been able to keep up with little Anthony. He spoke good English and could interpret for the cook and owner, who spoke only Italian.

"I don't always get the consideration they give the mayor, but they pay me each Friday."

"Ain't Friday a great day? Why'd they have to go and put those other days in between the Fridays, can you answer that, Bill?"

He had begun to trust the city, or at least this portion of it. They were all jammed together in a great scramble of hurrying people who didn't seem to care a bit about each other. That was the big-picture look of things. But break it down into pieces, detach a detail from this great crowded scene, examine it closely, and you see people like Anthony, attending to others with earnest friendliness. The city may be hard-hearted, but every single day people offered help and friendship.

That was something he hadn't expected, definitely not the kind of friendship Virgil had offered. Did Virgil even realize what he'd given? Bill once had Frank, who was more than a friend. He'd had friends as a miner, for if a partner underground was trustworthy—and if you relied on him underground he'd better be—then he'd probably be a good fellow to pal with above ground, to drink a beer with, to grumble with about the boss. Trusted workmates, casual friends. In prison, he'd learned to size people up, to trust a few.

He hadn't made a decision to befriend the truck drivers and didn't have to. Amos picked him up and carried him away, as if without a word he'd understood what was needed. The drivers had delivered him before he'd even realized how much he trusted them. Like he was a parcel and it was their job to deliver it, and they needed to do it well. He enjoyed the ride. He owed them something he could never pay back. But the question of trust had barely occurred to him before the ride was over.

"Anything, else, Bill?" Anthony asked as he put a plate piled with eggs on the table.

"Olives and a slice of cheese, Anthony." He had a good appetite, especially for the hard, blond cheese that crumbled when you cut off a sliver. He liked to eat it following eggs and meat and with his coffee. Along with a handful of olives. That saltiness was a great thing. It helped him end a meal with something appetizing, a message to his stomach to not be depressed that a meal was ending but to think ahead to the tantalizing promise of another one, probably not too many hours in the future. Life hadn't always included a full belly. And might not in the future.

Anthony had never called him mister. Generally speaking, people didn't. Michael was the exception. Bill didn't have that breed of face. Even people who bowed slightly and called each other mister didn't call him that. Some of the bosses called him Mr. Waite as did the paymaster. From them it had a mocking ring. Mister was too large a term to fit, like a big brother's hand me downs. Too loose on him. He didn't have that kind of face, not the eyes looking down on you of a man high up in the world. But a good face where a shy smile might eventually appear. The fact that it finally showed up on those flat, noncommittal features told others that genuine contact had occurred. Without conscious effort, he won people over, all except for a few wiseacres who thought him simple and made comments behind his back.

Virgil was shy in his own way. He fixed everyone with an accepting gaze. Brown eyes probing for answers, investigating the universe and every creature within. When Bill disclosed secrets to Virgil, it was as though he already knew them. He'd shown Bill what to say, who to watch out for, how to be accepted on the Lower East Side.

A leisurely breakfast was a good occasion for random thoughts. He'd first come into this place attracted by the large sign on First Avenue, just down from the corner at Fourth. D'Allessandro's was a name to spread across a twenty-foot sign. But the inside of the place had only five tables. Much of the business came from the sale of groceries and carry-out lunches for laborers. They'd take off the lid of a lunch bucket and Anthony would ladle in pasta and sausage. Bill was surprised at the number of Italians who frequented an eatery in this neighborhood. Apparently, it was not as exclusively Jewish as it had at first seemed.

He was a poor guesser on the subject of nationalities. Some of those he thought were Jews might turn out to be Italian, Ukrainian, or Irish. A Turk or an Arab might pass for a Jew but not a Chinese, an African.

He ate breakfast late, so D'Allessandro's was relatively quiet, with most of the noise coming from Anthony and the cooks as they got ready for lunch, clattering dishes as they stacked them, joking. As he sipped his tea, the din pleasantly in the background, he realized that something was about to happen. An instinct told him to look toward the front door, which soon opened, as if on cue. He saw her before she saw him. Rosie was dressed for her part-time job, wearing a light pink blouse and a gray skirt that seemed to billow below a trim waist. She was a bookkeeper at the bank where her brother, Paul, also worked. How could this fierce, competent woman not be a sharp bookkeeper?

Rosie was someone who worried, and it was a mistake to relax with her until you learned what she was worried about. Now, however, she smiled without a trace of the tension that normally gathered across her brow.

"If you order me a cup of tea, I'll give you some news."

He didn't have to place the order, for Anthony was eavesdropping close by. He quickly cleared breakfast plates, all except for the one containing the remaining cheese and olives, and brought a second cup along with a fresh teapot.

Then she cleared her throat. "I'm simply the messenger," she began mysteriously. "Pushy is the one to thank for this news. He was talking to Mrs. Hollowczek this morning, about installing a new tub in our kitchen, and she told him that the Bassios were moving to Brooklyn on Saturday, leaving with only three days' notice. They must be moving up in the world to forfeit their deposit. Mrs. Hollowczek was in a state, to be losing a tenant so late in the month."

So 7C, above the Shulmans, would be vacant and they wanted him to move in. Like their apartment, it would include a kitchen with stove and sink and a front room with high windows. The small window in the kitchen, which opened on the airshaft, would offer a little cross-ventilation. Before moving in he'd have to get locks for the front windows, which opened to the fire escape, or else anything he bought would be stolen. Thieves watched Fourth Street pretty close and made note of anyone carrying packages home. They kept an inventory. Some residents complained

105

that thieves knew better what was in their apartment then they themselves did. Theft was like the weather. People complained about it, but what could they do? Window bars and expensive locks were as much good as leaky umbrellas. At present, all Bill owned could be fit in the galvanized tub.

He was hesitating because he'd grown attached to his basement room. And Rosie was quick to pounce on this. "Come on, Bill, you know it's the place for you. You'd freeze this winter in the basement, and just think how Sylvie would love having you so close."

It was a great opportunity, and Rosie was disappointed that he was pausing to consider it. She put her hand on his and he felt the warmth as she squeezed it impatiently. "Mrs. Hollowczeck will discount the rent if you move in right away, without her having to arrange for the cleanup."

He moved his hand so that she had to lift hers away. She didn't mean much from the contact, he reasoned, except a demonstration of trust, but the warmth burrowed into him a little too much. Women were comfortable with a great range of emotions and demonstrated them in a confusing way.

"I'll start the clean up Saturday, unless we're scheduled for work. But I'll have to buy a bed, or at least a mattress."

"Pushy will gladly help you move it upstairs." She was quick to volunteer his services, which might be needed. Carrying a mattress seven flights was more than anyone would attempt by himself, even a sandhog.

"You'll need a lot of other things, too. You've been living like a hermit in the wilderness." Hermit sounded better to him than some things. He laughed to himself at the picture that came into his mind: Rosie, the city-girl, friends with a wilderness hermit.

**

As Sunday began, Bill would not have imagined that today he would unintentionally cause a hurt to his dear friend. He and Virgil bought a mattress on Hester Street and took a cab to Fourth, mattress on the top. They each had an arm out the window, clutching it, balancing it around sharp turns and quick stops. Because of his own poor skills Bill always admired anyone, like this cabby, who could drive on such crowded roads. High speed frightened Bill, but didn't it correlate with superior skill? Even so, this cabby drove much too fast. If the mattress sailed off and landed in the filthy street, Bill would've left it there and gotten a new one. And if they somehow got through to East Fourth Street, mattress intact, he would give the driver a piece of his mind. When they arrived what he said was, "Thank you and keep the change." He gave him $2. Too much according to Virgil.

On the sidewalk, Virgil thumped his chest. "You do most of the bull work under the Hudson, but this is my street. I'll push up from the bottom while you guide from the top. You need to save your energy."

"I see you're snorting to go," Bill said, but knew Virgil was wrong. Pulling a mattress is harder than pushing.

They stopped for a rest on the fourth-floor landing. "To a sandhog, this air is light. But Christ's sake this mattress sure isn't."

From the way Virgil was wincing and rubbing his back, maybe pushing from the bottom was harder. Bill was concluding that two men can't easily move a mattress, especially if one of them is Virgil. He crouched down and put the mattress over his head and shoulders and walked it up the remaining stairs by himself.

By that afternoon, the new apartment was pretty well set up, and he was resting on his new mattress, listening to the sounds from the street below through his open window. Then someone knocked at the open door.

"Can I have a look at your new abode?" Rosie entered his kitchen and gazed down at him, sprawled on the mattress in the front room. He jumped to attention. "Still Spartan, but new curtains and a few knickknacks will help."

He stood there, waiting to hear what was on her mind.

"Come over for soup, Bill . . . He's hurt."

6.

Yom Kippur, 1923

"You have probably learned that today is Yom Kippur," Virgil began, as he stood by the table and poured two cups of coffee. He often began a conversation while doing something else, tilting his head toward whomever he was addressing while striding rapidly over the sidewalks of Lower Manhattan. Or as now, with coffee pot still in hand.

His back, bent like a question mark, was still bothering him.

"On this day we Jews are supposed to abstain from the pleasures of food and drink, from all enticements, to atone for transgressions of the previous year." He could have told Bill that on Yom Kippur Jews swim naked in the East River, for all he knew of Judaism. What did he know about any religion, for that matter. He dimly remembered the Methodist Church in Oklahoma where his parents occasionally took him.

"Unlike Christians, Jews do not have a savior to carry our sins. I have looked at the image of Jesus and felt the pain of the crown of thorns, the warm blood running over my eyes." These words were not in character with the cheerful, even-tempered man. He put people at ease. He was a man of graceful, easy conversation. Bill wished he could do something to deserve Virgil's warm-hearted acceptance,

109

but an opportunity for that had not arisen. Might never, he thought. Or, more likely, it would arise and he'd miss it.

"I have looked at the paintings of the man on the cross and felt the brutality of it. Do Christians take comfort in that image?" He waited for an answer. The wispy brown hairs stood out on his head.

Bill shrugged to show again that not being a Christian he didn't have a ready answer to this question. Virgil nodded and continued. "Think of the crude thick nails they had 2,000 years ago driven into the open flesh of the palm."

He paused long enough to put the coffee pot back on the stove. Bill hadn't realized until then that Virgil had been holding it all the while. Then he took a rag and wiped at some spots that had dripped on the white enamel. With his other hand he braced himself. He couldn't stand straight because of the bad back, which made him appear older than he was. But his voice was strong.

"Was Jesus a Christian? Most Jews think not. On the day Jesus was murdered, the Romans crucified hundreds of others. They were poor Jews, mostly. Not one of them had the comfort of thinking he was the Son of God. To my mind these humble men are the true martyrs of the story."

These words were worth a carefully considered response, but all Bill could manage was a measly thought, which he blurted out: "I remember hearing that the Jews killed Jesus. Ma didn't tell me that, and seldom sent me to church. It was something the other children said."

Virgil knew from previous discussion that Bill's mother claimed Cherokee lineage. Most people from Oklahoma claimed some Cherokee blood, unless they hated Indians.

There were a lot of them as well. "Of course, your mother didn't like such talk, because she knew how remarks like that, stupid and petty, can become terrible factors causing immense harm to innocent people. Little children learn not only that the Jews killed Jesus but that the only good Indian is a dead Indian. Such bloodthirsty sentiments are not so popular today, but they have not been extinguished. In fact. they are pretty well baked into the way of the world. How can you get rid of these poisoned loaves without abandoning the old recipe and working from scratch on a new one, a recipe based on a more humane vision? Yet those who prescribe a new recipe are shunned as a danger to the established order . . . which, of course, they are."

Neither of them spoke for a few minutes. Maybe Virgil wasn't sure where these last thoughts were leading him or maybe he thought it was better not to go wherever that was. At least not yet. He poured a second cup of coffee stronger than the first, although that had been stout enough. He and Rosie bought it at the Italian grocery at the corner of Second Avenue and Fourth Street. The smell of good coffee fills a room—without the smell, coffee is just hot water.

They took a few sips, and a trance-like silence descended over the room. It was broken when Virgil reached across the table and seized Bill's hand. "Today might be the Day of Atonement, but what do we have to atone for? Have we Jews not suffered enough at the hands of those who do not atone? Or you, Bill. Aren't we both, as honest workers, more sinned against than sinners?"

His face brightened like a child's as he continued, "If you have no objection, you will join me on my annual

Yom Kippur observance. But first we need to fortify ourselves with a late breakfast and a libation at Mr. Flynn's speakeasy."

Bill sometimes had to puzzle over his friend's ideas. Not this one. Instantly, he stood up and carried the two coffee cups to the sink. He was ready to go. He didn't need a jacket because the morning was mild. A little gray outside, but quiet and easy.

Shoes ringing on the stone steps, they went down the six flights and entered the holiday quiet of Fourth Street. They turned west, which was pretty much the only direction open to them unless they wanted to walk into the East River, and crossed First Avenue, where few shops were open. The chickens that usually squawked from small wooden cages on the sidewalk had been removed from the front of Meyer Fischer's Market, which was closed. During a shopping day, after these noisy fowls had been blessed by a rabbi, the butcher would place their necks on a scarred block and raise the heavy knife high above them. Or maybe they were blessed after they were packaged for the customer. But today they would get a stay.

Virgil had warned Bill that his ideas about religion weren't shared by all Jews, and he now launched into more thoughts on this topic. "Many are observant, some sincerely so, some even zealously. But being Jewish isn't like being Catholic. If you're Italian and at some point reject the ideas and observances you were raised with, you can end your connection with Catholicism. With a few exceptions Jews don't end their connection." He paused and put his hand on Bill's shoulder. "Unless of course you succeed in assuming a new identity, changing your name, and joining a Christian church and exclusive club. Then you might escape into a new life free of the inconvenience of listing your Jewishness on job applications. Your children would be free to apply to the college of their choice. With a daughter at Bryn Mawr and a son at Princeton, you will have become free and clear of that baggage, a true and trustworthy American. Unless one day you meet someone from the old neighborhood."

Then his face took on a baffled expression. "For various reasons Jews feel a deep connection to our Jewishness, with the result that we don't walk away. Or maybe we can't because society won't allow it. I'm not so sure that, as presently constituted, society will ever accept us. We're marked for life. Not in the same way Negroes are marked—and we're not as badly off. At least for now, in this country."

Then he fell silent and the silence of the street was testimony to the prevalence of the holiday observance. Bill appreciated what he was being told but had no ready questions or comments. If he would have spoken, it would've been in a whisper. But Virgil's voice rang out, clear as a bell. "Today we will exchange notes on somber chapters of our lives. I know you have experienced such moments, no doubt more than I have. Hard to live through and tough to recall. Very tough, without the aid of the liquid that Flynn dispenses."

Bill let these words float off into the gray clouds, not very far overhead. He didn't have to grasp them because he knew they were hovering just overhead until Virgil needed to make use of them again. By then they'd crossed to Second Avenue and gone a little south to a sign advertising

NEXT DAY LAUNDRY APT 1A. Below this was a short flight of gray stairs with a shiny railing. It was brass, not the usual black iron, and glimmered in the basement shadows.

"Here it is, our portal to a world of once-yearly atonement. Follow me closely if you want to gain admission."

The door didn't have an outside handle, but it did have an eyehole. The individual on the other side must have recognized Virgil, a fact impressive to Bill. In a moment the heavy door opened and they left the world of prohibition behind. Once his eyes got used to the shadows Bill took note of the lavishly polished wood, the bright glass shelving, the shiny brass trim everywhere. Behind the bar were rows of bottles bearing unfamiliar labels. No doubt they were quality spirits bootlegged from Canada. A quiet dignity reigned. Two men chatted by the bar and turned toward them with mild, gentlemanly curiosity.

Even before sitting down, Virgil told the waiter, "I'll have eggs, rashers, black pudding, and whatever else comes with your deluxe breakfast."

Bill ordered hash and eggs, "But a little extra hash, please."

"I often wake up with an acid stomach," Virgil said, after ordering ale. "Rosie frowns on beer for breakfast, but it's by far the best thing. And today I have a burning that needs to be drowned."

He pulled a cigar out of his shirt pocket. "Care for one? It might keep you from starving to death while we wait for breakfast. They are sure to delay solid food while we spend a small fortune on beer."

Bill had never enjoyed cigars, although in prison he often thought it would be nice to try one. Behind bars a great many things you can't have inside seem nice, even those you never particularly wanted when you were outside. He held up his hand to decline the cigar while Virgil bent over a match and breathed a red glow into the tip.

"Long life," Bill offered over the first beer. After the third round, he was no longer on the edge of his seat waiting for Virgil's confession, for surely he was going to confess something. Then the two breakfasts came out, plates piled high with eggs, not overcooked, a touch of orange in the yellow. Bordering the eggs, like foothills, was the corn beef hash. A very thin coat of oil moistened everything, but not so much as to make it greasy. A sliver of pickle that still had a little cucumber inside it was on a small dish beside a jar of mustard for the hash. The shreds of beef diced among the tiny cubes of potato were delicious. They were salty, great food to wash down with ale.

"These mugs are short," Bill grinned, after their fourth. By then he'd accepted the offer of the cigar.

"They meter them out. Irishmen know how to be tight," Virgil whispered, and both of them laughed. They fell into a quiet spell. Virgil brushed off the end of his cigar, and the glow died in the ash tray. "At certain moments, the human comedy is revealed," he sighed.

"A round of whiskey," he then called to the waiter. "And bring me the check."

Bill made some clumsy efforts to take charge of the bill, which Virgil easily soothed. When the whisky arrived, "Here's to Sylvie—and Rosie," Bill offered.

**

Outside, the sun had burned through the mist and the afternoon light was blinding. Bill shielded his eyes with one hand and grasped the brass railing tight with the other. Now Virgil's posture was upright and his gait pain free. Manhattan is a great place for aimless walks. If you want to keep track of how far you walk, you can easily do so because of the numbered streets, though they were not in a mood to keep track. Bill knew, however, that Virgil had a plan for the rest of the day, and more than aimless walks would be involved.

Virgil tugged at Bill's shirt so that he wouldn't walk into a large planter outside a hotel near Times Square. "Listening to men chat on the Lower East Side, you might think Jews are all great comedians. But we steal our material from Yiddish Theater. Yiddish is where our genius comes from. I never understood the purpose of keeping Hebrew alive. We should insist, instead, that our children study Yiddish. Along with that language they would absorb self-effacement and irony, not to mention a wonderful sense of timing.

"You don't have to be either old or raised in the Old World to enjoy it. We bring Sylvie to shows and she laughs with everyone else. Although quite possibly it is the laughter of the audience she loves, and the spectacle of a grown man making a fool of himself, someone besides her father."

They walked down 42nd, which was squealing with traffic, especially when compared to the Lower East Side, then turned south on Broadway. By then, it was late afternoon, and the elm trees and electric poles cast shadows over the wide macadam. When they arrived at Washington Square, the sun was setting behind a line of buildings on the west side, and the leaves of well-trimmed bushes were already in shadow.

Virgil put hands on hips and craned his neck to look up. "There it is," he muttered almost to himself. He stared toward the top floors of the building facing them.

Bill followed him across the street to a park bench, glad to get off his feet. He waited to learn what "it" was.

"You may not have heard of *Triangle*."

Triangle—Bill knew from the way he said this word that Virgil didn't mean equilateral or isosceles. His mind wasn't working quickly, but he finally made the connection to the Triangle fire, which took so many sewing machine girls. The miners he'd worked with in Montana were well aware of workplace disasters, and some compared this 1911 fire to Butte's mine fire. That year, 1917, had been a time of disturbing images. He'd had to sort through them in prison—and had tried without much success to forget them ever since.

Virgil lifted a hand from his knee and gestured upward. "A great fire breaks out on that floor. The girls—and I pick the word with care, for more than half of the females on that floor were in their teens—they had no way out because the doors were locked by their employer to prevent stealing. There was a fire escape, of course. That is required by city code. But inspection of it isn't required. As soon as a few of those nimble young girls scrambled through the window, it fell away from the side of the building. It should have had a sign on it—*Fire Escape, For Small Fires Only.*

117

"If you would have been living here then, taking a late lunch in this park on that day, March 25, 1911, you would have heard the sound of girls and women falling seven, eight, or nine stories. The unsuccessful attempt at flight. And the sound of them hitting the street. I am not sure what that sounds like. Perhaps it was like a package landing next to you on the sidewalk, a heavy sack of goods."

"So many of us die at work . . . " Bill coughed before continuing. "I've seen men crushed and burned, both. To be burned alive is worse . . . "

"You are right. I think about it more than I should because out of those 146 women there were several I knew. I was a boy of 13 with many friends in the neighborhood. I was not a perfect youngster, and some of those women had to give me a scolding as I ran about like a little madman. Not all of them treated me fairly. Such a death makes good women of them all, at least in my mind, brave and good. I would like them all to be back here again, even if it meant another beating, a good sound beating, however unfair.

"I learned in the days following March 25 that one of the measures of friendship is the service of grief. A heavy lesson for a boy. My two best friends lost mothers. The terrible thing about a boy's grief is the look on his face. It begins in the eyes, sometimes without warning, and reaches to the mouth. A quiver, a desperate attempt to stave off crying. At every turn, tears press against the belief that we must behave as stoic little men. The fact that we do not think we should cry is what breaks your heart. With a girl, grief is in the heartbreaking sound she makes. In boys, it's the attempt not to make a sound.

"I walked back to my family's apartment on that early spring day, and as I mounted the steps in our building, I heard little girls, several of them, crying behind the doors to their apartments. During those moments, I was still ignorant of the blaze and not so affected by the sounds. Boys have the feeling that the world would be a better place if little girls would learn to shut up. Of course, I no longer think that and seldom tell Sylvie to shut up and wouldn't dare tell Rosie."

Virgil smiled after the last remark and paused. Then he turned away, hiding his face. "My mother was not due home from work for another hour, and I was hungry and wondered if there would be anything to eat in the apartment, in our poor little apartment. I threw open the door expecting to have the place to myself until Momma came home, when a surprise greeted me. My Aunt Liz was there, standing over Poppa, who was slumped in a kitchen chair, head almost to his knees. He looked up as I burst in but didn't utter a sound. His eyes told me everything."

Bill's own thoughts hurried ahead. He was calling up images and was not sure how much of what he saw in his mind he was putting into words as he was sucked into the flames. Fire was everywhere, carried on every wind. Combustion lives in every particle without exception and is feared by all beings. It hurries throughout the universe, threatening to burst out, even where darkness prevails, burning with an intense orange, then sizzling white, dissolving the outlines of surrounding space, the terrifying speed of it as it changes, ejecting great tapering flares from its broiling center, each flare the seed for another hungry, existence-devouring swarm of furies, until there is no place left on this earth that is not a remnant of ash . . .

The flames exploded into Bill's thoughts and ate into even those secret places he tried to keep sealed and safe from the harms of the world. *But no place is safe.* That's what terrified him beyond all accounts, beyond any words he could put to it. Anyone who has lived through a disaster knows that fear resonates in every recollection of it. And in the case of a fire, it's a nimbus of smoke surrounding all images, a hint of the flames that might rekindle at any moment.

This terror thrived on Bill's thoughts, behind his unblinking eyes. He'd never been able to speak of it. He'd been working in Butte for several months while Frank was on the road organizing. And on June 8, 1917, an electrical cable the size of a man's leg ignited oily timbers where hundreds of men worked. It spread to the adjacent shaft, warping heavy lift buckets, turning steel cables into bright wicks.

Bill escaped and was part of the rescue, the failed rescue. At that point the scope of it hadn't sunk in. It would become widely known as the Speculator Mine Fire, one of the worst disasters in all of mining, an industry where accidents had already claimed tens of thousands of lives. *Accidents,* they called them. Surely accidents happen. But when so many lives were lost and sensible precautions not taken, can these things truly be called accidents?

They found some bodies perfectly intact, huddled against those concrete bulkheads, intact except for fingers that were worn down to bone scraping against a last barrier as lungs filled with smoke.

Bill had worked for many days laying out what was left of the bodies. They carried stretchers to several churches because the Butte city morgue was overwhelmed. Some were light as a feather even with the remnants of more than one man. They couldn't tell how many were jumbled together. They laid these feathers out on cots, trying to allot a cot for each, though in some cases they could hardly tell where the remains of one man began and another ended. They examined strands of clothing or tried to guess from the shoes. If they were ash also, they looked for other clues, a belt buckle, knife. Even tags and lamps were twisted by heat and sometimes unrecognizable. They did their work with care. Good guesswork was their only pride.

"That last number on the tag is a three, so it could be McSorley's number," Emil Jokinen whispered into the afternoon shadows of the church. "And his widow has given up hope."

"It's her Henry, all right," Bill answered. "She will at least have his remains to put in a coffin." Was the certainty in his voice a mark of loyalty toward Henry McSorley or a terrible sin against him?

Those ashes were mixed with bone and other bits. They sometimes appeared like ordinary fireplace residue of coal or wood. But they were different, of course. No matter how cold, they glowed with a departed life.

He and Emil worked slowly for several June days following the disaster. They had no idea how many of the 164 men who died were carried by them to that church. It could have been only a handful or the great majority.

"Now what," Emil's voice rang out in the large stone chamber. They had run out of cots to put the men on. Bill could see the problem but had no solution.

"There," Emil said, pointing in the direction of the pine benches reserved for the congregation. A red velvet rope stretched across the aisle from one brass balustrade to another and blocked their way.

"This church is called Our Lady of Perpetual Help." Emil's voice had adopted the tone of a patient scholar, clearly to hide the emotion he felt. "What a lovely thing to think about, a mother's hand helping you forever. Our Lady is the Italian church. Maybe we Finns lack the sense of beauty that Italians have. St. Andrew's is the Finnish church I go to. Just St. Andrews. And I doubt any of us ever thought to give it a poetic name."

He winked at Bill and took the red velvet down. "We will rest these poor men on the congregation's benches. I don't think the Italians of Perpetual Help will mind."

Then he tried to spread the drop cloth over a row of benches only to have it billow in the air, one end sliding to the floor. He gestured for Bill to take hold and pull. They snapped the cloth between them, let it float a little in the air and stretched out the last of the wrinkles.

Bill didn't know how long he was absorbed in these thoughts. The images were sharp in his mind as if he was again a witness, describing the events to Virgil. Had he spoken out loud? Was he in such a state that he couldn't distinguish between what was passing through his mind and what he was saying?

He could feel Virgil beside him. Their sides pressed against each other on the bench.

"And your brother?. . ." he heard Virgil ask. With that another flood of images coursed through his mind, of the angry strike and the newspaper attacks that vilified Frank, its central leader. At first the strikers mocked the attacks, most of which were ridiculous lies. Frank wore them with pride. Pride and sarcastic humor. But little by little the lies took root and some of the men became disheartened. Despite the horror the miners had lived through, public opinion was beginning to brand them as enemies of public order. But the more they were vilified, the more a kernel of the strikers persisted, with Frank in the lead. How could they go back to quiet times after what they'd lived through?

But no one foresaw the brutality of what was to happen August 1. The vigilante attack on Frank altered Bill's world. Frank had been a respected man in certain circles, though ridiculed and feared in others. Feared no longer.

Bill lapsed into thoughts of his parole. Maybe Arnoldson was one of those who thought Frank had gotten what he had coming to him, or even rejoiced in the murder. Parole was a time during which he was always torn between wanting to act on what he truly believed—or on what his parole master required. That month had seemed like an eternity. Inside, he was raging with anger while having to maintain the countenance of a convict groveling for forgiveness. He'd gone to church with Arnoldson, said grace with him, thanked him for food and shelter. To Arnoldson, Bill was a project. A man who could be remade. But remaking, was that something one man could do to another?

He thought back to a typical dinner at Arnoldson's. The food was fine, a bowl piled high with potatoes, another of apple sauce, and a dish for bread and butter. The dish for ham held only two small slices, but they were red and dripping. A metal pitcher sweated beside two mugs. Arnoldson folded his hands and checked to make sure that Bill did also.

"Our Father, who art in heaven, hallowed be thy name.... " Did all who repeated that word know what it meant? Who was supposed to do this *hallowing?* If the people of this wide world were supposed to hallow their father's name, why just a name? Why not the whole of his creation? The earth was hardly a hallowed place, not anymore. As a miner, he'd lodged blast after blast in the bowels of the earth. And when the earth suffered, human beings did not fare too well. What did those who repeated that word know of an underground fire and the miners who couldn't escape?

"Give thanks, and help yourself, son."

"Thank you, Mr. Arnoldson."

Bill had been paroled early from a life sentence. That early parole was another mystery. Surely Arnoldson had something to do with it. Some of Arnoldson's neighbors might not have thought Bill had such a bad deal. Release from prison, honest work, plenty to eat. Only two meals a day, but they were good ones. Meanwhile, Bill often felt that he was the object of an experiment. But he was on parole and couldn't assert himself. What would have become of him if three truckers hadn't come to the rescue?

Bill yanked himself away from these thoughts, realizing that his friend had poured out his mother's story, and he'd answered only with confused thoughts of his own misfortunes. If the service of grief is one measure of friendship, as Virgil had put it, what words did he have to offer? Some men would have responded with a rush of helpful and buoying talk, but Bill wasn't such a man. His face tightened and twisted with frustration, but no words came.

A moment passed, a thousand years in his life.

He put his arm over Virgil's shoulders and pulled him close. This friend's whole life was there, gathered inside Bill's arm, a boy's life, that wonderful little thing that cries out inside us and battles to hold back its tears.

How long they stayed like that on the park bench, one man embracing another, Bill didn't know.

Then Virgil gave a low chuckle and straightened up. "My friend, the world needs our understanding, not our tears." He reached into a pocket and thrust something into Bill's hands, cold to the touch, a steel capsule. It was a flask. "We will sit here like old beggars and sip until we come to grips with the strange way of the world."

As the moments passed, pigeons gathered around their bench. Apparently, they thought that where humans shared a drink, crumbs might also appear. As the shadows advanced across the park, a briskness entered the air. The drink felt good, burning as it went down, warming them against the coming night.

Then Virgil made a sound that at first might have been mistaken for a cough, "*Tsedekah.*"

"Tsedekah," he said more clearly. "It is an old Jewish term. It refers to our obligation to right the injustice of society. I feel that obligation but don't always know how to let it guide me. What use is the feeling without the guidance? Maybe that's why so many refuse to recognize their tsedekah. Perhaps that feeling is not useful, in itself. But I trust no one who does not feel it burning inside them."

Bill took another sip and handed the flask back.

"Asch," Virgil pronounced. Again, he had emitted a sound that didn't at first make sense. "That was the name of it, the Asch Building . . . not spelled like what floats in the air after a fire but pronounced the same.

"The company that employed those girls and women was owned by Max Blank and Isaac Harris. They did not install sprinklers because it would interfere with a right they had exercised on previous occasions, of torching the property to collect on the insurance. This fire was not intentionally set. They were acquitted of any criminal intent. The flames were the result of a criminal system, but the greed of these men was the primary accelerant. In that regard, very similar to the fire in which you lost so much.

"On this Day of Atonement, I address God, I address all the gods man has ever believed in, that may or may not exist: you ask me to atone, you ask my friend Bill to atone— What is the meaning of this?"

7.

Unless they do something stupid, men have nothing to fear. His ma taught him that, with an emphasis on the *men*, possibly because women wouldn't do anything stupid. At least not the same kind of thing.

He remembered these words because he *had* done something stupid, and it had cost both of them dearly. In 1917, after Frank's murder. He was in a desperate mood and had thrown caution to the wind, because how could things get any worse. He should have known, things can always get worse. Especially if you do something stupid.

Which was what Bill did when he threatened the two most powerful figures in the copper industry, John Dennis Ryan, the Chief Executive Officer of the Anaconda Copper Company, and John D. Rockefeller, the baron of all copper barons. These two John D's were not well liked in Butte. In fact, it would be no exaggeration to say that after the Speculator Mine Fire and during the strike that followed, they were intensely disliked. But the murder of Frank Little, the strike leader, put a damper on things. Gradually, following August 1, hatred turned to fear.

Some brave souls continued to protest, foremost among them the brother of Frank, James Little. These protests weren't in themselves unwise. The exercise of free speech is held in high esteem, though not always in a mining town.

127

But in his grief, the younger brother was about to blunder into a trap.

"I hold you John D. Rockefeller, and you, John Ryan, responsible for the murder of 164 miners on June 8 and of my brother on the early morning of August 1." James, alias Bill, read these words from a sheet of paper handed to him during a small rally before the offices of the Anaconda Copper Company. "And since Montana authorities won't indict you, a sentence of death will be enacted by local men brave enough to carry it out."

It was a small gathering where police outnumbered union members. The statement he read had been handed to him by an agent provocateur. The angry tone may have been Bill's, but not the words. It would be all the evidence needed to convict him of attempted murder. Before his blunder, Ma had been a healthy woman living in the young state of Oklahoma, generous and well thought of. Not long after hearing of her first son's death and the other's life sentence—near a creek that fed the Cimarron River, in a cabin that had always been well cared for, she died of despair. Porch and kitchen contained the uneaten meals brought to her by neighbors seeking to return the generosity she had often shown them.

A stupid thing, a mortal if inadvertent wounding. And the guilt that follows from such an action never goes away. But it does diminish, at least a little. What began as a sharp stone cutting at his heart had worn down over the years to something else, like the pebble that aggravates your foot. You take off your boot and remove the pebble, but before too long, you notice it again. Bill would argue with himself that he, along with his ma, were innocent victims. This argument may have been valid, but it didn't change anything. The stone always came back.

**

Unless Bill did something stupid, he had nothing to fear. Something else stupid, like jumping parole and inviting the pursuit of Jacob Arnoldson. But now he could finally relax in Apartment 7C, his nest, his place of safety. A modern notion, safety, because for most of history and for all of prehistory, humans feared each twig cracking in the night. They kept dogs to warn them of the approach of a wolf. But in the middle of a city, who can hear the snap of a twig?

**

The Lower East Side would've fit within the borders of Arnoldson's 500-acre farm, depending on how far north of Houston you defined this district by, and how far west, to Second Avenue or The Bowery. But however you defined the area of this slum, you could have multiplied it several times and still fit it inside the borders of Butte. But land area gives a poor accounting of the size of a place. The Lower East Side with its density of souls was the most gigantic place Bill had ever experienced. On weekends he explored it and found it a monumental adventure. Virgil had said that this region, only a few square miles in size, was the portal through which humanity entered the Twentieth Century. Although you might never draw a clear bead on what this thought meant, it was a stupendous thing to roll around in your mind.

It was a life, and he was thankful for that. He loved the crowds, the way bodies teemed and veered around him, the sweat, the fast talk he could never keep up with, the cardboard signs in five different languages, the boys coughing and hawking up gobs into the gutter and sometimes at each other, the girls cursing and gossiping on their way to a day in a sewing shop. And the elms towering overhead, their autumn leaves whispering quietly in the breeze—as if they were, like him, dazed by the spectacle taking place around them.

**

Sounds came back slowly, sounds he didn't usually notice. Through the plaster walls, a sudden ocean of sound, playful shrieks, whining questions, a blur of rising and falling notes, none of the words distinguishable. Of course, these were the little ones watched by his neighbor, Mrs. Levine. Their voices were pleasant in the way the chaos of the Lower East Side could be pleasant, because it was a part of his new life, a part he didn't have to take responsibility for. He liked the sounds of children, especially in someone else's apartment.

How many did she care for? They were generally dropped off long before he awoke. Little things carried to the door, eyes still full of the gook of sleep. But Mrs. Levine would expect them to wake up and walk across her threshold, through her kitchen, and into the front rooms. She would let them nap and play, some on floor cushions, some on her bed. There were toddlers, but some as old as six or seven, from the sound of them. Beyond that age although not all would attend school, all would learn to take care of themselves without Mrs. Levine's careful watching.

They might not obey anyone else in the world—might grow up to defy parents, teachers, bosses, and cops—but they surely obeyed Mrs. Levine. He'd been given orders by her as well.

On his first week in this apartment, he'd been sitting in the hallway closet on his porcelain throne—not really *his*, of course, because he shared it with the other three apartments on the seventh floor. As Virgil pointed out, "The porcelain isn't personal." This was a statement that he liked to repeat to annoy Rosie. She would respond by shaking her head sadly and asking god, a god she didn't believe in, why on earth she was stuck with such a *nudnik* husband.

He pulled the wood knob—carefully, since it was attached to a flimsy chain and often came loose from the flush lever. The rush of water from the tank announced to the silent building that on the seventh floor someone had completed a task familiar to all. On that occasion, at the same moment as he stepped out, Mrs. Levine stepped from apartment 7B, a gray woman, short, wearing a faded housedress. The two doors opening simultaneously shocked him more than it shocked her. She turned her face to look up at him, a hard, triangular face, but still handsome despite the lines. She didn't say hello.

Mrs. Hollowczek and Mrs. Levine were both important figures in the life of the building. These careworn ancients were not so easy to tell apart, but to Bill, Mrs. Levine struck an even sharper, more commanding image. Doubtless her little charges saw her as wise and strong, and Bill was sure they had good reason for this respect. Her expression was acutely suspicious. Was there an old woman on the Lower East Side, or even a young one, who wasn't? And often with good reason. He later met her many times and finally she'd begun to return his nod. Over time, smiles became part of their greeting. Could she speak English? On that first meeting, she'd pointed a forefinger at another closet in their hallway. He opened the door and saw a broom, really a broom handle with a head of frayed and broken bristles. This broom was a dumb fact, but the bucket and mop spoke volumes. More tools, speaking in a language he could understand. The old woman's eyes drilled into him, but it was the tools that gave the orders. He began to sweep the seventh-floor landing, then the toilet room, and the flights of stairs leading up and down.

"Good," she grumbled. She knew that much English.

He looked up from the mop bucket but she'd already retired to her apartment. He cleaned hall and steps from then on.

**

At first, he didn't know someone was there. He'd been climbing stairs, and the rays from the skylight were bright in his eyes. He stepped into the shadowy alcove where his door and Mrs. Levine's angled together. Someone waited there, a rustle among the shadows, waiting for him to pass. When he unlocked his door, light from the front windows leaked back through his apartment to the hallway, and a young woman stood in the sudden wash of illumination, so close he flinched. She smiled, then walked casually away from him toward the stairs. The skylight lit her ruffled blouse and the firm flesh of her arms. A little taller than average, he realized. She put her hand on the balustrade, turned around, and smiled as if she knew exactly who he was.

"I'm sorry if I startled you," he said.

"I heard you climbing seven flights—you didn't startle me at all." She peered at him as if there was something humorous going on, too subtle for him to grasp, and then added. "I'm the one who should apologize."

She was on her way to work, skirt cinched around her waist by a leather belt, wearing gaiters and sturdy shoes. She continued to peer at him, her eyes dancing, lips still pursed in an ironic grin. He felt she would say something to him. He strained his ears for it. Then she turned and walked down the stairs, the rustle from her skirt sounding up the stairwell, the short heels tapping swiftly. Far below, the whisper of the heavy front-door closing behind her.

Are women ever anything but composed?

**

"A little taller than average," he told Rosie the next day. "Brown hair, our age. When she smiled I thought she was laughing at me."

"You could be describing 100,000 women who live in the Lower East Side, and they aren't really laughing at you. Tell me this, Bill, was she attractive?"

"It was dark. I couldn't see very well."

"Did she have a cute figure?"

"Like I said, Rosie, I couldn't see her."

"You shouldn't lie to me, Bill, you shouldn't even try." She was laughing at him as he grew more and more uncomfortable. "You saw her well enough, especially her figure. That's the first thing men see."

"Maybe she had a streak of silver in her bangs?" This was something he'd noticed—a stripe of prematurely silver hair as she smiled back at him in the shaft of overhead light, a distinctive feature in a young woman.

"You tell me, Bill, you're the one who saw her."

His face had grown hot from Rosie's cross-examination. All he wanted was to go back up the stairs—with or without the woman's name. Then Rosie burst out laughing and reached for his hands, clasping them tightly.

"Bill, does she look a little like me except for the silver in her bangs and the fact that she's far prettier?"

"Like you, but not prettier."

"So, she looks like every other Jewish woman except far prettier and with the silver streak?"

"I don't know," he said, in a defeated voice. "What does 'Jewish' look like?"

"I'm getting under your skin," she said playfully. "I want you to know that because you and I are best friends I'll tell you exactly who she is. Her name is Hannah. We grew up together and people have often said we look alike. But Hannah *is* much prettier, that much is certain."

Rosie was a pretty woman, maybe not beautiful. Although she never seemed to think of her appearance, Bill knew enough not to agree with her self-belittling comparison. He'd done stupid things in his life, but saw no reason to do this particular stupid thing. Rosie was a woman with sparkle but this woman, Hannah, was beautiful.

"Of course, she's prettier. For all the good her looks have done her. She's my friend. I've known her since childhood, although she has too many burdens to visit with me as often as I would like, with her job and little Ruthie, who has no father. No father because the word father should be a term of respect, and the man who left his seed in Hannah and abandoned her doesn't deserve the term."

She stared directly into his eyes, long enough to make Bill wonder if she meant to embarrass him. Then she continued, "Sperm are slimy cells. They have nothing to do with respect. That man—and I know who he is—has done nothing to deserve the honor of being considered little Ruthie's father."

Rosie's vehemence was not aimed at Bill, but he felt like the recipient and made a quick inventory of his prior life concluding that he was relatively innocent— relatively, if there is such a thing as relative innocence—and didn't deserve any share of the blame that Rosie was heaping on someone else.

Then in a voice with less anger: "Her mother worked at the Triangle but escaped and is your neighbor, Mrs. Levine. When you encountered Hannah, she was probably dropping off her child on the way to work. A few don't treat her well because she had a child out of wedlock, a few dark souls. I like having a husband, but I don't care a bit who has one and who doesn't."

Her face brightened to let him know she was about to trust him with valuable information. "She lives across the street. Her address is 122 Fourth Street, apartment 2C. I already told you her name is Hannah."

8.

They got off on Canal, near a hot dog vendor. A briny smell came off his cart. Bill ordered ten dogs, five each, and was ready with the dollar, so for once Virgil would not get to pay. They sat on a bench, their plan being to have two each now and three for lunch under the Hudson. Plodding through 25 psi would give anyone an appetite.

"You have to gird yourself for this work." Virgil grinned and raised the hot dog in a toast. "Here's to Nathan Handwerker, the inventor of this delicacy. *Zie Ga Zink.* Good health to you, Nathan, wherever you are."

They munched the salty cylinders of what was advertised as kosher beef and enjoyed a moment of contemplation that Virgil was sure to develop into an interesting piece of conversation, and did. "We prepare ourselves by entering an air chamber. Orlando pumps up the pressure. But it's the mental pressure we need to be pumping up now."

"It's a helluva job." Bill agreed. After a weekend, they were going back into the jaws of a beast they didn't understand or trust. Virgil had worked a full week without mentioning his back, but it was still bothering him. Bill could feel his friend's anxiety and knew it would increase as their shift began with a hiss of air. The pressure would increase, slowing their breathing. The hissing would seem to fill their

137

veins with lead, with the feeling that something unnatural was happening inside their bodies.

The work itself wasn't so hard, at least not for Bill. Their boss O'Dell had noticed the way he took to it and one shift had asked if he could set a charge. He wasn't sure he should answer yes, still not wanting to call attention to himself. But he'd learned the blasters trade pretty well in Butte and would rather do it himself than have to worry about someone doing it poorly. From then on, when their crew encountered rocky earth that the shield couldn't break through—and the regular blasting crew was for some reason absent—O'Dell would ask him to step up as blaster. This also meant a raise to $7.50 for that shift and an upgrade to $6 for blaster-helper rates for Virgil.

But on that day, they were weary even before the start of their shift, anchored to the bench as the crowds streamed around them: office workers, bank clerks, shoppers. Virgil and Bill were invisible to these people. But not to the pigeons, who took a great interest in the hot dogs. He tossed bits of a roll to them. Those solid, land-loving birds didn't fly so well but somehow were always present wherever a morsel appeared.

"I sometimes think of the intricacies of this job and the marvelous science our safety depends on." Virgil often discussed the work of the engineers, who tested the river-bed slime and gauged the depth and weight of the water. Memos were dispatched, voices full of static came over telephone lines. Orlando and others were at the other end to decipher these messages and dial in the right air pressure. Then sandhogs were sent out to do heavy work in an artificial atmosphere that was the creation not of god or nature but of other men.

"Speaking of engineering, I need to tell you something." These words got Bill's immediate attention. "Yesterday I went into the personnel office and applied for a position as a trainee in the engineering department. I studied engineering at City College. I'm also a draftsman, based on my experience in the apparel business."

Bill was thrilled at this news. If only he could keep him alive until Virgil's application was accepted. He stuck out his hand, "Congratulations, my friend."

"It's too early for congratulations, but the first hurdle has been cleared. At least the application didn't contain the warning, 'Jews and Irish need not apply.' Now all I have to do is convince them that designing trousers is pretty similar to tunnels."

"When will they let you know?"

"I've been told that an application can gather dust forever on the third floor. So, don't worry about losing a partner. I don't expect to hear until the main work on this job is complete."

For a perceptive man, Virgil missed a lot, like the fact that his friend wanted him out of the tunnel and in an office as soon as possible. In the meantime, the problem remained: Virgil wasn't cut out for this work. With Bill's help, he'd fooled everyone into thinking he was a competent sandhog. Only Rosie and Bill knew what a klutz he was.

Virgil continued, as they still had time to kill, "The human body lives through a million tiny developments we pay no special attention to. If any of them are out of kilter with another process, we die. Just think, for example, of what happens to the blood as it travels through the body. Billions of microscopic processes take place on cue in order for you to inhale the rich oxygen of the world into your inner core . . . Or to exhale, to burp or expel it back into the atmosphere in a variety of ways, not all of which are pleasant to imagine."

Virgil was right that Bill seldom thought about the journey of the blood—through lungs, heart, liver—and wasn't that interested. But he paid attention, now, knowing that his friend was getting to something and taking his time, as usual.

"Perhaps we have a right to grow accustomed to these millions of processes. They are our most essential belongings. An uncle may have given me cufflinks that I value because he wore them to weddings in the Ukraine. I keep them in a wooden box and never tire of studying them. The glint of the gold, the weight of it in my hands. But those are not the true gems of my existence. It's those biological processes I'm hardly aware of. I can't hold them up to the light or weigh them in my palm, yet they sustain my life and are truly precious and unique to me. We are unconscious of them, at least for most of our lives. We take them for granted. But I have never taken for granted Mr. Holland's elaborate mechanisms. I know just enough engineering not to."

To add an endpoint to his statement, he shrugged, the same what-the-hell gesture Bill remembered from when they were sitting on a bench being oriented into their new trade. That was more than four months ago. Fear was still there, only masked a little better.

"Imagine, the two ends of this tunnel will actually meet, like lovers, joining in the darkness. In the great underwater night, they will establish a seamless union. Decades from now, if all goes according to plan, folks from Manhattan will drive their autos under the river, all the way to New Jersey, and never guess there was a spot where two identities merged."

Bill broke in, "Virgil, if they don't make you an engineer, they should create a new job for you, Professor of Sandhog Philosophy."

Virgil chuckled politely and continued. "Building this tunnel is the adventure of a lifetime. What a stupendous thing to work on this project, even though you and I will never use it. Unless by some miracle we become wealthy enough to buy an automobile. A marvelous privilege to hoist muck all shift with that roaring in our ears. A marvelous privilege, after the first wave of terror and nausea pass over us and before the tedium sets in."

"Let me treat you to another dog, a small price for such grand philosophy."

"No thanks, my friend."

In fact, Bill was no longer hungry either. Something about a meal of hot dogs. It may leave you still hungry, but with the passage of a little time, another hot dog is unimaginable.

Virgil's mood had shifted from pensive to apprehensive.

Not able to think of anything more helpful, "Helluva job," Bill muttered again.

"I give you a *megillah,* and you respond with two words. Is that an equal friendship?"

"No, but if you don't move your *tukhus* we'll be late for work."

"At any given moment in New York City, many thousands of people are using Yiddish words. You are the only one to beam with pride when you do so."

9.

An emergency shatters the crust of routine, exposes what was latent, the inner workings of the human mind. After it occurs, people crawl about in the dark with only their instincts to guide them. Do they think first of rescuing others? Or do they panic from the din and disorientation and forget everything but their own insubstantial lives?

Bill was awakened from a deep mid-morning sleep by a bashing at the door. He thought immediately of Arnoldson and his large fists. At last he had found me and was announcing himself with door-splintering blows. Who else would create such a commotion, a noise that would carry up and down the stairs, frightening tenants to death? But the voice that pierced the door wasn't Arnoldson's.

"Come, Mr. Waite. Open!" It began as a tearful bleat and was repeated over and over, louder each time.

Bill pulled on pants and shirt in a single motion and ran to the door. When he opened it, he saw Mrs. Levine poised to deliver another blow. But her face had been transformed. The eyes that had seemed so strong and austere were now wide as wheels. Her lips seemed to have frozen, not able to shape words to fit the urgency of what she needed to say. He wasn't used to thinking of his tough neighbor as a helpless old woman. Never good with English, now she was

143

pathetically speechless. Her whole face strained while her eyes pleaded. But to do what he didn't yet know.

"You must help." Finally, the words were spilling out, telling him in the little English she had that her daughter, Hannah, had been hurt and was in Bellevue. Then she placed her hands on his back and pushed him with sudden strength into her apartment. "Watch them," she said, as the door slammed.

He stood in her kitchen, which was a duplicate of his own—including tub covered with sideboard—but with old-lady touches, including a nice china set and a row of matching bowls and cups. Surely too many for an old woman. He saw no one in the kitchen but sensed that he wasn't alone. As he stepped forward toward the bright windows in the front room, he became aware of tiny breathing creatures. It was like stepping into a barn where a litter of kittens waited in a dark corner.

Then he saw three children on a couch and several more on the floor. But he didn't think of them as helpless kittens. Instinctively he knew they were wise in the ways of childhood, for that was their domain. He knew that they expected something from him and were waiting to see if he was capable of delivering. Their eyes winked from the shadows, full of the knowledge that he had no experience with children. And Mrs. Levine hadn't left him with a plan, what games to play or songs to sing, what kind of food they ate or when mealtime was supposed to be. Or nap time. For them to be tired and sleep until Mrs. Levine returned— that would be wonderful. But he doubted it would happen and didn't even know when she'd return. His start time at the tunnel was four, and he had to allow at least an hour to get there, not counting time needed to buy lunch and for additional pre-work routines. Being a good worker meant you allowed plenty of time for routines. Routines are written in stone.

Why did she pick him? Why not a housewife? Many were at home in the other apartments. Women speak the language of children. They have an authority that little ones understand and respect. The way Rosie spoke to Sylvie, knowing with total confidence that her words would be obeyed. Or Ma, raising two wild boys. She was a soft-spoken woman but somehow maintained order.

Mrs. Levine may have had other options, but in an emergency the first door you come to looms large.

"Let's get to know each other, my name is Bill," he began, realizing as he spoke it the falseness of his assumed name. He couldn't pronounce it with any conviction. He'd used it over and over since his flight from Montana. It was as much his real name as the one his parents had given him. He'd identified himself to police, employers, shopkeepers, and ordinary friendly adults, without the falsity of it striking him. It was the name Virgil and Rosie used, even though they knew it was an alias. But surely these little ones had guessed in a flash that Bill wasn't his real name.

After a long moment of silence, they began to recite their names in loud clear voices: "My name is Morris, but you can call me Mo." For some reason this seemed absurd, to call a child of no more than eight either Morris or Mo. Bill smiled and nodded to the next child.

"My name is Edward, but everyone calls me Beale."

"My name is Walter, but my parents call me stupid *putz*." Several of the children tittered. He wasn't sure if they understood what this expression meant, but he knew Walter had to be called to order, whether or not his parents called him that. Teaching and calling to order were not his strong points, but he had to give it a try, venturing forth like a man eyeing an aerial wire, about to deliver a faltering lesson to a little boy named Walter.

But rescue came in the form of a little voice. "My name is Ruthie."

His mouth dropped open as he made the connection: this was the granddaughter of Mrs. Levine, whose daughter Hannah now lay injured at Bellevue. Yet Ruthie seemed happily unaware of her mother's situation. Of course, she was no more than six.

Without thinking about it, he hoisted her from the carpet and hugged her, feeling the starched dress pressing against his chest, and beneath it the beat of a heart. She folded her little arms around his neck so that she had to be pulled free in order to be put back on the couch with the other children.

"You live across the street, don't you Ruthie?"

"Yes, my address is 122 Fourth Street apartment 2C. Momma and I live there."

He was trying to think of another question for Ruthie when Walter interrupted. "Bill, we get a slice of cake."

Bill decided to counter this request with a hard line. In all probability Walter was respected by the other children because he knew how to put adults ill at ease. "If Mrs.

Levine wanted me to give you cake, surely she would have left it out where I could see it."

At that, Walter hopped off the sofa and walked to the kitchen, pointing to a shelf above the sideboard, to a box with the words *Lansburg and Sons Baked Goods.* He didn't seem to gloat over this piece of evidence but stood there pointing, a solid little boy, while the other children nodded, adding silent emphasis to Walter's argument. It was clear that he had to serve them cake, or whatever was in the box. It turned out not to be a sweet cake, more like a loaf of buttery bread with powdered sugar on top, and barely large enough for one slice each for the six children. The cake made them relax. They were very interested in what it was like to work under a river and chattered away with him, until one by one their eyes grew heavy and they nodded off. Was this really such a frightening business, making small talk with children? He dozed off a little, also. Several times they woke up, and he had them sing songs. But at two he started to wonder what he would do with them when he had to begin preparations for his shift.

Another hour passed before he heard a knock and Rosie's voice booming out, "Your relief is here!" She stood in the hallway, Sylvie trailing behind her.

As he backed through the doorway saying goodbye to the children, Ruthie slid off the couch and ran to him, hugging him about the knees.

"I see you've won another admirer," Rosie said.

He went next door to get ready for work, realizing a more important job had already been done.

**

Mrs. Levine visited her daughter at Bellevue, but not every day. She had children to watch, and Bill took Ruthie on visits. He'd gotten directions from Virgil. "You're the only person in the city who doesn't know where Bellevue is. You can't miss it—a monstrous brick building on a short tree-lined drive. But beware: that building dwarfs everything else, including the spirit of those coming to visit."

They lurched up Second Avenue on the crowded streetcar. When they arrived at Twenty Sixth Street, Ruthie jumped out, and he panicked as an auto car sped within a few feet of the shocked little girl, who froze and looked back. The terror in her eyes fastened on to the terror in his. She seized his hand, a huge ham-like thing, squeezed it tight.

"We're here to see Hannah …" He hesitated, unsure if the last name would be Levine. The old woman at the reception desk stared from behind a plaque reading, *Visitors' Information*.

"Levine," Ruthie spoke up proudly. "My momma is Mrs. Levine and I am Miss."

"She has been here recovering from burns." Bill added in a whisper, not sure how much the little girl knew of her mother's condition.

"What a good girl you are to visit the hospital," said the old woman, ignoring him entirely. She kneeled so her eyes were level with Ruthie's. She held out a white-gloved hand containing a small dish of lemon drops. Ruthie had made her selection, and the old woman reached out for Bill's help in straightening up.

148

"In the Psychiatric Ward," she whispered and pointed down a very clean hallway with polished wood floors to another set of doors. All over the city, from Bill's limited experience, doors were made like these, of frosted glass reinforced with chicken-wire. They entered the ward and saw another old woman, very small and frail in appearance. She was sitting in front of a wide curtain. Her penetrating eyes told him that he'd better have a good reason if he hoped to be ushered through that curtain. She was Annabelle Fisk, according to the placard on her desk.

"We're here to see my momma," Ruthie proclaimed, and apparently this was good enough for Annabelle Fisk, who parted the curtains to reveal an enormous room with three rows of iron cots. A depressing gray light came in through the windows of the high-ceilinged room. Apparently, these windows were made of the same frosted glass.

Ruthie ran ahead, passing the blank stares of gray-faced women buried under starched white sheets. Bill hesitated to follow, for he really had no business there. But he couldn't leave the little girl alone in the eerie silence of this room. Ruthie had no trouble finding her mother, at the end of one of the rows, lying on her side. His first sight of Hannah was shocking. Could this be the same woman with whom he'd had that momentary encounter, when she stepped from the shadows and surprised him outside her mother's apartment? That self-confident woman with the ironic smile had been replaced by someone whose face was partially masked by a large bandage that covered her left cheek and extended under the sheet. His heart sank as he realized that the change in her went beyond that. Her eyes were no longer bright and her facial features seemed to have been deflated. The female quickness and insight at play in her face—that had previously fascinated and intimidated him—were now missing entirely.

The nurse who'd been seated by the bed stood up to greet them, intervening when Hannah spread her arms toward Ruthie. "Since you're a good little girl and want your momma to get better, you must do as I say. Give her a little kiss on the right cheek where there is not a bandage then sit quietly."

The nurse placed the little girl on the bed. Then Ruthie leaned over and kissed, as directed. The nurse acknowledged this good behavior with a nod and continued: "And please, please take great care when you touch her. If she hugs you it will hurt her very much because of her burns. Remember that you mustn't let her hug you no matter how much she wants you to."

"I can't hug Momma?"

Hannah's eyes shifted toward her daughter, a mute begging.

"Soon she will give you the biggest hugs in the whole world, and it will be worth the wait." The nurse looked intently into Ruthie's eyes, establishing a gentle authority that Bill also responded to. He wouldn't have disobeyed one of this nurse's orders for the world. Her nametag said Hannigan.

Bill began to turn away from them. He had no right to involve himself in the private life of Hannah Levine, a woman he didn't know at all.

Meanwhile, Hannah had not acknowledged him in any way. Her eyes held a hint of life when engaged with Ruthie; otherwise, they were blank. Her face was gray in the dim light of the ward.

"You're not the husband," Hannigan guessed. "It's perfectly alright to leave them here. I'll be watching. Come back in thirty minutes."

He walked past the rows of iron cots and out of the enormous, gray room, through the long spotless halls that smelled of hospital chemicals. He pushed through the front doors and out to the tree-lined lane. As he walked, Hannah's situation weighed on his thoughts. That roomful of unfortunate women was a world he'd known nothing about. Would any of them truly recover? And what about the effect on Ruthie of her mother's injuries, body and mind? But it would be a mistake for him to become a busybody and involve himself in Hannah Levine's affairs. She deserved privacy not curiosity.

The spring air still held a trace of morning fog. He decided to turn down Twenty Sixth toward the East River. Bellevue had been built near the river because in those days the choppy gray water would have been the quickest way to transport emergency cases, and many emergencies had resulted from the construction of the city's giant projects of steel and concrete. Fatalities and crippled bodies would make this city the greatest on earth. He stared at the river and specters seemed to rise from the water. It was his own nightmare vision of the bodies that the great earth coughed up from the mine fire on June 8. After his crew had come back up the ladders from their rescue attempt and recovered from the inhaled smoke, he and young Tim Brady set off down what they hoped was an entrance to the disaster site. The area under Butte was honeycombed with shafts, used and unused. They headed down a steep incline that they hoped would lead them into the adjacent shaft, possibly to survivors. As they made their way down this dark incline they were struck by the cool, clear air. They broke into a run, eager to reach miners spared by the fire. Until a concrete wall blocked their path. Young Tim understood before Bill what this meant. His eyes darkened, as if at that very moment the boy was losing his youth. The wall had aged him. It was from the change that came over Tim's face that Bill finally grasped what those bulkheads meant.

That's how some people first understand the world of emotions, from the reflection they cast in the eyes of others. The overwhelming sadness of those June days was unlocked by the crestfallen face of that mining boy.

Unlike what happened during the mine fire, what happened August 1 had an instant effect. He held Frank's suspended body in his arms, trying to comfort this poor, tortured thing. Surely, a brother's loving embrace would be a help, even now after all life had ebbed away. He had to be pulled away, and it was only when the other fellows went up on the trestle and cut the rope that he began to see Frank's body as a lifeless thing, now crumpled on the ground.

But this was all wrong. The older brother was supposed to shelter and comfort the younger. The defender had vanished. Despite the punishing years of prison and parole, Bill had moved on in his life. But part of him would always be back there, the trestle above him, silhouetted against the dawn sky. The horror had the capacity to paralyze his thoughts, even years later. But in the years since he'd begun to ask the obvious questions: who had done this? Who had given the orders? The fact that he had no answers deepened the wound.

Virgil had once probed into this mystery. They'd just concluded a large breakfast at D'Allessandro's and Anthony had refilled their tea cups and walked away. Virgil looked over his shoulder and, satisfied that the boy wasn't in range, asked in a hushed voice. "You have no idea who Arnoldson is?" Bill pushed his empty plate to the side and leaned forward as Virgil continued with another question, "Do you know about a 1919 incident in a town named Centralia?"

Bill shook his head. He'd been in prison, where there'd been a grapevine and where newspapers occasionally passed from cell to cell. But no, he hadn't heard of a town named Centralia and he'd have remembered a name like that.

"An armed conflict broke out between vigilantes and a labor rally. A war veteran was captured by the vigilantes and lynched after being horribly mutilated."

The word mutilated stirred a moment of nausea in Bill. His first thought was that Virgil was ruining an enjoyable moment after a good meal, but he knew something more was involved.

"I remember a newspaper account from that time period that may relate to your situation," Virgil continued in the same hushed voice. "I apologize for keeping this from you until now. The article included a disturbing conjecture: the Centralia attack was carried out by a shadowy vigilante network operating throughout the Northwest. I don't know what intelligence this speculation was based on, if any. Maybe you know how to evaluate it better than I do."

Bill stared at his friend, pondering the implications. Was Arnoldson more than an influential farmer and parole boss? But there were no facts here, and he wasn't going to jump to troubling conclusions based on a vague conjecture in a newspaper account from 1919.

"Would you gents like a sweet roll?" Anthony's question broke into the silence of the empty restaurant. The boy hovered over their table, dying of curiosity, and received blank stares but continued, "A little extra energy might be just the thing for two men about to spend a grueling shift under the Hudson."

Bill put a dollar on the table to cover two breakfasts and a tip. Should he draw Virgil out on this shadowy network? But what more could be added, besides guesswork? Some disturbing issues would have to be pushed aside, especially those he couldn't do anything about. He was fighting to make something of himself and had to protect his new life. Like any other young plant, a new life can be choked by weeds. Or disturbing thoughts.

**

He turned swiftly from the wide gray water of the East River, and in that abrupt motion the gloomy images that had been before him shattered into a thousand pieces, a puzzle of tiny surfs and tides, mysteries and lives.

He had to hurry back to Bellevue, for he'd promised to take Ruthie to lunch on their way home. What about the responsibility he was taking on—for he'd be expected to take her on future visits to that gloomy ward. He knew very little about children. What was she allowed to do? What should she eat? But if he'd asked for Hannah's guidance, she'd only turn a blank, uncomprehending face. No, the responsibility had fallen to the one man in the whole world who was least qualified for it.

For some reason what popped into mind was the vision of the three girls he'd seen the day before playing in Fourth Street. Behind them was a spectacle of overflowing trash, of hurrying, distressed adults, including no doubt a few gangsters, of filth and dismay everywhere. Yet those three girls all had bright smiles as they sang in perfect unison and danced in a line, kicking their feet in the air as if they were performing in a chorus line:

Oh, boy! Tip your hat!
Oh, joy! She's the cat!
Who's that, Mister?
Ain't no sister—
Sweet Georgia Brown.

**

Ruthie's eyes lit up as he approached, but the person she'd been chattering with was the nurse. Hannah had turned away. All he could see were the sheets flowing over the contours of shoulder and hip. He wanted to step up to the cot and shake her, shake her until the woman he'd once met peered back. But that woman was in hiding. Women and men disappear second by second into places no one

155

can map. And the way back can be hard to trace, and has its dangers.

"Ruthie had a nice chat," Nurse Hannigan said. "And your timing was perfect because just this moment her momma let us know she needed to rest."

**

He was suitably dressed for *Schraft's*. If he'd been in work clothes, the waitress might not have had such a friendly smile as she ushered them to a table through a lunchtime crowd of shoppers and office workers. They sat on plush chairs and put their hands beside placemats, white with scalloped edges.

"I want blintzes," Ruthie announced before he had a chance to read her the menu.

"Are you sure that's what your momma would want you to order?"

"She wants me to order blintzes with strawberries, like that lady." She pointed to an elegant woman at the next table, who paused, fork in the air, on hearing her lunch referred to. Bill nodded to her and noticed how elaborately she had dressed for lunch, with several semi-transparent but colorful scarves wrapped around her neck and a crescent-shaped felt hat pinned to hair that looked like it had been baked in place. She looked like a piece of sculpture beside the candied berries topping her blintzes. She made an effort to smile at the little girl before guiding a forkful of buttery cheese into her bright red lips.

"Would you like to split a pastrami sandwich with me before we have our blintzes?" Bill asked.

156

"Yes," Ruthie declared. "But I need my own blintzes."

The waitress took the order according to those directives and was about to leave. "Momma wants me to have a slice of tomato with lunch." The waitress added this to the order and turned back to the kitchen.

At least he didn't have to worry about the way he was dressed. He'd bought this jacket several weeks earlier, thinking he'd never use it. His shirt looked like silk though it was only Egyptian cotton. "Everyone admires a shirt with a sleek finish," the salesman had said.

The low hum of so many conversations provided a kind of quiet space for them to converse in. She told him about her school, which she attended two mornings a week, around the corner on Avenue A.

"I don't like it. I already know how to read and figure. And all the boys are bad." She put all the force of her plump little being into those words.

He told her about his own schooling in Oklahoma, skipping over the tutoring from his father, the doctor who'd run off, like her own father. But he mentioned the old schoolteacher who'd taught him. "He was a famous soldier before he came to Oklahoma."

"We went to Coney Island four times last summer," Ruthie interjected. "And Momma took me to Hoboken once. Is Oklahoma near Hoboken?"

"A little further west," he said. It was only at that point in the discussion that he realized what he'd been revealing to Ruthie, telling her where he was from and other things that only Virgil and Rosie knew. And he had wanted to keep it that way.

"Oklahoma is our secret."

Her eyes closed joyfully over the revelation. All things of interest are secrets. They are revealed once, just for you. When children first learn about secrets, there's nothing else worth knowing.

She told him her own secret, which she'd been keeping for over a year because a magician, of all people, had insisted on it. At a show on Second Avenue, he'd jumped down from the stage and walked among the audience carrying his magic box. He turned it upside down and nothing came out. Then he put it on the floor and winked at Ruthie. "This is our secret," he'd said. When he waved a handkerchief over the box a rabbit jumped up.

"I felt the fur before Momma made me give him back. But it's my secret, and you have to promise not to tell." So, the magician had shared a secret with Ruthie, as well as the rest of the Second Avenue audience. And the rabbit, of course.

In growing up, the joy of a secret eventually turns into the weight of maintaining it. There's not much magic left, unless you can pass it on to someone else.

**

The very next morning, as he was waking from the deep sleep that followed his labors, he heard a light rap on the door. Ruthie stood there, her grandmother just behind her. Bill had earlier been struck by Mrs. Levine's intelligent gray eyes, set deep in leathery cheeks. When she smiled, her face was pleasantly alert, reminding him of Hannah's playful glance on their first meeting. But today Bill was greeted by a mask of suspicious, care-worn features. She muttered in broken English something to the effect that this was Ruthie's idea, not hers.

"We'll have a little breakfast. Then I'll bring you back to your grandmother."

Mrs. Levine eventually accepted the fact that Ruthie liked to come next door to visit—grudgingly, and only after first checking with Rosie. Everyone first checked with Rosie, and not only the women. Among the dozens of families that lived on that block of Fourth Street, she was known as a reliable judge of character by all except those whose character she didn't like.

**

On the second Sunday in May, he and Ruthie emerged from a crowded underground passageway and walked down Bedford Avenue to the entrance of an edifice of brick and glass. The immense face of the building towered over a bank of wood turnstiles where a mob of excited people lined up. The sweep of it was breathtaking and a little incongruous. How had this awe-inspiring monument taken root on such a shabby street, beside a dusty subway entrance?

The crowd writhed and squirmed with anticipation. The men had rolled up their shirtsleeves in the heat; some wore straw boaters but most were in billed caps like the ballplayers. Women pushed and shoved for a place in line along with the men. The younger women wore shifts without a waistline. They smiled boldly. Some looked quite dashing, wearing the same boaters and caps as the men. Thirty minutes early, and fans were already pouring into Ebbets Field to see their beloved Brooklyn Robins play. Ruthie was thrilled by the huge modern building and the excitement of the crowd. The stadium was said to hold well over 20,000 fans. No doubt it would be full by the first pitch.

Arriving at a ballgame was a thrilling experience. From her expression, Ruthie shared in the excitement. They pushed through the crowd, eager to catch a first view of the perfectly manicured field, wide and green. He'd played baseball at every opportunity—even a little in prison—and watched countless games. But that was out west, on rough fields with dried-out grass and plenty of bad bounces. This field was how a baseball diamond should look, a green ideal, lush but perfectly trimmed. Ruthie was fascinated by the work of the grounds crew as they finished chalking the two foul lines that radiated from home plate.

Thousands who were trapped all week in a squalid city came here to worship rural life. Not the reality of back-breaking farm work and harsh weather, but the pastoral ideal.

They found their seats, and he hoisted the little girl for a better view of the first pitch.

"Who's your favorite player, Bill?" She asked, after the game.

"I guess I'd have to say Zach Wheat. Wouldn't you say he's our best?"

"He got three hits today," she beamed. "But next time Zach will get ten hits and our redbreasts will win."

"*Redbreasts* is a nice nickname, but no one calls them that. Do you know why?" He explained that Brooklyn's team name, the Robins, came not from a type of bird but from the name of the manager, Wilbert Robinson. Years before, Robinson had been a great catcher for the Baltimore Orioles. Bill knew something about all the teams but didn't say any more about the Orioles so as not to confuse her, since that team was, in fact, named for a bird. Nothing about baseball made sense, unless you grew up with it. Now, Ruthie would grow up with it.

The games averaged almost two hours, and there were 154 in a season. Patience was required. But what could prepare you better for the long road than being a fan, the loyal supporter of a team, and the many ups and downs that this entailed?

Along with thousands of fans, they jammed into the subway for the ride home. Like them, they were exhausted from cheering. Even though the Robins lost 5 to 4, they felt satisfied. Not mere spectators, this crowd had played an active role, rallying the Robins, booing the umpires, unmercifully heckling the other team. It was a good game and they'd done what they could. They were humble people and had already learned that some things in life were beyond their control. Like the lineup of the New York Yankees.

**

On Tuesdays and Thursdays, he escorted Ruthie to the hospital and usually went for walks while she visited her mother, who continued to ignore his presence. Meanwhile, the little girl seemed oblivious to the fact that Hannah turned away when he was there.

Annabelle Fisk had become more accepting. And nurse Hannigan—Miss or Mrs., he never knew—was always friendly. "You probably can't see it, since you come here so often, but she's made a great deal of progress. Her burns are healing, and she's healing inside as well."

The nurses saw him often and were never sure of what to think of his relationship to Hannah. Not a husband or brother, but someone who cared, possibly a boyfriend. But the sad fact was that he didn't know her at all. They told him more about her condition than she herself knew, probably more than they told her mother, whose English was limited. The old woman visited often as well, but she never asked Bill to accompany her.

"The pain is a little like the trauma of the fire and will die down. She will get used to what remains," said Hannigan.

"What remains …?"

"The scar tissue covers a delicate area. For some time, the skin will be dry and numb to the touch. That is what burn victims tell me." When she looked intently at him, he could see that years of nursing hadn't extinguished an almost girlish optimism in her eyes. "You must have patience and support her in everything. And don't doubt her for a minute. All of my patients are strong women. I have faith in them."

She spoke with experience concerning the devastating impact of such burns. The Lower East Side was an overcrowded tinderbox. Injury and death by fire were commonplace in homes as well as factories.

"The cough will disappear. What is important is that you not disappear. Don't hesitate to visit us if you have any questions. Good luck. Everything will be ok."

But what was he to do with this secret knowledge about Ruthie's mother? He wasn't entitled to it. How was he to support Hannah, as Nurse Hannigan seemed to be asking, when he himself meant nothing to her? And the same was true of Mrs. Levine. He hardly even dared to talk to her about ordinary things let alone what the nurse had just told him. She would certainly resent the fact that a stranger had become so involved with her daughter's situation. And wouldn't Hannah resent it, when she learned that this man she didn't know at all was in possession of such personal details?

Because of his earlier discussion, and the great embarrassment it had caused him, he didn't raise his predicament with Rosie. But he did question Virgil about it. After telling him that Hannah appeared unable to relate to anyone, Virgil had asked, "Not even to Ruthie?"

"She does relate to Ruthie. Now that the nurses permit it, they'll sit on the cot, her arm around her daughter. They're sitting like that when I leave and when I return. But Hannah never says a word, at least not that I hear."

"Many Jewish husbands would welcome such a condition of wordlessness. But such men are silly because they don't realize that the joke is on them. In Yiddish we call them *shmegegges*. In fact, they expend more words on this overworked topic than their wives expend on whatever they have every right to discuss." Bill always listened devotedly to his friend's sometimes lengthy explications of Jewish lore. Such insights were welcome, for he lived surrounded by these people and sometimes felt like the only non-Jew inside a nation of Jews.

"You see, Bill, some unfair stereotypes can be communicated in the course of very funny jokes. Here's one example:

"A Jewish boy comes home from school and tells his mother he has a part in the play. She asks, 'What part is it?'

"The boy says, 'I play the part of the Jewish husband.'

"The mother scowls and says, 'Go back and tell the teacher you want a speaking part.'

Bill stifled a laugh.

"You see what I mean? Jews love their stereotypes and entertain each other with them by the hour. It's all very well and good to have a good laugh, and who can make you laugh better than a Jewish comic. But we should always keep in mind that the watchword of such comics is: Never let reality get in the way of a good joke."

This conversation took place over coffee in the Shulman's kitchen. In the background, Rosie and Sylvie were chattering away in the front room.

Virgil fixed his friend with a significant gaze and returned to the question of Hannah's mental health. "Are you frightened of her? Most people find mental illness very disturbing, because they can't understand it. The most terrifying Jewish myth is that of the monster *Dybbuk*, which inflicts a broken soul. Dybbuk seeks to attach itself to healthy souls in order to appropriate the wholeness that it lacks. No one wants to lose their mind to such a creature, especially not Jews, who have a prickly regard for their own sanity."

"But Hannah isn't a monster like this Dybbuk," Bill offered.

"Of course not, but she is a broken soul," Virgil stopped in mid-sentence, alarmed to find that Rosie had come into the kitchen and was listening.

"Hannah's soul has been wounded but not broken," she interrupted. "Pushy, I know exactly what you were going to say, and I agree with it, except for this: you're trying to use my friend as an example of how poorly the mentally ill are treated in this society. But there's nothing *meshugina* about my friend, and she is no victim. She's a strong woman. She'll get better because she's a mother, so she has to. But also, for herself. She's not done living, just because you see her as an example of someone to take pity on."

"My God, Rosie, I know that Hannah will get well. I remember how, in this very kitchen, the two of you spent hours together, talking and howling with laughter. But it makes me extremely sad to see such a fun-loving girl become so depressed and withdrawn. When I said she's broken I didn't mean she would never become whole again."

Virgil looked first at Rosie then at Bill, pleading with them to understand what he was trying to say, but Rosie changed the subject. "Pushy, if you have any of that good schnapps left, let's drink a toast to Hannah. She'll be released from Bellevue next Saturday.

**

Bill watched from the front window of his apartment as Rosie, Mrs. Levine, and a nurse helped Hannah up the stairs and into 122 Fourth Street. Around them, boys careened down the sidewalk, screaming at the top of their lungs; girls played hopscotch on squares they'd chalked onto asphalt; two derelicts sat on a stoop, shoulders hunched together; and a knot of housewives examined the turmoil and found everything in good order. And Hannah paused on the top step, her hand on Ruthie's shoulder. Was it his imagination or was she peering toward his window?

He couldn't be certain from that far away but it seemed to him that a smile crossed her face. Was it the same supremely confident smile he'd once seen? Hannah's return was good news for mother and daughter. Surely it was good news, even though it might spell an end to Ruthie's visits.

The next day he waited for a knock. He fiddled with the laces of his new work boots before leaving for D'Allesandro's for lunch.

"Your little girlfriend isn't with you," Anthony said.

"Her momma's back from Bellevue, so I doubt she needs me anymore."

Though only a youngster, Anthony had learned to summon a philosophical tone. "You were a good father to her, while it lasted . . . How about eggs over easy with some hash?"

He got up the next day, Sunday, feeling washed out and exhausted from the extra shift he'd worked the day before. Every blood vessel in his body had been stretched beyond the point of fatigue from the constant pumping and deflating they were subjected to during a week under the river.

But it wasn't just from the end of another week and the great weight of the air. It was because he usually spent Sundays with Ruthie, and now he'd have to make another plan, maybe to have a beer with Virgil. A talk with his friend was overdue. He'd kept hoping he would become more skilled, with months of experience under his belt. But over the past few weeks Virgil seemed to have lost his focus, had become more of a *klutz* than ever. On their Saturday shift, he'd stumbled near a cart. These were slow-moving, but the wheels could pinch a foot against iron rails and break it.

"Another accident sidestepped," he'd joked to Bill afterward. "I must be improving. This time you didn't have to spring to my rescue." Self-effacing chatter notwithstanding, Virgil didn't understand the danger he was putting himself in—and sometimes others.

As he shaved, he caught himself smiling as he thought of Ruthie. Her visits had given him something to look forward to. But maybe it was a good thing that he no longer needed to look after her so his attention could return to Virgil. He thought of how the two of them had hurried to the tunnel with the fat barker in the lead, and how he'd instantly known Virgil was a talker. How true that first impression was. And how Virgil had taken him home and given him a future—and a past. He couldn't live with himself if that kind man was hurt at work.

But without her, how far down would he sink? Maybe he had a little of the Dybbuk spirit in himself as well, and it was a monster only a brave little girl could vanquish. He'd done a good deed, and now mother and daughter were together. He toweled his face, folded the straight edge and put it on the counter beside the sink.

Then he heard a soft knock on the door and a voice whispering through it, "Bill, we have to see the Robins play."

A typical only child, he laughed to himself, always expects to get her way. He pulled on shirt and trousers and flung open the door. "Aren't they playing out of town today?" He teased, knowing full well they were in Brooklyn. The hint of a pout showed on her face. In his mind's eye he saw how that expression would develop as she grew to become a teenager then a young woman.

"Don't you know, Bill," she burst out, "they're playing the Pirates at home!"

The game today versus the Pirates was one he particularly wanted to see, but he wouldn't have attended it without her. "What's the name of that fellow who plays for the Pirates," he asked.

"Pie Traynor, everyone knows that," she replied impatiently.

"But what does your momma say?

"She already knows," Ruthie said. Was this a bad sign? On her first day back from the hospital she was sending her little girl away for the afternoon.

After the game, they walked from the subway, down Fourth Street, a little subdued by another tough loss. Everyone was out in the street, enjoying a warm evening, with the full heat of summer a few weeks away. The sidewalks and steps were full of lounging adults, and the street was packed with girls jumping rope and at least two different games of stick ball. The boys darted about fielding grounders, oblivious to the fact that they were constantly interfering with the graceful swirl of the ropes.

Then Ruthie stopped. "Do they have big trees like this in Oklahoma?" She asked as she pressed a hand against one of the great elms and held it there, like it was the forehead of a friend.

"Cottonwoods are as big," he said. Then he looked around, a little too furtively. "But Oklahoma is our secret, Ruthie. Don't you remember?"

With that her face fell, even more than it had when the last Robins batter had grounded out to end the game. He hoisted her up on his shoulders and reversed his steps, walking back toward First Avenue, where a little shop sold ice cream.

"One vanilla and one chocolate. It's for my momma," she explained to the clerk. She carried it with pride, while Bill watched to make sure no one bumped her as they threaded their way back up Fourth Street. They entered 122 and he followed her, entering this hallway for the first time. It was the same as the downstairs of his building, though not as well-cared for, the tiles not polished. Apartment 2C was in the back of the building. They stood at the door for a moment until he realized that it was up to him to knock, since Ruthie had her hands full with the cones. Would Hannah invite him in or just smile and say something like, "Hello, again. Nice to see you, and thank you for taking Ruthie to the ballgame." He straightened himself as he heard the clunk of the lock being thrown. But when the door finally opened it was only far enough for Ruthie to run in. He heard a few whispers as the door closed. At least she'd enjoy the chocolate and vanilla.

Rather than head directly across the street to his building, he wandered to Tompkins Square Park, where even more children were at play and adults smoked and chatted, enjoying the last few moments of their weekend. The scene outside apartment 2C had saddened him.

A week later Mrs. Levine confronted him in the hall: "You don't like to see Hannah? Afraid of burn?"

10.

No one wants to go naked into a room of daggers and hard stares.
But what if safety exists? What if there is no need to carry a shield?

When he first arrived, New York was noisy and shriek-
ing, a total shock. But as he grew used to it, he saw how
life here was similar to life in the West. He made a list to
compare them:

1. general squalor—the same although less extensive
    in the mining towns of the West;
2. violence—legendary in the West, but the Lower
    East Side was violent enough, not only because of
    the Irish gangsters feared by his truckers but also
    Jewish and Italian mobs;
3. the cops—protected no one and bullied many, the
    same;
4. sex, this was the difference.

In the West men and women lived separate lives. Many
western men didn't have families and lived in cheap hotels,
boarding houses, mine or ranch bunkhouses. This rigid
separation was the rule during a good bit of his life, six
years of mining, six of prison. Before prison, he worked
ten- or twelve- hour days, and if he didn't have a landlady
wherever he was staying, he might go a week or two without speaking to a woman. Two separate colonies existed,

as in *Reuben, Reuben,* a song that played through his mind although he hated it—

> *Reuben, Reuben, I've been thinking*
> *What a fine world this would be*
> *If the men were all transported*
> *Far beyond the northern sea!*
> *Rachel, Rachel, I've been thinking*
> *What a fine world this would be*
> *If the girls were all transported*
> *Far beyond the northern sea!*

In contrast, men and women lived crowded together in the Lower East Side, in one violent, undignified mass. But even here walls and strict borders were erected out of the need for privacy. And loneliness in crowds was one result. Where crime and violence are rampant, intimacy is suspect and many are doomed to lonely and secret lives. The same here as in the West.

From conversations with Rosie, he gathered that every Jewish wife longed to leave the Lower East Side. If not for the West then at least for New Jersey, Long Island, even Brooklyn. These neighborhoods seemed distant from the violent and filthy warren they toiled in, better places to raise children. As Virgil was so fond of repeating, the Lower East Side was the most crowded spot of real estate on our planet, despite increasing competition from parts of India and China.

**

He'd never studied a naked woman, a woman he'd just made love to. In western mining towns a reverie based on trust is seldom permitted. The brutal business of mining stamps men in its own image, angry and rude. Women maintain their guard, are sometimes as brutal as the men. At best, men and women are cautious and distant. Despite all this he fell in love with Dorothy, a telephone operator. She was intelligent and very ardent. He told her he loved her and she responded with a hug and warmth but said nothing in return. The hint of a smile played at the thin line of her lips and something danced in her cautious brown eyes. They had a few good weeks, much of it hemmed in by their jobs.

One Sunday they went on a picnic. It was Dorothy's idea. When she first proposed it, he thought she was crazy because the area around Butte seemed like the most unfriendly place to walk and relax in. But after quite a long stroll they escaped the smoke and smog, and what a beautiful late May day it was. She led the way along a fast-moving creek that was bright silver in the distance, close up a chain of deep green pools linked by shoals. Although the countryside was rocky and barren, trees lined the creek. They put the basket Dorothy had prepared down on the earth and sat back against a tree, shoulders and arms touching. Gazing at Butte from several miles out provided a spectacle of the hellhole they lived in. From this vantage it was striking: the smelters and refineries, the furnaces spouting fire, unleashing brimstone from the depths, as if the earth's molten core was finally breaking through the crust. A terrible scene, but fascinating, like a detail in a painting of the end of the world.

But here, far from stacks belching fire, from the rasp of gears and belts and iron wheels, they had trees and clear water running among the rocks, and their own voices.

"Aren't you glad I convinced you to come on this picnic?"

"I wouldn't have believed what a spectacular place we live in. Do you bring all your boyfriends here?"

"I'll answer your question—after we've known each other a little longer."

He took that response to mean that it was her business, in other words, you're not the only one I've taken for picnics. Their lives together were shaped from such small words. Small words, not always understood.

Then actual flames, the mine fire close-up, Frank's murder, his arrest. She waved goodbye as he was led off by the deputies, a brave smile mixed with tears. When he studied her image, as it remained stored in his memory, he saw what a striking woman she was. Her hair was thick, often unruly, not truly strawberry but pretty close, her eyes cunning, her smile restrained. A face that didn't usually reveal much emotion except that her cheeks always seemed about to turn pink. Very alluring, partly because of the restraint. Tough and lovely. From the distance of years, he saw something else in the lines of her face: tenderness. Maybe only a hint, but as time passed and he reflected on Dorothy, that hint became what he dwelled on. When they were together, he was afraid to see much tenderness just as she was afraid to show it.

After his jailing they exchanged letters once, and he wrote several times more but heard nothing. Then two years of silence. He became used to the idea that she'd moved on. A young woman shouldn't have to carry a pledge for the duration of a lover's sentence, not a life sentence anyway.

He shouldn't have felt angry, but that's how he felt, sitting on his bunk, putting aside a shabby novel from the prison library. He stared through the faint light of his cell, and images passed before his eyes, of walking with her to a tavern, later making love in her apartment, grabbing his clothes to hurry off for work. Or—after making love she jumps out of bed, laughs, and begins to button her underwear. He gets up and tries to help fasten the brassiere. Women don't really need such help, a fact men don't like to admit. What he longed to do was reach around her back and take her breasts in his hands. Feel the nipples that almost matched the color of her hair. But she twists away and pushes him back into bed. She pulls the sheet over his own nakedness. He lies there craving something more than their love-making. Craving their nakedness together.

Dorothy wasn't shy but had learned to guard herself. Propriety is a type of armor, and many people can't let it go, even in the most intimate moments. He wasn't the same in this regard. Had he seemed pushy or immodest to her? During the first several years of prison he played the scenes back through his mind and concluded that he hadn't. He was different from her but not rude.

To a convict, daydreams can be a kick in the teeth. Memories based on nothing but the past, having no traction in the world outside the jail cell, become a mockery.

But with time his thoughts of her lost their sting. He didn't forget her, but her image began to fade. He tried to make her fade. That's all inmates can do, to soften the hurt. But he couldn't control when and how she came back. Several more years passed before he learned that she'd died of influenza shortly after her last letter.

A dead-end, a live hurt.

Montana State Prison wasn't immune to the Spanish Flu. Inmates came down with it and died, if anyone cared, although not at the same rate that people died in big East Coast cities. As the year 1918 was drawing to a close, a guard caught him talking in dinner hall. This was out of character for Bill. By that time he'd learned how not to be caught. Most inmates were merely warned with a finger to the lips. But he served more than a week in solitary, isolated from the disease while fellow inmates were contracting it. So he'd benefited from a harsh punishment, on this one occasion at least.

Meanwhile, the flu struck the Butte telephone operators hard. They were a tight-knit group. Their solidarity had often helped them in the past. On this occasion, it meant that almost all came down with the disease and nearly half succumbed.

**

Very few can completely hide their thoughts. Despite best efforts, feelings leak out and show themselves. That was certainly the case with Bill, as he walked several times around the block, heading north on First Avenue, where he caught a glimpse of a frightened man in the mirror of

Levenson's Yard Goods and Dress. He tried to compose himself as he turned east on Fifth to Avenue A, and south again toward Fourth, all the while practicing an expressionless exterior. He'd come full circle, again, without establishing any equilibrium and contemplated another procrastinating walk. But no, he had to pull himself together and began to hurry to 122 Fourth Street and down the hallway, all in a rush before losing heart. He tried to gather himself together before the door to 2C but before he could knock the door opened and Hannah stood before him. A smile crossed her face as she guessed at the turmoil taking place inside him.

She may not have been quite her old self, but on this day she was doing a much better job of coping than he was.

"Do you mind if we walk this little fuss-budget over to her grandmother's house?"

Ruthie, who'd been standing beside her momma, begged to go out with them, so Hannah had to resort to the argument that "Bubbe will be so glad to see you. And since it's Sunday, she'll probably be baking."

As a result, the first part of their date was scripted by a stop at Grandma's. This was a big relief to Bill. He wasn't surprised when Mrs. Levine gave her daughter and grand-daughter hugs, but he hadn't expected the old woman to smile and open her arms to him. He was shocked but also warmed by the way the old lady reached around his waist and briefly nestled her head on his chest. He hadn't thought of it before, but the touch of an old person has a special feeling to it, a feeling he'd missed.

They descended the steps to Fourth Street. He'd prepared himself with several suggestions as to what they should do, assuming that this responsibility was up to him. Going for a late lunch was one.

"A walk is the best thing for me," she said. "I haven't gotten out much, as I know you're aware. And it's a lovely afternoon."

It was a little bit on the warm and sticky side, but the sky was high and blue. The tops of the elms tossed gently. Her initiative was a relief, even though it meant a more physically demanding afternoon than he would've chosen for his Sunday off. They made for Union Square and headed west from there. Though neither of them spoke, she turned and smiled at him several times and then paused.

"I want to thank you for caring for Ruthie, but you might not find me as entertaining a companion—or as interested in the Brooklyn Robins."

He wanted to assure her that she was a fine companion, but no words came. After what seemed like an endless tongue-tied moment, she seized his arm. "Let's walk—it's easier than talking."

They continued west, crossed Eighth Avenue, and at Gansevort Market found a fruit stand open and picked up a couple of apples. Perhaps they weren't the freshest, so far out of season. His mind wasn't on the taste. They walked on in the Sunday silence of the waterfront. The only sounds came from the two of them munching their apples, which made them laugh. They strolled down West Street, gazing at the moored ships through the iron gates of the piers. The gray hulls towered overhead, huge and peaceful, no longshoremen hustling up gangways, no screeching cranes.

They came to a gap in the fence where they could walk out to a dock, which jutted into the water. Here, away from the forest of buildings, the spring breeze circled their bodies. He lobbed the apple core into the river.

"My, what a strong throw. Did you play baseball as a boy?"

"Of course, don't all boys play baseball?"

"Tell me, Bill," she said, abruptly changing the subject, "could a woman do the kind of work you do?" This question caught him off guard. Wasn't it absurd to even imagine such a thing? Then he tried to play this question back and respond as he imagined Virgil might have.

"Put a woman under the Hudson and she'd clean up this filthy occupation and make it safer." This answer was exactly as Virgil would have delivered it. "But why would a woman want to?" He added.

"For the money. I was a garment sewer, one of the fastest in our factory, and made good money, better than many unskilled men, but far less than you and Virgil make at your tunnel work . . . But don't worry," she laughed, "I'm not about to join you in that unsanitary river mud. Rosie has told me about the filth and the high accident rate.

"Virgil is a good worker. I don't have to do much to help him." He winced at the lie.

Then she levelled her eyes at him. "You're careful at work? I couldn't stand to be friends with you if I had to worry all the time about your safety."

So, they were friends, and she was gripping his arm again.

Hannah held his chin in her hand as they sprawled in bed. "Are you afraid to look at me?" She raised his head so that his eyes scanned her thighs, swept her stomach and the tight crease that deepened into her navel, to her breasts, hanging marvelously before her ribcage. Then to the discoloration. It looked like a filmy rose-colored shawl draped over her upper torso. Part of her left breast was covered by the burn. Where the flames bit deepest, around her neck and collarbone, was an area of scarred, glossy skin. Her left cheek, beneath her eye, also held a blush.

"Not much," she shrugged, when he'd finally asked if the burn still hurt. With a quick movement of her head she tossed her hair back off her face. It flowed behind her shoulders in a long wave, brown, now mixed with a little gray. Were there as many gray strands before her injury? The shock of silver in her bangs, the birthmark, brought out the whites of her flashing dark eyes. They were wide-set, dominating her face, laughing at him just as they had when they'd bumped into each other in the hallway months earlier. But something else was in her eyes now: an awareness of the scar. And with it the need to have it accepted. Not just the damaged skin but the whole episode, which had bitten deeper than the flames.

She'd emerged after those months of withdrawal during which only Ruthie could reach her, and not always her. She wasn't a self-conscious person, but a notion of her own vulnerability had invaded those laughing eyes. She needed to be accepted, and Bill was the perfect man for that. He accepted her with an innocent and profound love based on years of loneliness. She loved this man because he was what she needed. He'd perceived in her a great need to rely on him. At first, he thought her feelings were based solely on the fact that he'd proven himself trustworthy with Ruthie, and of course the little girl was crazy about him. How could this woman who was not only beautiful but witty and discerning have fallen for him? Gradually, however—and in spite of bouts of insecurity—he'd become convinced that her need for him was as deep as his for her.

When he was with her, he sensed beneath the unruffled demeanor the deep wounding. She'd been an invalid, drowning in pain and madness, until she began to seize pieces of her shattered existence, seized them and steadied herself for the sake of her child. The strong, laughing woman had returned because she didn't want Ruthie to see a scarred and scared one. What a great and lonely effort resurrecting herself must have been. For a few months in the little girl's life, two other adults became central: her grandmother and Bill. But now wasn't the mother a larger woman, a more fascinating presence because she'd lived through a fire? Ruthie found something magical in that. She wasn't the only one.

Children on the Lower East Side, if they were lucky, learn to be cheerful yet wary. A mood of tough good humor shows in their faces. If all goes well it lasts a lifetime. Hannah had that toughness, the upward tilt of her features, the nose turned up, eyes bold and laughing under the strong line of her brow, the look of someone who was always on top of her game, whatever game it was, about to break into knowing laughter. But during her long convalescence her mouth had drooped, the skin lost its color and sagged from the bones of her face making her look much older. Ruthie must have noticed the change but never mentioned it or expressed disappointment with her mother. Somewhere inside maybe the little girl was wounded as well. But the scars became strengths as mother and daughter became strong together.

**

"I'm not surprised," she'd said, when he'd begun to explain his flight to New York. "A little birdy told me who you are." Of course, the little birdy was Rosie.

They were lying in bed after his shift. "Some people on the Lower East Side may have heard of your brother from an old headline." She spoke in an uncharacteristic whisper, surrounded by the hush of the sleeping tenements. "No one but Virgil would have made the connection to you."

Frank Little had enjoyed fifteen minutes of fame, at least in the West. He'd led free speech fights with some outrageous tactics. He'd read the entire Declaration of Independence to an Oregon sheriff who was threatening to arrest hundreds of striking loggers.

"No one remembers the hobo agitator," she whispered. "But you must have been proud of him,"

"He had the biggest funeral that part of the West has ever known," he added with pride, remembering the thousands of miners and others who accompanied the casket to the cemetery. "Famous—forgotten pretty fast."

"You have every right to be bitter. But the right person remembered. Virgil is a genius, however much Rosie complains that he sometimes acts like a *shlemeil*."

"When has he acted like that?"

"Bringing an unknown man home last summer, for one, especially such a strong and mysterious one. I'd give almost anything to have that strong man's arms wrapping around me right now."

Bill learned how to make love from her, not the physical act—not simply this—but how to enjoy it as part of an intimate relationship. Loving expressions, pet jokes. With every act, and by this one act especially, they were inventing a love neither had ever known before.

**

That morning, Ruthie was across the street at her grandmother's, and they were in no hurry to get dressed. He leaned against the wall while Hannah sat facing him in the bed, legs folded, feet toward belly, heels almost touching the triangle of hair.

"How can you sit like that, in a position that would ruin my back and haunches if I tried it?"

"Women can do many things you can't, just in case you hadn't noticed."

"You have a good strong voice. You'll never need to buy a telephone," Bill had commented, not for the first time poking fun at her clear, strong voice.

"Very funny, Bill Waite"—she always called him by this name. She'd said that it suited him better than his birth name, and he wasn't sure how to take that. "The fact that you're not Jewish isn't the only reason you're not a Jewish comic. Don't quit your day job—I mean night job." Her face glowed with the fun she was poking at him. If he cared very much about his dignity he would've refrained from banter with her, for she always came out the winner. "As a humorist, you couldn't even compete with that dumb-bell Jack Benny, and don't criticize my voice. My mother raised me to speak so I would be heard, which is how all Lower East Side girls are taught. Do you think I care if Seth Seidman has his pimply face glued to the wall? I'd like to give him an earful but he's probably heard it all before, from some other loud-talking woman."

**

This smart woman, whose eyes were always laughing at him, had an inkling of the fear and guilt he carried. His inner strength, like hers, had evolved from a deep and unjust wounding. He might survive the injustice, and that would be his triumph. But the injustice was a fact and the triumph still a question mark.

What neither spoke out loud was that if he was still hunted, he might be found. And might pose a threat for all who sheltered him. But that risk was small. Hadn't love inoculated him against such dangers? He felt stronger now than he'd ever felt. Even the exhaustion caused by his work had lessened. He would come home, and the grueling shift made his joy all the more palpable. He was home with Hannah, a man at the end of a journey, sitting on the bed, smiling, laughing.

He was curious about her Jewishness. But this was a topic she couldn't say much about, because she'd never known anything else and found his efforts humorous.

But he kept probing. "I can see why Ruthie can consider herself one of the Chosen People, because I *chose* to take her to ballgames. But did I ever *choose* you?"

"I may be one of the Chosen People," Hannah responded. "Unfortunately, I'm also one of the Chosen-by-Blockheads people. The Chosen People never got to do much choosing, and it appears that I'm no exception."

He enjoyed being her straight man, and what a wonderful escape her laughter was from any shadows that pursued him, from mysteries and conjectures. On one occasion, after work, he'd tried to tell her how much she meant to him. But the results were less than articulate, and she burst out laughing.

"I'd say you picked up too much dialog from those ladies' novels you were forced to read in prison." Then her voice softened. "But in case you didn't notice, I've already thrown caution to the wind." She avoided his eyes. "I have some reason to be afraid, maybe as much as you." By *afraid* she could have meant a fear of trust resulting from the blow to her life from the man who'd abandoned her, pregnant with Ruthie. Or that late May morning at *Myerson's Shirt and Tie.* It was a second-floor factory near the corner of Third Avenue and Second Street, without a sign on the street, a place where expensive items were crafted, one of many sweat shops on the Lower East Side. Hannah had just discovered a rent in the fabric she'd been sewing. In these sleek men's ties, that would never do. She was carrying it back to the cutters to make sure they were aware of this defect. They should have been, since they examined the cloth as they spread it over the long tables, three, four or five-ply, before superimposing the almost translucent paper patterns. Then they'd take their electric knives and whirr away at the fabric. Their work was no more skilled than that of the sewing machine operators but paid a little better by virtue of the fact it was performed by men. Apparently, they'd missed this flaw, which might extend through a whole bolt of material and could mean a lot of wasted work. Thank you, Hannah, that's why everyone in the shop calls you Sharp Eyes!

In addition, she needed an excuse to stretch her legs, cramped from a morning of grinding away at her machine. She was lightning fast and could afford a moment away from the grind. And her friend Elizabeth Lobman worked in the back of the shop near the cutting tables. Elizabeth was a lot older, mentor as well as friend. Her smile was a rare thing on a sewing room floor, where women strained every second to boost their piece-rate earnings. A wink from Elizabeth helped pass a tiring shift, and a wink was about all Nathan, the floor boss, would permit.

When she remembered that day, she'd hear the machines growling at an earsplitting rate. Hannah was fast and the work came easy, less of a grind for her than some of the others, who scowled as they worked. She felt like the queen of all creation for a moment, to breathe deep and leave her machine for a stroll, her eyes roaming the shop, glowing with that cunning and laughter. Then she saw something out of place, a flickering among the shadows. She'd told Bill how the incident at first revealed itself, before she recognized that this was a fire, how the strangeness of it distracted her. A moment of brightness, something exciting during the long hours trapped indoors. Maybe a tiny blaze, something to talk about over lunch break, anything to relieve the boredom. Then the flames seemed to explode toward Elizabeth, who brushed at them with her hands like they were rambunctious puppies.

"When I think back to that moment, I see her exchanging a wink. But I know that could not have been the case."

Men's ties required a shiny coating, brilliant and highly flammable. The fire, such a small thing a moment before, attacked in a rush, feasting on scraps of glossy material and spreading to the flimsy cotton of Elizabeth's blouse and skirt, then to the flesh underneath. Hannah leaped on her friend to smother the fire. The rest of the shop must have stared dumbfounded for a moment before rushing forward to prevent the flames from going out of control. Their efforts helped Hannah but were too late for Elizabeth. By then, the smell of burned hair and flesh filled the shop.

A cigarette flipped into a box of oil-soaked rags stashed near the tool crib—and near Elizabeth's machine—may have provided the initial spark. Those rags, the oil, and the sporty polish of the ties. The shop had no fire extinguishers and its employees had no fire training. This was not unusual even following the Triangle Fire, especially in small shops.

Rosie as well as Hannah had looked up to Elizabeth, an older woman of proven experience and courage. It was Rosie who'd told Bill how, as a little girl, walking a picket line with her mother, she'd witnessed the slightly built Elizabeth in action. A crowd of half-drunk thugs began to assemble in the street and hurl insults and threats, fueled by free drinks provided by the struck shop's owners.

"Hold the line, girls." Elizabeth hollered. Then she walked from the sidewalk into the street and bellowed even louder at the men who towered over her, "If you half-drunk bullies want to beat up on women, you can start with me."

But courage has its limits. Elizabeth survived longer than expected, and for almost a week the two friends lay in side-by-side beds in the burn unit at Bellevue. Heavy doses of morphine, which was all the mercy the doctors knew to provide, did little to suppress Elizabeth's pain. She moaned and cried, lapsing into words that made little sense, except to question the right of that thing called life to keep her within its horrid kingdom. Finally, the doctors realized the devastating effect this was having on Hannah, who could do nothing for her friend but was chained within earshot of the tortured rambling.

By then Hannah had already withdrawn and her mental wounds had become more serious than the injuries to her body.

"The scar tissue will be dry and numb to the touch." Hannigan had said. "All my patients are strong women. I have faith in them . . ."

**

Hannah waited up for him, after his shift, shortly before dawn, she'd prepare a plate of something cold, cheese, olives, pickles, maybe a sandwich. After he finished eating, she'd usher him through the blue canopy and begin unbuttoning his shirt and jeans. "It's time for your examination.

I need to see if Mr. Holland's hot showers have turned you back into the clean little boy I sent off to work."

Any showers on the Lower East Side were makeshift devices of rubber hose and sprayer. The fixtures for these contraptions could be purchased at one of several hardware shops. They worked well enough but couldn't compare in pressure or hot water volume to Mr. Holland's showers. Tunnel workers also had access to endless supplies of soap, which these families couldn't afford. Bill enjoyed those steamy waterfalls—and afterwards her fascination with his clean skin. When they lay next to each other, the length of her skin had a coolness, and the difference in body temperature gave him the thrill of a shared boundary—until she warmed to his temperature and the border dissolved and they flowed into each other and were one riotous pounding of voice and flesh and, finally, laughter.

They had the run of two apartments, with Ruthie's grandmother for a babysitter, so they had a great freedom shared by few couples on the Lower East Side, lovers deliciously alone with each other. What an absorbing life this was for him, a simple man from the West. Late night and early morning and the days off, which might be spent shopping or exploring the city with Hannah and Ruthie. No worries, beyond an occasional bad dream.

She needed to learn more about his ma, but his recollections came slowly. At first, he dismissed questions, stating that "she was an ordinary woman." But what boy's ma was ever ordinary? Speaking about her made him uncomfortable, based on the conviction that his stupidity had caused her death. Finally, Hannah coaxed him past his feelings of guilt, and he began to describe her more freely.

One recollection summed up the kind of woman she was. In Oklahoma, hunger was always in the background of their minds. At first the settlers weren't sure they should accept her help. They were too proud to take a handout, especially from a woman. Bill could see it in their faces as he went with her to their cabins, a little boy stumbling beneath the weight of a sack of potatoes. How heavy it was, how he loved the hard and lumpy burden as he stepped up to the front door.

"These will only go bad," she explains. "I don't like the smell of bad potatoes." The little boy releases the great weight on to the porch. The sound of the bag falling on the boards, a drumbeat muffled by burlap. He savored it, that clattering in the dry air of a clear Oklahoma evening. Mrs. O'Hare didn't have to say thank you, for it was not a gift. *Mine* and *yours* are only words. *Hunger is something we feel.*

Hannah relished such images of Oklahoma. She could feel the sack thudding on the boards. She heard it and pictured in her mind the boy stepping down from Mrs. O'Hare's porch. Then she saw him walking home with his ma. The big brother joined them, walking ahead. In the summer, some of the runs would be dry but not the main creek that ran past their farm and emptied into the Cimarron River. Purple blanket flowers were beginning to fade in the long dry days and the rising heat.

Childhood returns to us in moments of safety. Safety was Hannah's apartment, as well as his own nest, as long as she was there. Especially during their long talks in the early morning hours.

Hannah's recovery was by now almost complete. She'd learned to live with her scars. She planned to return to work, though not to Myerson's. She'd find someplace else needing skilled sewing machine operators—plenty of such outfits remained in the Lower East Side. In the meantime, they lived well off Bill's income, occasionally dipping into her small savings.

Despite their happiness together, he had to acknowledge that Hannah was truly herself only with Ruthie. He belonged with them but not in the same way that they belonged together. One afternoon, as he was absorbed in packing his lunch in the kitchen, he happened to notice that they were engaged in rapt conversation in the front room. What struck him was the look on Ruthie's face. Her eyes glowed, and a beam of light seemed to connect mother and daughter. The room was in shadows except for their gleaming faces. Hannah wasn't speaking much above a whisper, but her voice was clear and echoed with conviction as she recited the story of Ricky Ticky Timbo. There are many versions of this story, set in different lands, but in the one Ruthie was hearing, the unfortunate child with a great many names had the last name of Schultz.

When Ricky fell into the well, Ruthie inhaled sharply.

Without realizing it the unfortunate boy had doomed himself by insisting that his playmates must repeat his full name, every syllable, without shortening it at all. And so, each time the children approached someone for help in saving Ricky they had to sing out, *Rickytickytimbotimbotimboala montipentagobenascoschultz.* The grownups couldn't believe what they were hearing and asked the children to repeat themselves, and, in accordance with Ricky's wishes, they didn't shorten the name a wit. Several adults had to be consulted and each one had to hear the entire name. Hannah prolonged the story until, finally, it was too late for poor Ricky. Seeing the little girl's consternation, her mother hugged her tight.

"But don't worry, *Bubala*, you'll never fall down a well. Not to mention, I wouldn't ever have given you such a long name."

"But what about Bill?" Ruthie's outburst told him that, despite his efforts to shelter her while Momma was disabled, she still saw him more as trusted older sibling than parent. There was only one adult in the world. He accepted this as natural, but always hoped for something more.

Hannah cushioned Ruthie's head against her hip. "Don't worry about Bill. He might fall down a well, but he has a good short name."

**

Hannah rose from bed and took a step through the afternoon light, toward the kitchen. Then she twirled around and caught him staring at her back. She waved her index finger and laughed. "You're naughty—and I like that in a man."

The layout of her apartment was the same as his, but since it was in the building opposite and at the back, the large bedroom windows opened on the air shaft not the street. The first time he looked out from these windows, he was surprised to see sumac leaves and overgrown brush pressing against the glass. In the summer, even in the heart of the most crowded city in the world, weeds grow wildly. That green jungle would have partially obscured their images from any spying eyes. During the dark early mornings, they'd be framed in light, but visible only sketchily through the weeds.

Among these tenements, where they were crowded together with so many other insignificant lives, who would be out there to notice?

He must have dozed off again and hadn't heard her running a bath, a noise faint enough even though the tub in the kitchen was only a few feet from the bed. He turned toward the sound in time to see her stepping over the rim. She held it, balancing for a moment as she brought the other foot over and slipped into the water, which she'd already let cool in the tub. Lukewarm, easier on scars, she'd said. She lathered the soap into a rag and began to rub it over her skin. He got up and walked into the kitchen and sat in the chair as she rose to her knees and rubbed the soapy cloth over her crotch, grinning at him all the while. Then she bent forward and swirled her head in the water. Her hair floated, became waterlogged, and sank around her face. When she looked up, squinting through soapsuds and matted hair, she was not the woman he explored the streets with, neatly dressed, hair curled and brushed. But soaked hair and eyes that winced from soap were more alluring even than that well made-up woman.

It seems a law of memory that the most important images fade most quickly. For whatever reason, this picture was saved, of Hannah squinting over the rim, and her matted hair.

11.

When one enters a setting and senses that all is familiar and as it should be, a feeling of peace and good order settles in. Unless something catches your eye, a detail is out of place or untrue. At first you can't tell what it is, then the whole scene begins to unravel and sprawl into a disorder to which there is only one answer: escape.

Just a puddle, at first, nothing unusual in that. Under a river moisture is everywhere. Bill went back to shoveling the muck that oozed endlessly from the tunnel face. When he looked up again, the puddle seemed to have widened, a bright sheen beneath the arc lights. Soon, the iron rails were under water. Michael was working with Petey, who propped his shovel against the cart and stared at the widening surface. It glistened like a satin bed spread.

"Leak!" Michael hollered, his voice sounding meek and boyish in the din. Petey began lumbering toward the steps. When a call to retreat was raised by one, the rest had to follow. The crew had a code, and they weren't going to work until the leak was stopped, which was a good safety measure as well as a way to get out of work. Anyone who worked as hard as they did had a right to look for excuses. They sat on the steps hoping the operators could deal with the leak without greatly increasing the air pressure. No one looked forward to that.

They were glad for the rest, frankly, but by now the puddle had spread over both sets of tracks. The two black men had come down from the scaffold, leaving the giant two-man wrench on their perch high overhead. Virgil and Bill waved a greeting to them as they climbed up the steps. They knew their names, but because Lorenzo and Victor spoke English with such strong island accents, they kept their talk with them pretty simple. And simple talk is sometimes just the thing. The rest of the crew had left their work stations—the blaster and his helper, as well as an equipment operator, an engineer, a surveyor and his helper. And O'Dell himself. They descended from their platform at the tunnel face, down an iron ladder and waded to join everyone sitting on the steps. Some of these skilled men and supervisors weren't used to getting even their shoes wet let alone their pants. They sloshed through the liquid, almost at their knees now, annoyance registering on their faces. Now it had expanded across the whole floor, shining under the arc lights, the brown glow filling the cavernous room with a dancing and rising illumination.

Then something happened that can only be described as a sighing, a relaxation of the mud and stone separating workplace from river. The walls were surrendering. River water lapped in like a great animal, happy to find itself inside the house. O'Dell and the other men broke into a stumbling run toward the steps as the pool rose quickly. The crew climbed the stairs to a platform above the shield, which was a steel flooring that was supposed to protect everyone from floods such as this. Up there, perched on a section of stairs just below the door to Orlando's lock, they watched with increasing alarm.

O'Dell picked up the phone outside the locks. "Not an emergency, Orlando, but pressurize, and get ready to let us in." No one was in a panic about a flood, but a little worried about a rise in air pressure. If the pressure in the section began increasing before Orlando could raise the pressure in the locks, then they'd get the bends. They knew Orlando was pretty good at such judgments. They counted on it. They stared down the steps, toward their tools, which leaned against mud-filled carts whose wheels were well under water. It was no longer a workplace; it was a lake. A nervous rustling took place as men grinned nervously at each other. O'Dell stood on the steps and counted heads.

Where's Michael?" Virgil asked as O'Dell counted a second time.

Had he become separated from the others in the retreat? Everyone assumed he was with them since he was the one to first sound the alarm. O'Dell counted heads a third time. Everyone else scanned the slime and darkness hoping Michael would appear. He was known as a daydreamer, not so out of the ordinary for a boy that age. Except for Petey, they weren't panicking. As Michael's partner, he should have kept track of him.

Concern mounted in Bill and Virgil as well. If you didn't look out for your friends, what good were you?

A rescue would surely not be necessary, but sooner or later, someone would have to get wet. So, Bill descended through the shield, almost to the bottom of the stairs then looked back in case Michael had reappeared from a hiding place, maybe laughing at what would have been a poor joke. He tried to take stock of where the boy might be. Most likely in the vicinity of the cart he and Petey had been filling. He stepped into the slime, uncertain of its depth. When his feet hit the bottom, he realized the fluid was up to his waist and chilly. It was like walking into a river because there was a current to it. The Hudson was a mix of gushing tributaries and underground streams, and the water he was sloshing around in seemed a conflux of currents and tides pressuring him this way and that, upsetting his footing. He knew how to swim but didn't want to lose his balance and float off among augurs and other unseen equipment, some sharp enough to hurt and draw blood. Half floating, half stumbling, he bobbed along, wondering if this was such a good idea, to come down here without a plan, plying his way through the muck-filled water, dazzling arc lights overhead. There's not much thought involved in an emergency, and about the only thought he had just then was that all this was happening to someone else. Someone without a plan.

And beyond that, on the perimeter of consciousness, panic was beginning.

To calm himself he tried to imagine what Michael might have been doing. And the thought struck him that Michael probably didn't know how to swim. Many Manhattan boys didn't, although they lived surrounded by water. The most likely explanation was that he'd slipped and knocked himself unconscious. Bill crept around the cart, which was the most likely place for such an accident. He tried to peer into the water, but it was muddy. A viscous tan swirl met his eyes. Gripping the lip of the cart, he swung his foot back and forth, hoping to make contact with Michael that way. But in the steadily rising current, the boy could have been almost underfoot, drowning, and impossible to find.

Bill was beginning to think that he had to cover the whole bottom systematically, futile as that seemed given how large the area was and how easy it would be to come within inches and still miss the boy. With each step he hoped his boots would find him. In his mind's eye, he saw the youthful eyes staring at him. "You're a great man for this work, Mr. Waite," he'd once said, some wonder in his voice. He'd put great trust in this Mr. Waite, who was now failing him. If Bill would have been fully aware of his thoughts at that moment, he would've acknowledged that this task, which had at first seemed hardly even necessary, had changed from urgent to hopeless, all in a matter of seconds.

The water was numbing, and the relentlessness of its rise was frightening. The other men sat out of sight above the shield, no doubt thinking that he had the situation under control and would come back with the boy. But Bill was botching the rescue and now feared for his own life. Or maybe Michael had already plodded up the stairs, grinning sheepishly at the crew. Maybe the crew was waiting for him, delaying the evacuation until he came back. How long would they wait? The wise thing was for him to give up the rescue. He'd search a little longer and then return.

The water was now to his armpits. What if the rest of the crew was already in the locks? In that case, at any second he would feel the crushing weight of the air pressure rising fast enough to stop the leak. Such a rapid increase made you drunk and disoriented, according to men who'd experienced it. But the decompression would be the real hell. Some brave men don't think of their own safety, he knew that from talking to rescuers. That wasn't the case with him.

Michael worshipped him and probably would've said, "Bill is just the man for a rescue, the strongest man on the crew, and calmer than anyone."

But at that moment, at least a few of Bill's thoughts were of his own wellbeing. Not just the risk of drowning or the bends but danger from the filth he was submerged in and the likelihood of infection from a cut on a sharp tool.

How miserable everyone would be to lose that smiling foolish lad. All Bill could think about was how the boy had admired his competence at this type of work—and how misplaced that admiration had been. Then the thought struck him, I might be inept, but no one else is out here with me. What choice do I have but to continue?

In the liquid expanse, the iron cart loomed large, something to hang on to, lifeboat to a drowning man. He half stumbled and half swam toward it. Then, as he neared it, he tripped on the submerged tracks. His ankle turned and he lost his footing, went down on his knees, over his head in the muck. He bobbed up, grabbing for the side of the cart, finding the rusty iron. He ran his hand up the rough surface until he could loop fingers over the brim and steady himself.

Hand over hand, he crawled around the cart, trying to feel with his foot and afraid this small effort was too late. His adrenalin was beginning to run out and he was getting woozy as he clambered along the side of the cart and almost went down again because he'd tripped over something large and soft. He ran his foot over the area again and whatever it was felt strange. When boot brushes against human flesh, it feels not at all like anything else. Michael was right here, but was he alive?

Now time was the only thing that mattered. He ducked into the swill, pulled the limp body up by the shirt, held him in his arms, squeezed him tight in a bear hug, yanking at the skinny chest. The compression produced a rumbling sound. To Bill, this was proof that Michael was alive. But the stairs were at least thirty yards away, and he had to somehow pilot the two of them through the swirling fluid.

At that moment someone dove off the stairs, Virgil, splashing toward them. The muddy features were grim and focused. The hint of fear that Bill often detected in his friend's eyes had been replaced by steely determination. The two of them fumbled with Michael, somehow supporting his sprawling weight as they struggled back. At the steps they realized how much the air pressure had already been increased. They had to drag themselves plus a sodden Michael up the stairs, one at a time, crawling like toddlers under the stepped-up weight of the air. Bill's muscles were almost too fatigued to respond. How they inched up the stairs was a foggy memory. Virgil's silhouette strained above, pulling while Bill pushed. Bill thought back to the mattress they'd moved up seven flights. There was no easy way to get a half-drowned man up those stairs. And when they neared the top, they saw they were alone.

**

"Oh, jeez, oh, jeez," he moaned.

201

"Headache?" the nurse, Barb, asked. She'd revived Michael, who had a bad knot on the head, visible from five feet away. She'd run to the locks after the night watchman reported seeing a huge plume of water over the river. No doubt treating cases of the bends was on her mind. The other men had gotten out before the air pressure spiked. It was a tough call for Orlando, who had to spike the pressure so the tunnel wouldn't fill and drown everyone.

"You're doing great, gentlemen," Barb said, as she directed the four men who were bearing the stretcher across the yard toward the stone building that housed the clinic. "Careful, don't trip on the cobbles, steady as you go."

Bill and Virgil walked behind the stretcher. Someone had a hand on his elbow, and he was thankful for the guidance because he was walking like a drunk. The nurse's silver-blond hair was framed in the dim lights from the windows as they approached the building. But how good it felt to breathe sea-level air! Bill swore he'd never go back under that river again. I quit, that's what he'd scream at O'Dell, as soon as he had the energy.

Barb flitted around Michael's stretcher and offered reassuring words to the entourage. Bill began to shiver and his clothes, wet and caked with mud, felt like they weighed a ton.

"Virgil, are you shaking as bad as I am?" The night temperature seemed to have dropped alarmingly, his body telling him how drained and spent it was.

"I can't hear a word you're saying," Virgil answered. "My bones are clattering too loud."

A hand reached up from the stretcher, from a mound of blankets. "Am I ok," Michael sputtered. "Did you save me, Mr. Waite?"

Bill squeezed the hand as he limped alongside the stretcher. That's when the idea dawned on him that the rescue had been a success. He'd done the right thing. Until then, it had all seemed like a sad comedy of errors and accidents. But Michael was okay. Bill would've done a jig if he'd had the strength—and enough Irish in him to know how.

Something important had happened—he was no longer a man of failed rescues.

The heavens were dark, but city lights produced a soft glow in the night sky. The lot surrounding the tunnel offices was bathed in pre-dawn stillness. After all that desperate thrashing, the scene seemed extraordinarily peaceful. Exhaustion and a little self-satisfaction had left Bill limp, tranquil, deserving. Like an old soldier, couldn't he retire from the rigors of daily life, a full set of medals on his chest? A few more steps and they'd be in the clinic with its promise of rest and warmth. The only unknown was the bends and how bad it would be. But he was strong, a hero full of confidence.

They'd nearly crossed the lot, and the last thing he expected was a man leaping from the shadows, "You survived a blowout," the voice rasped. "We already know about it at *The News*. We got people phoning us from Jersey. I guess they got a better view of that spout from the other side of the river."

The man with the voice thumped Bill's chest, almost knocking him down. "Tell me, Sport, how does it feel to save a life?" The reporter had stopped the entourage in their tracks and didn't appear willing to give way, not even for a nurse and stretcher. His hat brim was pulled down so that the hard angle of nose and chin was all that was visible. "You're the Man of the Hour, eh, Sport," he blared. "Quick now, what's your name and how'd you do it?"

Bill was frozen to the spot. The reporter snapped his fingers and another figure leaped forward, this one with a camera, and a great light exploded in Bill's face. He reeled backward, almost upsetting the stretcher. He regained his balance, still blind from the flash, when the whining, metallic voice came at him again. "I got you on the front page, you'll be everyone's hero."

As his vision returned, he became aware that the camera was operated by a woman, the famous camerawoman who worked for *The News*. Her photos were often on the front page.

"Hold still, Sport, where's the fire. Let's have a few words for your adoring fans." Even in his dazed state Bill found the reference to a fire humorous, having just emerged from a flood. "Let the little lady take another shot." The silhouettes of these two—camerawoman and reporter—were weaving before him when she raised her camera again, but not in time for another shot since Virgil was already pushing Bill through the frosted glass doors and out of danger.

**

"Your blood pressures are very low," Barb announced to all three as they sprawled on cots in the company clinic. "You poor wet lads will stay here until morning."

"I was hardly involved in the situation," Virgil spoke up, mustering a confident tone. "Thank you very kindly, Barb, but the best thing for me is a home-cooked meal and a cup of tea." He puffed himself up to add a measure of self-importance to his words. When Barb saw how vigorous his objections were, she consented. What she was up against wasn't so much Virgil as the prospect, looming large in his mind, of a fretful Rosie. Not hard to imagine her mood if she heard from someone else that he'd been hurt and was being treated in the clinic.

"I'll let Hannah know that our hero's ok."

**

As he lay on the cot, his mind wandering, he had a dreamlike vision that he was lying in bed with Hannah, and she took his hand and placed it on her belly. "Can you feel her move?"

He felt a pulse in the inflated skin at the center of his palm and a little kick. He leaned over and kissed the rounded belly and felt a thump meet his lips. He pressed his face to the spot and sensed the pressure of mother and child swelling beneath him.

"How can you be so sure it's a girl?"

"She feels like a girl, and her name will be Ruthie."

Was this dream telling him what he'd missed in not being there for Ruthie's birth? Being there would've been a grand part of the experience. The kick of an unborn child is an amazing thing. But Bill's life was giving him more than he'd ever imagined.

Then a voice from close by shook him from these thoughts.

"I'd just passed out," Michael was sputtering. "You wouldn't think you'd pass out when you're so scared." His voice sounded small in the high-ceilinged room.

"At times like that, we're all afraid," Bill told him. He felt too weary to talk but sensed that if he didn't try to steady Michael now, he'd get even needier over the next few hours. Clinics aren't soothing places, despite Barb's best efforts. The starched sheets on the rows of empty beds glowed eerily in the gray half-light.

"I can't get used to it—I was thrashing like a dumb fish and I started to die, that's what it was like—and now I'm here. I don't feel like myself, I feel like a ghost. All my emotions, everything inside me, gone. I know you're a great man for what you did, but I don't even feel grateful. There's not enough left in me to feel anything, even though I know I should feel it."

He held his hands up to his face. "I don't like the way I am right now, Mr. Waite." The anguished mood didn't seem to fit Michael, until Bill remembered back to the boy crumpled on the stairs, afraid to come down for his first day of work.

Bill had lost the feeling of euphoria and felt pretty rung out himself, as if everything was taking place at a great distance. Even his dream of Hannah and Ruthie had come to him from a distant world. "I know you'll feel better soon," he replied wearily. "But don't thank me. Virgil was the one who rescued both of us."

Michael made a dismissive sound.

206

"What about your grandparents?" Bill had never met these relatives, who'd apparently raised the boy. And Michael seldom mentioned them.

The answer came with surprising vehemence. "Oh yeah, my grandfather. He'll find out. 'I told you so,' he'll say. He was against me taking this job. But I had to earn my own way. I thought I'd gone to heaven when my aunt invited me to live downtown. But look at me now. I always screw things up. Without you and Virgil I'd never have lasted a day."

Bill was feeling queasy. Symptoms he didn't understand were stealing over his body. He was short of breath and smothering in the semidarkness of the room. Added to fatigue was a faint and distant feeling, not at all pleasant, an achiness, like having a headache in his whole body. And unease over the incident with the reporter.

"Maybe he was right," Michael sighed. "But I couldn't stay under his roof when I hated what he stood for. He wanted me to go into politics, because that's what he did, collect bribes and grease palms. Not one of those hacks had the backbone of the most lily-livered sandhog on our crew. I know he'll gloat about this accident and try to take me back under his wing."

To Michael, working on Mr. Holland's tunnel must have seemed a great way to strike out on his own. "I'll never admit to him it was a mistake."

"It wasn't a mistake, Michael!" Bill was surprised at the energy that had come into his voice. "There's nothing easy about this work, no matter how little your grandfather respects it. And you're good at it. You're one of the old timers on our crew. Everyone looks up to you. You, Virgil, and me—we're still the three champs."

Michael didn't respond, but his silence indicated he was giving some consideration to these words.

At that moment Barb approached their cots. "How are you boys doing?" The fact that the words were so ordinary didn't diminish their soothing quality. "How about some tea?"

It was comforting to hear her pouring water into a pot and setting it to boil on the small range by her station. Bill enjoyed the feeling of being cared for and the thought struck him that one benefit for the children of the Lower East Side, as a result of the cramped quarters, was that cooking, and the comfortable sounds that go with it, took place a few feet from their beds. Ruthie and so many others grew up, sleeping and waking, with their mothers only a few feet away, cooking, washing dishes, drying their hands on an old linen rag, humming to themselves.

"I made it strong." Barb put the two cups on a small table between their beds. "You boys will need the strength. People all over town will be talking about you."

"Barb, you're not going to let the reporters in, are you?"

But even if his story was on the front page, how could news about Bill Waite hurt him? If anyone in Montana read the New York papers, which was highly unlikely, they wouldn't know who Bill Waite was. The only worry was the photo.

"Those vultures won't be coming in here. Not on my watch. You boys need to rest. You both have family out there, but they can't see you either. No one gets in while I'm on duty."

**

Bill didn't know if his mood was caused by letdown or the first phase of bends. He'd hate to have a chronic illness and become an object of pity, a burden to Hannah. According to the papers, sandhogs rarely developed the bends and only mild symptoms at that. But sandhogs knew different. Even the supposedly mild cases were very bothersome. The symptoms might begin with headache and stiffness, go away in days or weeks. Or heart problems might develop. The higher-ups chalked this up to heredity, even in formerly healthy men. One man they used to work with, Jimmy, developed headache and joint pain so severe he couldn't work and was let go. His life became a painful battle. He and his wife and two children had to move in with relatives. He couldn't find a job. And when he felt well enough to apply for work, he guaranteed a poor response by telling the truth.

"I see you've had the bends, Jimmy," an employer might say with a sympathetic look—and Jimmy had a sad and earnest face you couldn't help but be touched by. In this world, sympathy might put some bread on the table, but never enough. About the only help Jimmy got was from the other sandhogs, gifts not from pity so much as the knowledge that they themselves might end up in the same boat. That, plus the sandhogs really liked poor Jimmy.

Virgil often read out to the whole crew newspaper accounts about how sandhogs were predisposed by heredity to heart disease and arthritis. Often, they were the only ones in their entire lineage to come down with an early onset of such ailments. Go back as far as Belfast or Cracow and such an ailment could not be found in the family. Such articles implied that sandhogs were lazy, full of excuses, and had other unsavory qualities as well. But one thing sandhogs never got credit for was their sense of humor. Those who publish learned articles about "the lower classes" don't understand them at all. Meanwhile, sandhogs understood the higher ups very well.

Their sense of humor helped, especially a sad case like Jimmy.

"Why don't you get off your tukus and find a job?" Virgil would ask Jimmy after bringing a bag of groceries for his family.

From the way Jimmy beamed, it was clear that this give and take was the high point of his week. "I hope you brought corn beef and potatoes, not that damn kosher food, crackers and salty stuff that tastes like you baked it in the desert."

**

He woke to the sound of a newspaper rustling and knew that Barb had been replaced. When Doctor Meyers turned on the desk lamp, Bill could see the trim moustache he'd once compared to Virgil's.

"You boys are famous," the doctor called out. He came over and dropped the front page on Bill's cot. The two patients might have expected that at this point the doctor would poke and prod and ask a lot of questions. Producing

210

discomfort was a sure sign that a doctor was doing his job. But all he did was return to his desk and adjust the gooseneck over the sports section.

The front page was upside down, but the headline was clear: SANDHOG SAVES MATE FROM TUNNEL FLOOD. The banner covered the entire front page. Below it was a large photo in which Bill was clearly visible as he blinked into the flash. He looked guilty of something, like a prisoner in a mugshot, even though the accompanying article saluted him as a hero. The article spelled his name Bill Wait.

"Your families are outside," the doctor called over. "But I can't let them in until noon. Company policy."

Bill started to argue with him, but Michael broke in. "If it's my grandfather, I don't want to see him." He was staring up.

"Won't your aunt be there?" Bill asked.

"I hope so. She understands why I wanted to get away from the rest of them and earn my own way."

"I admire you for that. You have guts."

"Do you really think so, Bill?" He was no longer Mr. Waite to Michael, but the hero-worship was still there.

"Of course. You survived a disaster. A lot of men can't say as much."

"Like my grandfather and his cronies." He smiled for the first time, as if he'd just understood something. "He's never worked outside an office—or a speakeasy."

They dozed off again but were interrupted by what seemed a small crowd hurrying toward the cots. A tall man with a full head of gray hair made straight for Michael. He was spindly but carried a belly round as a medicine ball. He was accompanied by a woman who took careful steps, and another woman who ran to Michael as soon as she saw him. The aunt of course.

The spindly man shook hands with Michael. "Glad to see you're recovering, son. And that you survived to learn a valuable lesson. You can do much better for yourself. I haven't withdrawn my offer to help."

"I owe my life to this man here," Michael announced.

"Bill is the bravest man in the world," Ruthie yelled. It was only then that he realized she'd come in with Michael's crowd. When he rose to take her in his arms, he saw Hannah, too, and Rosie just behind.

Bill was able to walk although a little wobbly. Before leaving the clinic, Michael seized his hand again. "See you under the river," he said, loud enough for his grandfather to hear.

Once outside, Rosie took him by one arm, Hannah seizing the other, as they helped him to the trolley stop on Canal. "Virgil's feeling pretty bad or he'd have come," Rosie said. "But he told me what to expect." She was referring to the rude reporter, who would've received a sharp elbow in the ribs had he been there to interfere with them. Apparently, he was taking it easy after filing his blockbuster story.

As the trolley rattled off down Canal Street, a full-scale headache was taking shape. But he was a lucky guy, surrounded by Rosie and Hannah, and with Ruthie on his lap.

**

He was out of work for a week, went back still with the headache, ate aspirin by the jarful until his stomach burned from those harsh little whites. But a headache is worse than a bellyache, so he kept taking them. Virgil was in worse shape and stayed home several weeks longer, while Barb sent aspirin via Bill.

"She didn't offer anything stronger?"

"I don't want to see you hooked on that dope," Rosie yelled. "We have enough dope-fiends in this neighborhood." Which was true. The "habit" existed on the Lower East Side. Funny to call it a habit, like it was a small thing—*I'm in the habit of taking a walk in the morning*—but it was a shock to realize that Rhonda and Mark Fine had gotten hooked. You could see it in their eyes, which were always darting away, and the way people started avoiding them so as not to get hit up for a loan that would never be repaid.

Rosie had taken Virgil to Bellevue, where she was told that there was no cure for the bends except aspirin or narcotics, which the hospital authorities offered but Rosie wouldn't let him take. That, and time. It would gradually get better, they assured her.

Meanwhile, Virgil continued to sit at home, holding his head and groaning.

"Take a cold bath, read a good book, or go out for a walk with Bill," Rosie said. She wasn't about to let Virgil weaken. But there was tenderness in her voice when she whispered, "Listen to what the doctor said. It'll get better."

Bill's own headache was not so bad that he couldn't work. And once he got into the mud and muck of another shift, he'd forget about his aches and pains. Michael had staged a remarkable recovery. With the strength of youth and no small amount of determination, he was back at work a day after Bill. He was no longer ashamed of having been rescued. In fact, he was quite proud of surviving the ordeal. "Sandhogs are tough," he told his workmates. "And Bill is the toughest one of us all."

His attachment to Bill had one uncomfortable effect. He insisted on plying him with his aunt's cures. "She soaked these almonds in garlic and ginger water. She says it's just the thing for a headache. Much better than aspirin."

Bill wouldn't have guessed that the professional-looking woman he'd met in the clinic was such a believer in folk remedies. He would have been just as happy to never make the acquaintance of soaked almonds. That mushy, salty gruel was work to get down. But the unpleasantness was a distraction, so at least in that way, it worked. And little by little the headache *was* getting better, and a pain that's going away isn't really a pain anymore.

Some of Bill's headache may have been caused by worry over the notoriety that came with the photo. Coworkers and acquaintances on the Lower East Side congratulated him on a job well done. Even Anthony declared that D'Allessandro's would treat him to breakfast every day of his life, an offer the head cook nixed after the first free platter of sunny-side ups. He shrugged off the praise and declined the free drinks. To his relief, such special attention diminished over the next two weeks. He comforted himself with the thought that Fame is fleeting, especially in New York City.

12.

On a fine Sunday in September, they were preparing to go out for dinner with Rosie and Virgil.

"Why can't I go, too?" Ruthie whined.

"Because Bill and I are going out, not you, you little fuss-budget," Hannah responded. "Besides, you and Sylvie will get to stay here with Bubbe, who always treats you like her royal highness. And if you're good she'll give you your favorite dinner."

In their home, blintzes and jam solved many problems.

They let Ruthie off at Mrs. Levine's and went downstairs to 7C for Virgil and Rosie. Virgil was still out of work.

"You kvetch about your aches, but then you tell me you want to go back to work," Rosie exclaimed as they walked down Fourth Street. "Without my help, your hand couldn't find its way into the sleeve of your shirt."

"Yes, but my hand can still find its way into *your* shirt." Virgil put his arms up to shield himself from Rosie's backhand feint.

He was better, maybe due to the fact that Rosie had been keeping him home. Now he stepped briskly along as the four of them headed for an early Sunday dinner at *Nom Wah Tea Parlor* on Doyer Street. It was a long walk down Second Avenue on a fine late summer afternoon. They wanted to arrive before a crowd of stylish, late-night people

215

descended on the place. Virgil and Rosie walked ahead. They often held hands or embraced in public—even while Rosie was scolding him. From time to time, he let her hand drop to laugh and gesture. He'd stop walking and wait for her response then pick it up again. Hands are full of fragile bones waiting to be held.

"Virgil is telling stories, and maybe some of them are true," Bill whispered to Hannah.

"And Rosie is encouraging him. But soon she will catch him in an exaggeration," she whispered back.

Which is what seemed to be happening, at least from the fact that Virgil looked flustered by one of Rosie's comments. Then Rosie brought his hand up to her lips and kissed it.

"Could the two of you not block the sidewalk," Hannah laughed. "For those who can't keep their hands off each other, a good many private rooms are available."

Meanwhile, Bill's hand stole around Hannah's waist. He had been learning how to conduct himself in public, when to hold her hand, when to pass a finger over her lips, and when to go further, to kiss deeply, to hug her so tightly he felt the pressure of her breasts and hips. Bill was cautious and followed her lead, over time taking more initiative. The Lower East Side was not a proper society, but it did have its conventions.

The tea parlor was a modest, low-ceilinged room with tables painted black, thickly lacquered. As they sat down at a table in the corner, Virgil pulled a newspaper from his back pocket.

"Put that away, Pushy," Rosie snapped. But Hannah had already snatched it from him and begun reading the front page.

A waiter brought tea. He bowed but kept a proud face. Bill was used to the manners of Chinese waiters from the restaurants in Butte. Some were coarse slop shops that served American food only. A few had Chinese menus similar to those in New York, but the food wasn't as good. He knew this waiter would be efficient but not courteous, would not say thank you when an order was placed. Which made sense. The waiter was the one doing the work—why should he thank them? Bill already knew he wasn't a king and didn't need to have anyone pretend he was.

"Okay if I order *dim sum* for everyone," Virgil asked.

"You want beef, chicken, prawn and fried rice." The waiter, standing just behind Virgil, phrased this as a statement not a question.

"Yes, please, and could we have flatware as well as chop sticks?"

The waiter said nothing.

"Tell me, will they come with rice noodle rolls?"

"Always with noodle. No other way for dim sum," The waiter turned abruptly from the table.

"*Tsk-tsk,*" said Rosie in response to Virgil's faux-pas.

"Someday I'll get past the rudeness and find out what makes these waiters tick."

"Do you really not understand him, Pushy?" Rosie asked. "He wants to do his job and go home without having to answer a bunch of silly questions." Virgil seemed so perceptive to Bill, but not always in the company of his wife.

Another non-Chinese came in and placed an order at the counter. He looked around and nodded at Virgil but didn't come over.

Virgil leaned forward and whispered, "I know that man from my old job. He was a salesman for Cohen Brothers. We only chatted a few times. He must have found another job after they closed. He's probably wondering the same about me."

All of them had looked over at the man, who nodded again. All but Hannah, who was absorbed in Virgil's newspaper.

"Those black women are persistent," she said, bringing their attention back to the newspaper spread out before her. "They're pushing for the anti-lynching bill again. The senators who refuse to consider it are lazy, fat old men, and they make me angry enough to scream." Hannah, often detached and sarcastic, was speaking in earnest, her voice trembling with outrage.

Virgil, who'd been trying to read it over her shoulder, suddenly looked away. He reached for the teapot and offered a refill to everyone though they'd only just started their first cup. His eyes met Bill's, and there was a desperate urgency in them out of keeping with the offer of tea. An awkward moment was transpiring, during which Bill scooted his chair next to Hannah's to get a better view of what she was so absorbed in. A photo accompanied the article, running across three columns. It showed a man who seemed to be slumped above a crowd, as if he was standing on an invisible platform. His head was slanted off to the side, turning away from the people. Then Hannah stifled a gasp and shut the paper.

Rosie had been reading the paper over her shoulder. "You're right, Pushy," she said abruptly. "Let's finish our tea and forget the news."

They were trying to distract Bill from the article, which only increased his curiosity. As he leaned over Hannah to see the photo more clearly, he realized why the man's neck was cocked at such an angle. Of course, it was broken. What the audience in the photo was watching was a lynching. The recently dead look so much like the living, but the slackness of their features tells all. They are blank and still, a silence amid the hubbub of time. But in this silence, he saw the persistent reality of his own grief. That elongated body with the bent neck was the haunting figure that had appeared to him so often, that last picture of Frank. But now that horror was captured in a prominent photo. At first, he was embarrassed for the sake of his friends because they were trying to protect him. He turned red under the weight of their concern. He knew they were straining to comfort him without knowing how. Not even Virgil had the words. Their silent efforts magnified his sadness. But for their sakes he couldn't break down and ruin the evening.

The tea shop was beginning to fill up. Now there were two waiters taking orders amid the din of dishes clattering through the open door of the kitchen.

He glanced around the table but only Hannah met his gaze, staring back at him in round-eyed desperation. Her concern panicked him even more.

What rescued Bill was a desire to learn more about this event. He gave the paper a tug to get it out of her hands and scanned the caption: "The body of Albert Williamson hangs from an oak tree in the square of this small town in Southern Indiana. Although illegal already, the proposed 'anti-lynching' bill would mean that the Federal Government could enter charges and aid in the prosecution of such heinous crimes. The bill does not have the votes to pass at this time, but its supporters say they will continue to push for its passage."

He'd heard people speak of such crimes. The hatred involved made him angry and sad, but he'd never drawn the connection to his own experience. It was something done to black people.

Albert Williamson wore a loose cotton shirt and trousers. He was dressed for work. When Bill had found Frank, he was in his underwear, because the vigilantes had dragged him from bed. He'd never realized how thin his brother was until he saw him hanging there, skin and bones stretched out against the faint light of dawn. Frank was the big brother. He was tough. He taught Bill to fight. Poor skinny Frank.

The crowd was no longer looking at Albert Williamson. They were milling around, getting ready for a picnic dinner, chatting with each other, maybe conducting the town's business. You could also tell something about the photographer. He was there to take a picture and nothing else. He was not the worst of the crowd, but he was one of them.

At first, Bill didn't want to view it as a photo of Frank. But there he was, for all to see. The fact that the skin was a different shade was irrelevant. His brother was Albert. And, strangely, it was a relief to know that through this widely circulated photo his brother's fate was on display for many thousands of readers. And to know that what those black women were doing had a connection to him. They were on his side. They may or may not have known who Frank Little was, but they cared about him and the little brother who'd survived.

13.

On Virgil's first day back from his bout with the bends, he sat in front of his locker, dripping with sweat. Although his physical health had improved, he was clearly anxious about returning to work. Bill had often wanted to read his mind but doubted he had the intelligence to do so. Unless you don't need to be brilliant to guess at the thoughts of a brilliant mind.

"Did you ever feel that the mud is a great slimy monster, and we're the knights tasked with combating it? It's a perilous duty, but somebody has to save the village." Talk was Virgil's tonic, but it wasn't a cure-all. A grin showed on his face, which was still sweating.

"It's a monster all right," Bill answered. He was dreading that shift—having to witness the efforts of his awkward friend, and know the stress behind the what-the-hell shrug and the soft, brown eyes.

He was also dreading lunch, when he'd have to gulp down more of the cure that Michael's aunt was still sending each shift. Although he'd been gratified to see how that frightened boy had begun to change into a dauntless young man. With surprising good humor he'd borne the jokes about his efforts to swim "in the deep end of the pool."

As they were all pulling on their coveralls, O'Dell came in with a mile-wide smile. "Shulman, it seems like us sandhogs ain't good enough for you anymore. I hear you've applied for office work. And the strangest part is they didn't toss the application in the garbage heap. That's what I would've done. I told them you were too damn lazy for *any* kind of work, office or otherwise . . ."

Then O'Dell seized Virgil's hand and began to pump it. "But like everyone else in this God-blessed world, those jokers paid no attention to me!"

He pulled a letter from the back pocket of his coveralls saying that Virgil had gotten the job he'd applied for weeks ago in the department of engineering and drafting.

"As a youngster, I played among Jewish fellows," O'Dell continued. "Most were as poor as us Irish kids, some poorer. I guess it's a fine thing, Pushy, that you don't plan to remain poor. Just don't get your nose so far in the air you pretend not to notice us working-class brothers."

"Says you, O'Dell," Michael shot back at him. "You're a boss, not a working-class brother!"

"Don't get me wrong," O'Dell sputtered. "I'm glad Pushy got this job." That was a fact of which they had no doubt. He'd been trying hard to hide his feelings. Not every boss on the tunnel felt so close to his crew. This didn't change the fact that they enjoyed seeing their boss on the defensive.

"And you're right, Michael, I had a chance to climb up and I took it, so I don't blame anyone else for doing the same. And I'll miss you, Pushy, and I hope you remember us sandhogs when you're in that clean office, drinking tea, hobnobbing with college men and pretty office girls."

When he'd applied for the draftsman position, Virgil had argued that he was qualified based on his experience as a garment designer. Of course, he exaggerated the responsibilities he'd had at Cohen Brothers. But he was smart and educated and could carry it off. He was being hired as a draftsman trainee and might become a qualified engineer before long. His starting salary as a trainee wouldn't be as good as sandhog pay, but he'd quickly make up for that. Rosie, never a big fan of work under the river, would be thrilled. Good news was a good cure for whatever headache remained.

The letter told him that in two short weeks, instead of reporting to the tunnel, he'd climb to the third floor of an office building, where he'd begin reading blueprints. Eventually he'd work with planners and architects on the road to an engineering career.

Change was in store for the rest of them, too. The two ends of the tunnel were about to kiss. The whole city— and New Jersey too—was waiting for the big event, set for October 29th. A ribbon-cutting wouldn't have worked. The ribbon, and the dignitaries, would have gotten soggy. But President Coolidge himself would detonate by telegraph the final blast connecting the separate ends of the work. If the engineers' calculations were right, that is. A foot off would be a disaster. The city held its breath. The long odds were saying a miss.

A lot of work would continue since the tunnel wasn't scheduled to open for traffic until 1927. But it would require different skills: putting down a roadbed; walling the tunnel; and finishing it off with tile, wiring, and ventilation.

Bill could set tile, bend tin for ventilation, and could work asphalt for a roadbed, though that was a stinking job he knew enough not to apply for. He wouldn't try to bluff his way as an electrician, but he could begin as a helper. He didn't want to spend the rest of his life doing unskilled work. Now was the time to get a skill besides mining and mucking. The world was changing, and those two trades, if you want to call them trades, were no longer in great demand. Bill suspected that the world would always have some need of miners and muckers, but let someone else try their hand. He didn't want to wait until he was too broken down to learn a trade. He'd seen fit men wear down and fall by the wayside. No one knows how many disappear like that. The scrap heap isn't well-publicized.

O'Dell would give him a glowing recommend. He owed him. His wife was close friends of Michael Kerrigan's aunt. The Irish in New York were a giant population, amounting to as many souls as in all but a couple of cities in Ireland. But it was still a small world. It would have been an inconvenience to O'Dell if Michael hadn't been able to stick it out as a sandhog—a bigger inconvenience if he'd drowned.

Sandhogs were infected by the excitement of the upcoming holing-through. They looked forward to a break from their filthy and grueling routine. They were right in the middle of the news that was being discussed in every workplace and on all the street corners. If a sandhog went out for a drink or a meal, it was often on the house. But most of them worried that the best-paying job they'd ever had might be drawing to a close. Men would be let go, some sooner than others.

As Petey had put it: "Quite a romantic event. New Jersey and Manhattan *kiss*—and I'm *screwed*."

**

That October was lovely, a high blue sky topped off the mild afternoons. Flame-orange leaves stood out against the sky. The elms in Tompkins Square Park swayed in the dazzling blue heights. Filthy walls of brick and stone were hidden by multicolored leaves. There, before the people of New York, was proof that this city was made for something better than to be a hole for roaches and rats. The human population might have built skyscrapers that dwarfed the great elms, might every day bombard the elms with bubble gum, spit, and worse—but the roots were a marvel. They held their own and pushed back—against footers and basements, subways and sewers.

Roots are a wonder, Bill thought. The fact that he 'd become separated from his didn't trouble him so much as it once had. Wasn't he putting down his own roots? Hadn't he begun to regrow himself on these crowded streets?

And these new roots were strong. To be torn away from them was such an unlikelihood it did not need to be considered.

Apparently chief engineer Holland was not as sturdy as these trees. The pressure of the last stage of the work had been too much for him. The papers told of a total nervous collapse followed by hospitalization and death. But the work was bigger than any one man. That was the conclusion everyone seemed to be drawing. Like ancient pyramids and the great cathedrals of the Middle Ages, this architectural wonder represented a triumph no matter what the cost.

Those whose friends and relations had been maimed or disabled on this job might not have held this view. Maybe the tunnels name should have memorialized others as well as the chief engineer. They could have called it the Sullivan-Robinson-Graziano-Lopez-Holland Tunnel. The other fellows had never been acknowledged as fatalities of tunnel work, but the truth is that the pressure of the job took its toll on many, from sandhogs to a famous engineer.

Poor Mr. Holland, a genius with a weak heart and a head full of worries.

Meanwhile, sandhogs were working six days a week. They may have basked in their celebrity status off the job but didn't welcome the pressure that the deadlines added to their work. Bill was still the best-known sandhog in New York or New Jersey, but more famous personages had stepped into the limelight, like the President. Coolidge had set aside October 29th for the holing-through, and no sand-hog, if he knew what was good for him, was going to keep the U.S. president waiting. By that date, the two ends had to be aligned within a fraction of an inch.

"The whole spectacle depends on us," Virgil had said over lunch.

"Listen up, the engineer is about to speak," Michael said. They were all proud of Virgil's promotion and viewed it as a collective honor. Which meant they kidded him all the more.

"American mythology is based on the taming of the West, the perilous journey in covered wagon, the danger of attack by Indians and bandits. But America's highway to the future is about to take place right here under the Hudson." Bill and the rest of the crew turned toward Virgil—Michael, Petey, O'Dell, Lorenzo, and several more. "Along this westbound trail, you won't see any hitching rails or watering troughs. This tunnel has one purpose and one only: to connect the most powerful city on earth to a future of high-speed automobile travel."

"You mean to say that we might be remembered along with Davy Crockett and Daniel Boone?" asked Petey. "How come not one of us pioneers has a horse or a covered wagon to his name, not to mention a new Rolls Royce Phantom?"

**

The Sunday before the holing-through was another spectacular day. Bill and Hannah went for a walk in Central Park with Rosie and Virgil, along with two chubby little girls. Just ahead, as they approached a duck pond, was a skinny fellow with a big head. He walked with a certain pomp, vaguely familiar. But only after they'd almost bumped into him did Bill recognize Orlando. He was the last person they were expecting to meet up with in Central Park, but there he was, with two little boys and a woman much larger than he was. He was smoking a cigarette and didn't appear to be enjoying the afternoon. But when he saw his work mates the brilliant smile lit up his face.

"Olivia, this is the hero. Remember I told you how he pulled that poor young fellow from the flood and sat in my locks, filthy and shivering?"

He introduced his wife and pointed to the two boys who cared too much for throwing sticks in the pond to pay much attention. They weren't twins but were close in age, about ten.

Bill introduced Hannah and put his hand on Ruthie's head. "And this is my daughter, Ruthie."

That night, as they lay in bed after making love, Hannah whispered, "That was good in the park today. About time you start calling Ruthie your daughter. I know she wants to think of you as her father."

The fact that Ruthie wanted this was something he hadn't dared to hope. He was as excited by this good news as any man when the nurse emerges with the news that he's a father.

"Is it a deal then?"

"Yes," he said. "It's a deal."

Would he be worthy of that name and the new status? Would this be an easy job, considering what he'd already survived? He'd had many names in his life: son, brother, copper miner, friend, convict, fugitive, sandhog, and lover. But this name, father, was different from the others. To be a father meant more than just rolling with the punches. It meant wider responsibilities, providing security for the future, which of course he couldn't see into.

14.

New Yorkers see winter as a threat. Winds knife the length of straight avenues and streets, swirling around the exposed legs of women, the necks of men who don't have a top button on winter jackets, freezing the hands of everyone who has to be out in the weather without gloves or mittens. During this season, the sidewalks are always in shadow, the concrete covered for days at a time by treacherous ice.

But just prior to the tilt toward winter, a wonderful neutrality fills the air. New Yorkers luxuriate in an in-between state, not sweltering and mopping sweat, not having to bundle up. They smile at each other as they walk about in heaven. The great stone apartment buildings have sloughed off the last of the summer heat, and darkness lingers in the mornings for a long time, in the mortar between cobble and brick, in the tar of the rooftops. The smoggy summer has been drained from the air, leaving clarity and crystalline perspectives, a sharpness even in the lengthening shadows of dusk and dawn.

The only irritant is that no one can complain about the weather.

His first fall in New York had been fair enough. But these days were putting that autumn to shame. Especially today, as he'd walked to D'Allesandro's to order a sandwich for lunch. The air had been washed clean of soot by rainfall the previous week. Almost like Butte on the rare occasions when the smelter smog cleared off. But instead of a ring of mountains, skyscrapers enclosed them. Instead of distant slopes shaggy with pine, they had elms floating up toward the roofline.

Bill expected to be pretty well insulated from the coming winter harshness, not only because his work kept him out of wind, rain, and snow, but because of the warmth of the apartments, whether they enjoyed the steam heat in 122 or 145 Fourth Street.

And he was safe in all these fine thoughts. That was his simple meditation on October 28, after having walked back from D'Allessandro's. His chief concern, so he thought, was which apartment they should give up, for it made no sense to divide their time at double the rent. Or should they look for a larger apartment? The other concern was the end of the baseball season. No more Robins games for Ruthie. That, and when would he start as an electrical helper, which was the job O'Dell had successfully promoted him for. It was his first choice. He was the luckiest man on earth. He was aware of the misery in which too much of the world toils. But the good fortune that he enjoyed was a fine thing in and of itself and need not be qualified by ifs, ands, or buts. It was enough for this one man to stare out at the future and see that it wasn't crowded by shortfalls and bad luck.

The two sides of the tunnel would meet and kiss tomorrow. The *Times* and the *News* had been dominated by this coming union. It was certainly the conjugal news of the year.

Arnoldson flickered only briefly through his mind. Maybe he should've asked Virgil his thoughts about the "shadowy network" of vigilantes. Apparently, Virgil thought he should investigate that issue. In the future he'd ask him for help with whatever research was involved. But too much was going on in his life. And enough history was being made in the tunnel without him having to look for any more. Every shift, in a little meeting before work, O'Dell would update them on progress, to afford them an insider's knowledge of the upcoming kiss. By the latest calculations they were on target.

When he first heard the tunnel union called a kiss, he thought of Hannah's lips and what was soft and pink and just a little moist in her. After reading about the kiss often enough that image had been erased leaving only the newspaper meaning. Of course, in the dark, Hannah and Bill weren't precise. If his lips landed on smooth cheek instead of mouth, he'd still be thrilled. Her skin was deliciously warm, every inch of it. He could kiss her right ear or her big toe, he was easy to please. But for the engineers, precision was everything. A few inches off was the same as a mile.

Sandhogs would be celebrating along with the rest of New York. They knew what they'd accomplished, so they didn't have to talk much about it. And their work these last few days was easy and relatively safe. The tunnel was complete up to the last foot or two and the works were now encased in steel and concrete, so no blowout could occur. They no longer worked in heavy air. Much of their day was devoted to clean up for inspection by engineers, planners, and occasional bigwig politicians. They were told to hide when the tours came through because, apparently, these upper-echelon folks were under the impression that the tunnel had been built by means of ingenious calculations and that human labor wasn't part of the equation. They did their best to get out of sight when O'Dell told them to disappear, so that these gentlemen might continue to remain ignorant. The sandhogs wouldn't beat their own drums because no one wanted to hear a racket like that. The reward might come, many years later, in a good story for their grandchildren. A great tale, fun to tell, even if the audience over time grew weary of listening.

Bill's preparations, his pre-shift routine, were light-hearted. They included a visit to the hallway toilet. His backside felt a little chill on the porcelain, no doubt from the long wait in between customers. When he was done, he'd grab the lunch he'd purchased at D'Alessandro's and take off for work, for an easy shift of staying out of sight.

His biggest concern just then was that he didn't have time before work to rush across the street and give Hannah and Ruthie a hug. But after work he'd put a kiss on sleeping Ruthie and drink a beer with Hannah before celebrating with more than a kiss. As much as he liked his own apartment, the other side of the street was even better.

If they gave both of them up, where would they find a larger one? Lower East Side apartments were pretty uniform, as if its planners were of the opinion that none of the residents would ever be able to afford something better for a large family, of which there were many. Did Hannah feel that they should stay on the Lower East Side, preferably on

Fourth Street? He was pretty sure she felt as he did about staying near Virgil and Rosie, but it was something they had to discuss.

Those were his thoughts. But he waited before his shaving mirror, needing to relax for a few seconds more before the race to the tunnel. He wiped off the last of the shaving cream and checked his face. His wasn't a job that required a stylish appearance—he'd never had that type of job and never would. The door to his apartment was ajar and, as he shut off the faucet, sounds emerged from downstairs. A door opening, a child playing in a hallway. Then a sound arrived that he couldn't quite place. Probably not important. But rather than grab his lunch and bolt out the door for work, he trained his ears.

It came again, a knocking, soft, not telling him much except that it was taking place on the sixth floor. Then Rosie's voice drifted up to him, muffled, probably asking who was there and not pleased to be disturbed. Then a brief answer, a latch turning, the click of a cylinder sliding free of the strike plate.

At first, he couldn't decipher the words, but something was being said to Rosie in a hard voice that got his attention. No one spoke that way to Rosie. As he listened intently, he understood what this voice meant for him long before making out the words. But the words themselves were enough to send him reeling. "I am authorized by the parole board of the State of Montana . . ."

This couldn't be happening, he whispered to himself. Arnoldson couldn't have followed me here. What clues would lead him to New York, of all the places in the world?

The front-page photo, of course. But with each passing day, Bill had grown less concerned by that incident. Even if Arnoldson came to New York, how could he have found Bill in this jumble of boroughs, among so many millions of walled-in souls?

He had no escape plan because the odds against being found were so high. He'd lost the outlook of a fugitive, the sharp attention and focused care. All his routines were based on being a father and lover in a secure nest.

He crept to the railing and stared down at the Shulman's door.

"To refuse to cooperate exposes you to a charge of contempt . . ."

Arnoldson didn't belong here, on Fourth Street, at his friends' door, just across the street from Ruthie and Hannah. For months he'd lived in New York, and it had become the only home he'd ever need or want to claim. He thought he had outdistanced this threat by many miles. But the past is always with us. Now his was reemerging with a fury.

He kneeled by the railing trying to see below, still keeping the banisters before him so he couldn't be seen. Arnoldson wasn't visible in the doorway. Apparently, he'd brushed passed Rosie and into the apartment. The caged strength of that man was inside there, waiting to be released, poised to destroy Bill's life. Unfortunately, Virgil was at work, having just started his new job. He was the only person he knew who might be able to come up with a story, a line of guff to deflect Arnoldson from his chase.

His first thought was that he should sneak through the open door and jump Arnoldson. With surprise on his side, he'd prevail. Surprise and the knife he had in his apartment. He was strong now, from carrying the great weight of the tunnel air. He tensed, ready for what he had to do to finish the battle once and for all. He'd imagined it for much of his parole, never followed through because he realized the fate awaiting a parolee who did such a thing.

He knew something else. Men were hard to kill. Arnoldson's muscles and bones would flail at him with life-struggle power. His great animal strength would be increased many times by the creature knowledge that survival depended on it. A mortal threat can detonate furious muscle power, especially in a man like Arnoldson, whose very existence was a tightly wound spring. Bill shivered with an expectation of the terrible strength he'd be taking hold of in that combat. But with the element of surprise and a knife in his hand, how could he not be the one to prevail?

Then caution began to assert itself, a mood he would later curse as cowardice. And a startling image, of Arnoldson lying on a bloody floor in the Shulman's kitchen, their apartment a shambles. Could they live where a killing had been committed, and with Sylvie a witness to the entire struggle? She would stare from behind her mother's skirt at the blood spilling from a man's throat. From then on, Bill would be the man who brought death into her life, the man with the knife.

He'd been convicted of threatening murder, now he must commit one. Except that it would end badly for everyone, especially Ruthie, who'd see her new father charged and convicted of murdering an officer of the Montana court system, and surely hung.

237

That last thought destroyed his resolve to act. He felt nauseous and had to grip the railing. In the Lower East Side, he'd fallen into a life he'd never thought possible. Prison and parole had given way to the love of his life and to a little girl who looked up to him as her father. His new life, which he'd imagined he could defend, was gone in a heartbeat. In its place was a total lack of options, a sickening vacuum. What he did next made little sense. He took two quick steps back into his apartment and grabbed the lunch he'd picked up at D'Allessandro's. Perhaps he needed his before-work routine as a refuge, as if carrying his lunch was a way to hold on to the everyday life that was melting into a pool of terror.

With the lunch bag tightly gripped he crept down the stairs, hoping Arnoldson wouldn't burst through the door as he passed. Then he realized that he couldn't go to work. That's exactly the place where Arnoldson was most likely to expect him. Bill would emerge from the washroom after his shift, the late fall breeze chilling his skin, and Arnoldson would seize him. He had no idea how or where to escape to but knew that first he must warn Hannah. Urgency and purpose reentered his life as he flew down the remaining stairs and ran across the lobby floor. He'd just seized the brass handle and was about to give the heavy front door a yank when, through the glass, he saw three men on the stoop, lounging like they had no business but to keep watch. They were within ten feet and could have seen him if they'd turned to look. Arnoldson had men with him from Montana, or New York police. Or both.

He turned from the door and his feet carried him downstairs again. It had been a long time since he'd descended those basement steps but the moldy smell was all too familiar. At the bottom was the small anteroom with the wheeled bucket and the janitor's sink. This was his first home, where he'd found what he thought was security. Whatever refuge it would provide now would be temporary. And here he'd be trapped, completely and totally. But where else could he go?

Next to the sink was the outside door, always locked. It would have opened to the airshaft. A dingy yard where walkways intersected, one to First Avenue, another to Fourth Street. He tried the rusty steel knob just to make sure, but the door wouldn't budge, as he'd expected. A weighty old door, the key long ago lost, for all he knew. His old room was straight ahead, where for a month he'd collapsed after every shift. A dead end there also. Going upstairs and over the rooftops might have made more sense, but now Arnoldson stood between him and that path as well.

He was staring at the janitor's sink and thinking of how yellow it looked in the shadows. When he lived here, he'd tried to clean it but it stayed yellow, like an old tooth. Mildew caught in his sinuses. He went into the room he'd slept in and remembered Rosie's visit and the gifts she'd brought. How did she describe them— "weapons for the all-out and endless war." Killing an army of bugs—if only that was the extent of his battle now. How that smart, tough woman had dazzled him then, as she stood in the midst of these dismal shadows in her fine bright blouse.

She'd pointed above the door, to the alcove he hadn't seen. "And don't forget to dust your perimeters." It was almost as if she was in the room with him, pointing overhead, laughing at him because he wasn't seeing it. But of course, it was there if you looked for it, in the shadows above the doorframe, the razor-edge line of the alcove. "There it is, dummy," she would've said.

He stood on his toes and ran a hand along the ledge. Barely able to hook on to it with his fingers—it wouldn't furnish a grip for chinning himself. But if he could balance on the janitor's bucket, hoisting himself with all his strength while kicking the other leg toward the ledge, could he somehow swing himself up? It would be tricky, but with good timing and a little luck, he might make it. Timing and luck, two things that had not always been present for him.

To a man with little to live for saving his own skin didn't seem much. But he had to go through the motions, and this alcove seemed his last chance. It was all but invisible, offering up only a faint shadowy line in the darkness of the room. Like a cornered cat he was drawn to this high place where, even if discovered, he'd have an advantage in a fight. He rolled the bucket under the alcove and remembered something. He still had the sandwich tucked in his shirt. He tossed it above, heard the thump. A good lunch from D'Allessandro's was waiting for him if he could clamber up the wall. That thump was nothing compared to the racket that would echo through the basement when he pushed off from the bucket and tried to hoist himself up with a kick. And probably fell to the floor on his back. Surely the whole building would hear it. He gripped the ledge, perched on the lip of the bucket, kicked while trying to chin himself at an impossible angle, clinging there, losing momentum. Then he thought of the lunch and kicked harder, finally swinging a leg up, heel catching the ledge, rolling up and over, the momentum carrying him into that dark, blind hole, where he panted in cobwebs and dust. He lay there, relieved to have made it but a little disgusted with himself at the thought that all he was doing was prolonging his own sorry existence.

He played the scene back and didn't think he'd made much noise. Of course, the bucket was directly below, a tell-tale indication of where he was hiding. But the mop handle was within easy reach. He grasped the smooth old wood and scooted it over the old cement floor. Its wheels carried the bucket through the doorway and into the anteroom.

This small, very small, triumph was followed by the let-down of his filthy surroundings, full of dust and small bits, probably left by mice. A year ago, he'd slept on the floor below after sweeping it well and knew he was sharing the space with mice, maybe even with rats. He hadn't minded it then. How quickly he'd become spoiled.

He'd have to be pretty hungry to eat the lunch he'd just tossed up, the cheese and tomato sandwich wrapped up with a few pickle slices. If he lived that long, he'd eat it. He knew from his time in the hole that while disgusting surroundings are a relative thing, hunger is an absolute.

Those who are cornered and trapped consider time their only ally. To delay the inevitable becomes the goal of a doomed life. To live a little longer. Life, a few moments more of it, is the objective even to a miserable creature without prospects. To be patient, to treasure the waiting. A trapped person can lose their nerve and do something rash, scream to relieve the tension of hiding. But that screamer, that wasn't Bill, at least not yet. He was overwhelmed with despair but clung to the habit of the next moment, of waiting, of wanting to travel a little further down the road, even if it was a road leading nowhere.

And a thought occurred to him. His friends needed him to prolong this final act. The more time they had, the better able they'd be to shelter themselves from the great wrecking ball that had entered their lives. "Harboring a fugitive" might be the next headline. His friends didn't deserve that. Virgil and Rosie might be able to defend themselves from the repercussions, but what about Hannah and Ruthie? A father had just entered their lives—how would they bear up under the disgrace of his trip back to jail? But with a little time on their side, Rosie and Virgil might be able to help Hannah dodge whatever bullets were likely to come flying out of this situation.

In his basement alcove, he had barely enough room to sit up but didn't want to. He lay on his back while a few minutes passed, possibly an hour, and still nothing happened. How could that not be a good thing? He tried to occupy his thoughts with something pleasant and trivial, like the last Robins game they'd attended, an exhibition with the Yankees. Hannah had begun to take an interest in baseball, although it still paled beside her daughter's fanaticism. But both had become fascinated by the phenomenal Babe Ruth.

No doubt, Mr. Ruth was changing the game. For Bill, baseball was a comfortable distraction. Having played it as a boy and young man, everything about it was familiar and calming. But wasn't it a momentous change, of importance beyond sports, what the Babe was bringing into the world?

Every moment of distraction came to him as a tiny victory over terror. He forced himself to submit what had been happening in baseball to a rational inquiry. The walls of a baseball field, of a good major league field, were constructed far enough from home plate to contain all the action of the game, the grounders, the fly balls, the running catches. That was the way things were supposed to be, the way of the world. Batters hit singles and doubles and occasional triples. The inside-the-park home run was a great feat, but a ball hit over the fences was truly exceptional. These were phenomenal hits that sailed beyond the confines of baseball as we know it, awesome hits, and a loss to the team owners of the price of a new ball, about 50 cents. But this year Babe Ruth had slammed 46 home runs, $23 to those writing the checks.

He wanted to cling to these reflections, as if no harm would come to him while he meditated on baseball. But he couldn't maintain the mood. His next thoughts were also of baseball but bitter-sweet. Ruthie and Bill had been among the "Trolley-Dodger" fans who thronged Ebbets Field every chance they got. To stare up at the great rounded letters outside the stadium and join in the excitement of tens of thousands pouring into the ballpark—never in his earlier life had he dreamed he'd experience Ebbets Field, and with such an earnest little fan.

He lost focus and studied the highlights playing in the plentiful dust motes. Then the afternoon light was gone.

Nightfall had arrived and, at the tunnel, another shift was underway. "You seen Bill?" O'Dell would have asked Michael, then Petey. He'd never missed a shift, except for the week he was out with the bends. They'd regard it as bad luck that their most stalwart sandhog wasn't there for "the kiss." His thoughts dragged on. He knew for a certainty that he no longer felt capable of running. He hadn't intended to flee from Montana. As wretched as he'd been under Arnoldson, that flight would not have occurred without Amos. Bill had awakened in the truck to the fact that he was free. In his thoughts he'd often thanked Amos and the other truckers. That thank you was one of many outstanding debts.

He'd never been a man to take much initiative. His greatest accomplishment was to step forward and help Hannah. His rescue of Michael was executed with a spur of the moment decision. Anyone else would have done it. Or so he reasoned. It did not count for as much as his commitment to Hannah. For months he'd given her and Ruthie someone to rely on. No, it was more than that. He'd finally developed the courage to call Ruthie his daughter. He couldn't back away from that. And as Hannah's lover he'd proven to her, at a low moment, what a desirable woman she was and that he was a man who would devote himself to her. But now, with Arnoldson in the picture, would they be any better off for such devotion? And his decision to become part of their lives, if it was a good thing, wasn't something he could take all the credit for. Wasn't it Mrs. Levine who'd given him the push when she'd asked, "Hannah not good enough?"

What with unhappy reflections, the time had passed. It was after nine p.m. He could tell because he was very hungry. Under the river he'd already have eaten his lunch. He gripped the wax paper package containing his sandwich, wanting to tear it open. Why wait? Arnoldson wouldn't let him enjoy it after arresting him, which was bound to happen soon. But his thoughts were interrupted by a sound on the stairway. At last Arnoldson was coming down the steps. How stupid to sit here all this time clinging to the foolish hope that he wouldn't search this crevice. Bill counted the steps until they reached the bottom and paused. The fierce eyes of this man, intent on reasserting his supremacy, would be sweeping the basement. The slow tread down the stairway continued, surprisingly light for such a huge man. Then the steps crossed the anteroom and came through the doorway directly below the alcove, where Bill held his breath. He hunched further back into the darkness.

He'd been a fool to hide here. Too late now, those three words, the refrain of those whose lives are founded on error.

But what could he have done differently? Could he have avoided having his photograph plastered all over the front pages? It never occurred to him to regret saving Michael. But at this moment what mattered were the muscles and sinews of the creature a few feet below him, breathing quietly, a soft wind that was sure to become a storm. Now the fight would take place, and surely, he'd lose.

Bill had never killed anyone, had never raised a fist except in defense of himself or others. He'd tried to save lives, in the mines, and helped save one under the river, but never taken one. And when he'd picked up his lunch, he'd left his knife on the counter. What sense did it make to bring the lunch he would have carried to work—and not a weapon? Unarmed, what chance did he have against Arnoldson?

As he sensed the impatient, stalking movements below, a rippling power in every step, Bill thought again about what kind of man Arnoldson was, to have such a dark power even over powerful men like Warden Middleton. "Do as he says and you have nothing to fear." Bill wasn't the only one to have been caught up in this man's web of fear. Amos, that hapless man of good nature, hadn't realized whose plans he'd foiled when he plucked Bill away. Or maybe he had. Maybe that was exactly why Amos did it and why the other truckers fell into line with the plan. They'd known he had to get away from Arnoldson. They'd known more about Bill's predicament than he had known.

Bill heard a click and the room below was suddenly flooded with light. He wanted to peer over the ledge but didn't dare. Arnoldson had apparently switched on a lantern-style flashlight and was moving it about the room, providing himself with a panorama bright as day. He must be standing at the opposite wall, holding it up by the ring handle, for the light shone into the alcove and almost touched Bill's shoulders. The beam played just above him as he held his breath. Then the illumination descended further into the alcove, touching the fabric of Bill's shirt, the blue cotton brightening momentarily. Arnoldson must have spotted the alcove and was standing on his toes, trying to gain a better sightline over the ledge.

If Arnoldson's eyes could penetrate as far within as the rays of light, Bill would now be exposed.

He waited for the giant claw-like hands to seize the ledge. Again, he regretted not having the knife. He could have thrust the point down through the meat of one of those hands. Without the knife, Bill prepared himself for an effort that wasn't likely to succeed. Then, with the sound of a shoe sole pivoting on the floor below, the light retreated and Arnoldson left the room.

**

Bill felt at the oil paper again but decided not to open his lunch. He breathed slowly and listened to the noises of Fourth Street. The stoop to 145 Fourth Street was directly above his basement perch. He could make out a babble of greetings, of happy yelps and angry growls, an explosion of laughter, and once in a while an automobile rattling past.

Ben Jacobs shouted a greeting to his nephew. Maybe the Fines were sitting on the stoop, almost directly overhead. They were sociable and greeted everyone. They acted like good citizens, although maybe they'd just stolen from some of the people they were greeting. Waiting for drugs, always living in that zone between desperation and self-abasement.

But the street offered up no report of his loved ones.

His thoughts gravitated back to Arnoldson. While on the farm, he'd been frightening, but the source of this man's power had remained a mystery. In truth, he hadn't done much to discover what it was, and such investigations would have been risky. He remembered once beginning to take just such a chance. He'd finished milking and took the large tin to the outdoor cellar, stepping down into the cool air and the smell of the dark earth. He enjoyed the feeling that he was insulated by yards of dirt, totally alone. But to linger would be a bad idea. Arnoldson surely had another task for him. That was to be expected. Bill had learned how to live under his control. He climbed from that dark hole into the harsh sun and took a deep breath in the yard. Arnoldson wasn't there, so Bill walked across the flat stones to the house, thinking he might find him doing paperwork at the kitchen table. He stepped into the shadows. Of course, his boss would be there, hunched over his work. Bill saw an empty tea cup on the table beside some papers but didn't see him. Was he in a corner of the kitchen, watching from the shadows?

Bill wasn't supposed to read the papers that were on the table. He took a step closer and saw that several pages contained the letterheads of the bank and the hardware company. Across the top of another sheet—ARNOLDSON PROPERTIES: Statement of Goods and Services. Below that "four bales" was written in Arnoldson's formal hand. That was a small order. The entry didn't list what kind of bales. But the price listed was '$180 misc.' Who would pay that much for *any* bales and why was it listed as 'misc'? These questions passed through his mind as he stepped further into the room.

Arnoldson wasn't in sight, but Bill was uneasy. Had he ever entered the house without Arnoldson's permission? Without knowing why, why on earth would he want to do such a thing, Bill took two more steps into the heart of the kitchen, across floorboards that creaked. The sound was sharp, like the noise wood makes when split by a maul. He froze halfway across the room, his ears tuned to the late morning silence. Then he noticed that the door to Arnoldson's bedroom was ajar. Why didn't he call out to him, to announce himself, to assure Arnoldson he wasn't trying to sneak about in the house?

He took another step toward the bedroom door.

He was out of place, especially on this man's farm. His skin crawled with the feeling, with the risk he was taking. He hated everything about his life, everything except the cool cellar and the steady work into which he could lose himself, if only briefly. Work and sleep. He hated the talk he was expected to share with Arnoldson. Every conversation they had gave testimony to the fact that Arnoldson was trying to shape him into a different kind of person. Reshaping: was that something one man could do to another? It galled him that Arnoldson had made it his business to root around in Bill's life, while he knew nothing about Arnoldson. And why Bill? Why had Arnoldson and the warden selected Bill for release when so many at the prison merited parole? Had Arnoldson known about Frank?

The door was ajar—it wouldn't have to be unlatched. His hand was inches from the knob. Whatever secrets lay behind that door exerted a force on him and drew him on. He stood at the door, listening for footsteps behind him, waiting for a rough hand on his shoulder to yank him away, slam him against the wall. Would he be sent back to prison?

He was suddenly aware of his hand on the doorknob, about to give it a pull, and froze. His head spun with the sudden knowledge of where he was and what he was about to do. Did he have time to reverse his steps before discovery sealed his fate? Hoping Arnoldson wasn't already behind him, Bill began to back out of the kitchen, across the porch, almost falling as he stepped down on the flat stones. He walked quickly around the barn and down the lane, breaking into a run at the stream. He looked back several times and didn't see Arnoldson emerging from the house. He breathed a sigh of relief as he kneeled in the dirt of the beet field, glad to have weeds to pick. Weeds are everywhere. The earth is full of them.

**

He must have slept for many hours. At one point, Hannah lay down beside him, spooning. But Ruthie must have been sleeping close by for Hannah turned toward him, finger to lips. All his worries had disappeared. Absurd to have gone to such lengths to avoid capture, when all he had to do was make a home for her in his arms.

When he woke, the basement was washed in a dim light. That meant the sun was up outside. Had he spent a full day in this alcove? He felt far from the life he valued, yet very close, only a few feet below the noise of Fourth Street. Like a spirit whose body was interred underground, he longed to return to life on earth. He thought of the song boys sing, the rhyme that fascinates them as they first become aware of death—

The worms crawl in, the worms crawl out,

The worms play pinochle on your snout—

Nonsense lines were enough, at that age. Death would be forgotten by those boys until they grew older. But it was no longer death he feared so much as the death in life that a return to prison would mean. A terrible restlessness of spirit, that's what prison would mean. And that's what he felt right now. Soon, he'd have to break out of this miserable hole and attempt an escape. But inertia had taken hold. To think of an escape attempt made him sweat. He felt the dust sticking to his skin. Coldblooded logic told him that to remain would mean discovery on the worst possible terms. Capture, a merciless beating. Virgil and Rosie would by now have formed a protective wall around their family and his. If anyone could do it, they could. In fact, at this point, his capture was what they needed. His friends would have been living under a siege. If he ventured out now, Arnoldson would have what he wanted, but the siege on his loved ones would be lifted. All he had to do was leap down from the alcove and make a run up the stairs into the arms of one of those thugs.

Or it might not work out that way. A fight to the death might ensue, right out on Fourth Street, on Ruthie's doorstep.

Would Ruthie go see the Robins this year? Would someone take her? In a few years, as she grew older, baseball would be replaced by other interests. He wouldn't get to see her as a young woman. How would that pudgy face glowing with little girl excitement change over the years? But he'd always see the little girl inside her. He tried to cling to the image of Hannah kneeling beside her, as they huddled in the kitchen, talking quietly, laughing.

The Lower East Side had been his orchard. All he had to do was reach up and pick the fruit. Why would someone seize him for possessing an apple?

**

How many hours did he endure of that restless, indecisive squirming? A lifetime by the clock of his spirit, not so many in actual fact. When he was first startled by the scraping, it sounded like a rat in the walls. When it sounded again, he could tell it was not from the walls, but from the other room, or beyond it, in the airshaft. It was the crisp sound of steady work, as if someone were trying to rake away the filth and rubbish of the years.

It wasn't his imagination. The sound was too conscious, persistent. He had to find out who was out there, so he got ready to descend from his alcove. Should he take the stale lunch? He hadn't had the stomach to eat it, and probably wouldn't, now. But the code of slum life was to never leave anything that might draw rats and bugs, so once again he tucked it inside his shirt. He perched on the edge of the alcove and tried to lower his feet slowly to avoid a fall. He landed in an ungraceful squat but managed to avoid injury. He crept into the anteroom, where he could see a little better in the dim light from the stairs. His eyes swept the area, from the closet full of mildew to the yellow sink. The corners were empty. He was alone except for whatever was making the scratching sounds.

He walked over to the door and put his hand on the wood. Someone was on the other side working at something. It was probably one of Arnoldson's men, but it could also be Virgil. Wouldn't it be just like him to lead Bill to safety again? He imagined looking into his friend's eyes and seeing, reflected there, wisdom along with that ever-present hint of vulnerability. The scratching stopped. Bill strained his ears and heard the click of an old spring and the rusty sound of a lock sliding free. Apparently, someone had the key to this old door, which looked like it hadn't been opened for years. Could Virgil have found a way to sneak unobserved into the airshaft with a key?

Bill felt for the knob and began to turn it and pull—when it came open and someone practically fell into him, and he could tell right away it wasn't Virgil. He looked down and saw in the shadowy stairwell a small, bent woman. The last person he would have expected was standing there, Mrs. Levine. Over the months, he'd realized how much like Hannah and even Ruthie she was. And was struck by this again as she stared up at him, her eyes wet and glowing, and pressed something into his hand and closed it tight. Then she seized his collar and pulled his face down to hers and kissed his cheek. "Go," she whispered.

**

He bought a ticket at Pennsylvania Station, aware of what he was leaving, probably forever. He was abandoning New York, fleeing again. This had become the habit of his life. He had fifty dollars; the money Mrs. Levine had given him.

"Next express train west," he said as he placed a $10 bill, one of the five she'd given him, on the hollow place beneath the ticket window. That wood had been worn to a shine by thousands of transactions, including, no doubt, by other fugitives. The bill sat beneath the glass partition for a moment. The hubbub of the station all but drowned out the clerk's voice, "We don't have an express until 4:20, but I can put you on a local to Pittsburgh, and you can transfer there."

He gripped his ticket, trying to orient himself as he stood in the huge cathedral-like room, He was in no mood to appreciate the majesty of the domed roof with its immense side windows. It was only noon, but light flooded through the glass to the huge floor, packed tight with determined, business-like people.

With difficulty he threaded his way toward his track and descended the stairs, a fugitive again. Only this time he had no destination. He was fleeing the only destination he could ever have claimed for himself, fleeing those he loved, for their own good. Even Mrs. Levine seemed to agree it was necessary. That his absence was what they most needed had been a terrible realization.

He arrived at the westbound platform to wait—or end it all on the tracks. Others had done that, maybe from this same platform. Most rail tracks have been christened by blood, or baptized, whichever is the correct term for it. Or maybe just greased. Maybe that's all such lives amounted to, in the end, a greasing of the rails.

That would be one way to escape Arnoldson. And no one would identify the remains. Just another John Doe.

Hannah and Ruthie would never hear how he'd ended it all, wouldn't have that grief to deal with. Nor would Arnoldson and the state of Montana get the satisfaction of crossing him off their list. Case closed for him, unsolved for others.

Then the platform began to pulse with the approach of the train. The steel rails vibrated, a mere three or four feet below where he stood. An easy jump. The view from down there would be very different from the view from above. He'd kneel beside the rails, ballast chips digging into his knees. Above him, a platform full of shocked people. Even further overhead, on the sidewalks of the borough, shoppers hurried, maybe some of the very same stylish people who'd surrounded him with snobbish indifference on his arrival in New York. He'd kneel there, running his hands over the shiny rails, studying the tiny spider cracks in the finish. He'd have a close-up of the solid wood sleepers securing the rails. They were the foundation of the travel and transport dear to so many thousands. The rails were held fast by mush-room headed spikes. But not too tight. They had to give under the great weight of the engine. He'd driven plenty of spikes in his time, on spur lines entering the mines.

If he were down there now, as the train approached, he'd wrap his hand around the icy rail, feel the vibration of what was coming, the anticipation of something he'd never known before and wouldn't remember for long afterward. He'd be unaware of the collective gasp from the platform, which would seem so far above. Not to worry, he'd look up and try to tell them with his eyes. This is a good thing.

Then the squeal and hiss of brakes filled his ears. He shook himself and hurried with the crowd and pushed like them into the nearest car, disappointed to be still alive. The moment was lost, although he suspected another chance to end it might arise.

There weren't enough seats so he stood in the aisle along with most of the other men. At that moment nothing mattered. Except that one fellow remained seated without offering his seat. Several older men and a mother and child had no seats and rocked back and forth in the aisle. An old woman caught his eye and it was clear what both of them were thinking about this man who lacked the simple courtesy to offer his seat to others. It wasn't until after several New Jersey stops that everyone found a seat.

He was in a daze as the train crept into the mountains of Pennsylvania. Now, they were buried in smog. A red sign for *Hazelton* was visible as the train slowed and the conductor droned out the name. A coal town, no doubt, grime and dust everywhere. People jammed the platform, looking for the face of a loved one. Bill wasn't their kin and Hazelton wasn't his town. Not far enough yet. Distance meant safety, so he stayed on and watched the little Hazelton station disappear. Once it had been a pretty station house, before coal dust had smudged the bricks gray.

The truckers had taken him to a world of good hiding. Now he was seeking another place to hide, but without the heart for it. The train strained up a grade then picked up speed. The old lady sitting next to him nudged his arm. In her hand was a handkerchief. At first, he didn't know why she was handing it to him. Then he began to dab at the tears on his cheek with the soft cloth. It had a refreshing scent, the kind old ladies wear. He wanted to break down and cover his face in that clean handkerchief with the minty smell.

"Thanks," he said, "a little hay fever."

"It's bad in these trains because the dust lingers in them," the old lady responded. "Maybe they don't clean them well enough. I feel it myself."

He tried to smile, remembering how Frank always had a smile on his face, even when he was upset. That had probably saved him more than once. Frank was angry and foolish and just plain funny. When the vigilantes grabbed him that last time, he probably grinned at them, convinced he could tell one more joke, sure he could get out of the rope they were placing over his head.

He'd never have let them see he was scared. If he was sitting here now, Frank would dismiss the vigilantes and their horrible work. "Those fellows had no sense of humor."

Bill emerged from these musings when the old woman nudged him again, pointing to a somber procession on the street next to the tracks. "These towns have their share of funerals. My little brother died of miner's consumption. A skeleton Edward was when we buried him. Wife had left him before they had any children. No one at the church but old workmates and me. They invited me out for a drink, which was kind, but I had no place there. It would only have made me feel old and alone."

She talked on, and he was glad for it. She was a lovely old woman. She helped him endure a few hours. But then her kindness plus the cramped quarters began to make him restless. He said goodbye at a town called *Rices Landing*. The sign spelled it without the apostrophe.

Bare bulbs hung from the peaked roof above the platform. As he walked away from the station, these lights faded out in the grimy air. He'd smelled coal dust and coke tar but not in such a heavy concentration. His mouth was gritty with the sticky powder, and the sweet stink caught in his nose. He didn't know where he was going, but as he walked uphill, away from the station, the air seemed to clear a little. He caught a glimpse of a splinter of moon above a steep hillside.

The first impression he had of Rices Landing was of great crowding—but not like the Lower East Side. Here, the buildings weren't tall, but they were stacked very close. Everything was cramped on the side of a hill. At the bottom, a river. Without seeing the water, he knew it was down there. Everything was wet from it, the trees, the rooftops and walls, the bricks and boards. He trudged further from the station until he saw a mildewed sign that said *Rice Hotel.*

Part III: Rices Landing

Greene County, Pennsylvania

16.

"You kin to the Waites in Morgantown?"

Gerald looked at him with the widest smile on earth. Or below its surface, because they were in a mine hundreds of feet under the main street of Rices Landing. Partners, timbering in a section of low coal. Never comfortable, this crawling and clambering in the muck. A sharp stone catching you in the kneecap was the least of it.

"You're not related to Charlie or Daniel?" Gerald had stopped work, as if they had all night to set timbers. He seemed to know everyone, and he referred to them by first name as if Bill would know them also. And he had a curiosity that burrowed into people, friendliness like an augur. And Bill with no past, none he wanted to reveal.

"Charlie's wife is Deborah. Last time I saw them she was pregnant and their other one, little Charlie, had just turned two, walking and talking like a fine young scholar. Good people, those Waites. But Charlie worked in Osage."

Gerald's words hung there. No clarification needed. Everyone knew about the explosion in the Osage mine, just across the border in West Virginia. It was now the end of November, 1924. Another gray and barren winter was on the way, especially for the family of Charlie, the Osage miner.

"He might've made it out ok," Bill responded, after a respectful silence. He'd learned that these miners clung to hope long after it was reasonable to do so. They were superstitious that way. Superstitious for a good outcome.

He'd told Gerald five times at least that he was from up north and not related to any local Waites. He was from up along the lake, above Erie, PA, he'd insisted. His people were farmers. He wasn't related to any Waites around here. But in this part of Pennsylvania, just upriver a mile or two from West Virginia, everyone knew everyone else. Especially among miners. And these were the most curious people he'd ever met, like friendly dogs, constantly sniffing at you. Wanting to be helpful and him not wanting to be helped. They'd marked him as an outsider right away, someone who needed their help.

On his first shift at the Dilworth Mine, when he was about to leave the wash room on a night that had turned cold and rainy while they were underground, Gerald called out to him, "Honey, you can't go out in that wind without a jacket." He'd never been called honey by a man before. "Take mine. You show up at your hotel in a wet shirt, and they'll think you're crazy as a pig at a pepper trough."

"I can't take your jacket," he'd said as Gerald thrust it on him. They were both big fellows, and the jacket fit fine.

At that point, he didn't even know Gerald. They hadn't become work partners until later in the month, when Bobby Crandall hurt his back. "Honey, could you take Bobby's place?"

In a span of less than two years, Bill had found a life in New York, thanks to Virgil. For less than six months of that span he'd been with Ruthie and Hannah. A child's temper tantrums, the mood swings of an injured woman—that's what real happiness is built on, the imperfections. The perfect world of dreams lacks the grit and richness of real life. His faults were much larger, especially after the vigilante attack on Frank, which had revealed all the weaknesses in his character. The foolishness that had cost his mother's life. As Hannah's lover and Ruthie's father he thought he'd finally put himself back together. Now, again, his life was a shambles, like the old mine ruins that dotted this part of the country. Old tipple, busted headframe. Sumac sprawling where his heart was supposed to be.

The vigilantes had destroyed his life. Revenge might have helped. Revenge against the "shadowy network of vigilantes," if Virgil was right. Revenge, finally, against the mastermind of it all. But they had acted in darkness, two thousand miles away. Even revenge seemed hopeless.

Now he lived in a cramped coal town bruising his knees and breaking his back in low coal. It seemed a fit life for a man without hope. He wasn't the only one in Rices Landing who'd led a rough life. On days when the coal dust suddenly cleared, he could see bare trees, the sky gray as lead. At least a river flowed through this town at the foot of these soaring hills, the Monongahela. Not many rivers in North America flowed north, but this one did, from West Virginia toward the massive steel mills that lined the riverbanks around Pittsburgh.

Bill grew impatient with this cramped world, the hopelessness he saw around him, and with the veneer of cheerfulness. Or were these people really happy? Were they idiots, to not admit to themselves how gloomy their prospects were? His coworkers acted like mining coal was a vacation in paradise. He bridled at the sunny optimism he saw all around him but recognized that these people were better than he was, Gerald especially, who'd given him the shirt off his back. Of course, it was a jacket not a shirt. Wool-lined, canvas shell. Perfect for cold rainy weather. It carried Bill through the winter.

But what he had less patience for was Gerald's talk about Charlie Waite, the man whom Gerald was convinced he was related to. Bill hoped Charlie had survived that mine disaster but was tired of hearing about him. He was tired of the lies he was telling. Tired of life, as he slid another timber off the cart, hoisted the end up under a roof beam, and held it in place with both hands. Reluctantly, Gerald picked up his four-pound hammer and a shim. Four blows thudded in the passageway, the shim was wedged tight, the roof secure. Gerald was a good worker and fast, once he got around to it.

"How about the Waites in Preston County. Them is farming people. They're a fine bunch for never shaving or bathing."

Bill wrestled with another timber, hard work in low coal, lifting and carrying on your knees. Keeping busy was his aim. He was a man who didn't want to think. He hurried ahead on his knees, mouth shut, while Gerald lagged behind still chatting about these other Waites. Maybe he was gently riding Bill, trying to coax a smile. Gerald cared more about that smile than he did about timbering.

"You're a fine fellow, Bill. But as stone-faced as a god-damn Indian."

Bill felt safe in this mine, which was a stupid thing to feel. It was the most dangerous place he'd ever worked, gassy and prone to explosion. It was amazing to think of these hills, covered with a carpet of trees—but underneath, all the noise and danger of a battlefield.

His thoughts always went back to 1917 and the underground fire, how he'd been working in the adjacent shaft and heard the siren. He and his crew ran to help. They clustered beneath the headframe and hoist, which the fire had disabled. They were eager to help but trapped in a nightmare of delay while the bosses argued about how to conduct the rescue. Finally, several miners began climbing the ladder, and he'd joined them. Only a few flights down and they ran into dense smoke. The men in the lead could no longer breathe, so Bill yelled for the procession to reverse. Like a single creature, they'd gone snaking down the ladder and had to go snaking back. Once in the fresh air they dropped to all fours, seized by coughing. They cried for the men they couldn't help. What did Arnoldson and his hallowing know of the 164 miners who died on that day?

He'd heard one miner, who'd served in France, say that a lot of soldiers hadn't faced as much danger on a battlefield as miners faced on a shift under the lovely green earth of Pennsylvania and West Virginia. From what Bill had seen, even the mines out west weren't this bad. Under these peaceful forests, explosions, war-like conflagrations occurred, and smaller hazards were an everyday fact of life. Even when the top might look sound, a section of slate could break off, leaving you crippled or dead.

Not to mention coal dust. It could kill you a couple of different ways: suddenly, when it caught fire and exploded; or gradually, by catching in your lungs and slowly strangling you. You didn't have to spend long in Rices Landing before you noticed the old men—at least they looked old—panting, without enough breath to walk off the front porch.

Bill was aware that being Gerald's partner had helped him win acceptance. His coworkers were impressed by how well he could do the work. It was a little different from copper mining, where the mines were roomier, with more secure tops, less gas, and a little more of what you might call amenities. Not good, not safe, June 8 was proof of that, but better than coal. But the big issues were the same: Can you work underground, go without seeing daylight for a week? Are you careful? Most important to these miners was the fact that he looked out for the other men. It sounds funny to say, but among these tough men, caring counted for everything. They were the only bunch, maybe in the whole world, who lived to the golden rule. At least towards their workmates.

He'd been there two weeks when a miner asked him, "So what brings you to Greene County, son?" He was dumbfounded. This was Greene County, the very spot that Virgil had invented for him.

He stayed for a month at The Rice Hotel, paying weekly rates. His wage from the mine was enough to cover it. Whether or not others thought he was a fugitive outlaw was no longer his prime concern. He had no prime concern. He cared about work, a habit he couldn't shake. Beyond that, he didn't have much caution left. He was at the mercy of anyone suspicious enough to wonder if he was on the run. There's a fine line between curiosity and suspicion. Fortunately, no one in Rices Landing had shown an inclination to cross it.

He moved out of the hotel in January and got a room with Mrs. Mac, a small room in a big house. In the coalfields, it was a lucky widow who had a large house with rooms to let. As her tenant, he received breakfast and lunch. For dinner she'd pack two sandwiches in his bucket, on a metal tray. Beneath the tray was water because there wasn't any in the mine. At Mrs. Mac's he had his own private room with a washstand, a basin, and a window, which needed washing. He'd do that in the spring.

He didn't need much. Except a hole to die in. The Dilworth Mine was perfect for that.

**

Inventing a new identity is a once-in-a-lifetime thing. He'd done it once, and didn't have the heart to do it again. He was Bill Waite. He'd stick to that name. He'd invented the story about a family up north, along Lake Erie. He didn't know the first thing about Lake Erie, which didn't matter, since nobody believed him anyway.

He was free, in a discouraging sort of way. Those he loved were hundreds of miles away, on the Lower East Side, or dead. What lay ahead was a continuation of the same dark story, but it was unlikely to involve the same type of loss. Losing isn't something that goes on and on. You run out of things to lose.

What he clung to was a primitive caring. He didn't care about himself but wouldn't let that disregard lead him to endanger others. That was a standard, maybe the only one he had left. On a dangerous job, your mates come first. Swirling around in Bill's confused and unhappy mind was another vague thought, a flickering carbide lamp at the end of a tunnel full of wreckage. Despite it all, wasn't he still a father? A father shouldn't do anything to disgrace himself.

**

Some of the people here were backwoods, like Gerald and the other Waites, the ones he didn't know. They'd lived here since Adam and Eve went to war against Tecumseh. A lot of Italians lived here, and some blacks; wherever there was dangerous work, the Irish showed up; but Bohunks outnumbered everyone. If you were a Pole, a Serb, or a Slovak, you were a Bohunk. And of course, Hungarians were Bohunks.

An echo of those origins survived. On Saturday afternoons, if he wasn't scheduled to work, Bill would take a break from Mrs. Mac's average cooking and above-average considerateness and go to a kitchen that served goulash. There, a handful of men would hold up their bowls to Mrs. Cerkvenik's ladle and receive chunks of meat with boiled potatoes and carrots all in a thick brown gravy. Not the New York cuisine he'd sampled with Hannah and Virgil, but rich enough. Meanwhile, Nowak and Sandor told stories concerning the persecutions of their families under the czar's domination. These stories reminded him that there might be a life harder than Rices Landing. Bill had heard stories like that in New York. They shook him out of his self-pitying mood, but only for a time.

He'd arrived in October and had made it through most of the winter. Only a few months, but they seemed like a lifetime. The steep hills and the shift after shift imparted a smothering sameness to the life. Nothing is going to happen in Rices Landing. Nothing but death in the Dilworth Mine. Or, Arnoldson might show up and arrest him. Or kill him. Under color of law he could do that, too. Would Bill fight like hell or was he past caring? Either way, this little holler would be the end of it.

On good days, the hours passed without much thought: the darkness of work and the darkness of sleep. Even the sun at mid-afternoon peaking over the hilltops meant only shadows. All winter, he followed the rail tracks as he walked with other men on the way to the mine, along the river, which was covered by a thin layer of ice out to where the channel water flowed. The wet chill ate into his bones.

At the beginning of every shift, Gerald would ask him, "How are you, Old Son?" He'd put his hand on Bill's shoulder, eyes searching.

Bill didn't like to be worried over, so he'd try to think up something cheerful. "Last shift was a piece of cake. This is the only job where they pay me for having a good time!"

"That's right, Honey, we got the world by the short hairs!"

And then it was spring. Bill's act was wearing thin, and he wasn't prepared for how the lush weeds and vines would affect him. The green on green of plants and trees multiplied, sprawled over the shambles of the old coke ovens, the half-destroyed brick footers of an outmoded mill. Around town and on the road to the portal, a jungle was taking shape, a luxuriance full of bright greens and lovely deep shadows. The leaves were coming out on red bud, hackberry, and maple. Undergrowth sprawled over hillsides, a confusion of sumac and mountain rhododendron. The brilliant greens clashed with his outlook. The beauty added weight to his sadness.

But most of the spring consisted of icy rain pouring from a lead sky. The days were oppressive when it rained, heartbreakingly beautiful when a rare sun edged above the rim of hills and poured into the valley. It was the type of loveliness you could drown in, cruel to an unhappy man. On late mornings, he got out and sniffed at the lushness— the dew on flat leaves and needles, perfect little drops of it shining in the sun like tears—and what he'd left behind knocked the wind from his chest.

**

He walked back along the river with a few other men, passing a row of coke ovens that smoldered, giving off a stink that combined the heavy odor of burning coal with the harshness of deadly chemicals. By now, he was used to it. Gradually, men left the group and trudged off into the darkness, for boarding houses or homes. Some tramped along Route 88 toward Crucible. Bill turned off and continued down Carmichael Street, then to Walnut Ave. and Mrs. Mac's. He put his hand on the top slat of the gate and stared up at the pyramid roof silhouetted against the night sky. She always left something on the counter. He appreciated the gesture, but that night the thought of her kindness depressed him. People may expend all the kindness they want on the lost. It doesn't change much. Another moment passed during which the neighbors would have glimpsed a man still as a statue at Mrs. Mac's gate. Then he pulled the gate softly shut, turned away, and continued down Walnut toward the river. He passed fences like Mrs. Mac's bordering postage-stamp lawns where spring grass was just beginning to emerge. The town was quiet, as if a thick blanket had been dropped over it. No sound reached him from the mine. Even the blades and bearings in the huge ventilating fans, buried in hillside forests surrounding the mine, could not be heard, although their vital work continued, circulating air through the mine. This part of town slanted steeply toward the river. Once, Bill had witnessed a man not really so old attempting the hill. He took a few steps and leaned on a fence post to catch his breath. Bill took the man's arm to help, only to have the man shake him off.

He turned left on Water Street and headed along the level stretch by the river. The air was a little cooler here, soaked in the mystery that lives along flowing water. A coal barge slid soundlessly by, not more than a dozen yards away, the belly piled high, a black hillside adrift.

The river glowed like foil spread out against the darkness of the opposite bank. He could make out the sound of leaves brushing against each other, featherlike in a soft breeze. As his ears strained, he realized he was hearing a louder more insistent sound. He looked to his left, toward

Pumpkin Run, which emptied into the river with a chattering, frosty chorus.

Except for a moment in the New York train station, he'd never been drawn toward taking his own life, never felt like that was something he could surrender to. In some people, it's a force that seizes hold and draws them irresistibly toward this act. What he felt at that moment was pretty close, an urge within him to embrace the chill of the water, to battle the depth and flow. To dive in and experience the tug of the current rushing with unexpected power below the tranquil surface, to experience the helplessness of muscle and bone caught up in the unforgiving flow. How could awakening to the slap of time and loss not be a good thing? The way seconds were linked together to form minutes had been choking him. The hours were choking him.

He stood on that terrace a few feet above the water and wondered at the fact that his life had veered so far off course. Yet he could do nothing to redirect it. The gulf between where he should be and where he was had opened like a wound. On the other side was James Little, a boy in Oklahoma, learning to read and write, to set traps, run around with Frank like a little hellion. He'd worked, been sent to prison and been trundled to that place where he'd become a husband, a father. His life seemed to have taken place without any conscious direction on his part.

Thoughts, if sincerely held, should be acted upon. Thoughts are what guide us into the swift-moving river of who we are. We learn nothing if we don't act decisively and put thoughts into action. But there is one thought that should never be acted upon. In the face of it we should be weak and compromising. Better to let your life slip by, no matter how unhappy, than to act resolutely to destroy it.

Besides, if he destroyed himself, wouldn't that be a blow aimed as much at Hannah and Ruthie as himself? Their lives would also be lessened by that action, even if they never found out. Maybe it was the idea that what he did in the present could harm the past, that this deed could reverberate back in time and discredit the life he'd had with them. For their sake, he'd fled. He had to survive for them, much as he hated it. What else did this wash of a life amount to?

The mine's floodlights were a faint haze several miles off. The only real light came from the stars and a sliver of moon and their reflection on the wide river. This glow lit the emerging grass in the municipal lawn that spread out between him and Pumpkin Run. He'd never paid much attention to this area and the two or three official buildings huddled there, dwarfed by flanks of the valley. The sound of the Run carpeted the scene with a drumming of water on water that was so continuous it was like silence, like a line of music that might play on through the night and through all the nights to come.

But there was another sound. As he listened to the water spilling through the night air, he heard a mournful whisper rising above it. It was surely just a reflection of his own mood. He turned toward the town lawn, where it seemed to be coming from. This time it lasted a little longer, still indecipherable. Like a sadness, a sadness through walls. Then nothing but the waters of the Run. His mind was playing tricks on him. He was hearing his own thoughts, nothing else.

Then he heard it again, speaking into the night. It seemed to come from a little brick building on the lawn over by the copse surrounding the Run. He remembered, now, that this building was the town jail, a miniature jail, apparently all that was needed for such a small town. Bill walked toward it, across the lawn, dew soaking into his boots. He approached the building's one window. The wood framing had been recently painted and glowed an eerie white. Iron bars crisscrossed the glass.

Someone was in there, not able to sleep—jail isn't an easy place for sleep—thinking he could cry into the darkness without being heard. Bill's first instinct was to walk away and leave the inmate to his private sadness. He took a step away from the building but heard the voice again, soft, quavering, almost like the mountain songs he'd heard from some of the miners. He leaned on the bricks and peered through the reinforced glass. Since the darkness inside was greater than outside, he saw nothing through the window, not even the cot he knew was there. Whoever was in there could see Bill framed by the window he was trying to see through.

17.

"Don't worry, brother, I'm here." Bill felt foolish, speaking to this unknown man, embarrassed both for himself and the inmate. There was no response to his words, but the soft crying ceased immediately.

"I was locked up once, two-thousand miles from here," Bill continued. "I lived behind bars for six years, but never in a jail this tiny. I wish I could shove something in through this window, like a jar of whisky, to share on a long, lonely night. But they have you locked up pretty tight."

In one sentence, he'd revealed more to this inmate than to anyone besides Virgil, Rosie, and Hannah. This lack of caution shocked him but he blundered on. "They say I plotted to kill some men, but I didn't. My brother was murdered by company thugs. If I told you his name, it might be familiar. Out west he was famous, or infamous, depending on who you talked to. I was caught up in a union-company thing. You can guess which side the law was on. They threw the book at me, but being stupid was my only crime. That's the worst crime a poor man can commit. Standing there, stupid before the law. But I'm not telling you anything you don't already know."

He stopped and waited for a response, but none was forthcoming.

"I'm a miner," he continued. "But being stupid is what I do best. Same for you, maybe. I shouldn't make assumptions, and you don't have to answer. I don't blame you for not being too talkative with a stranger."

Bill chatted on. He accepted the silence. The darkness of the night had lifted, or maybe it was only his eyes getting used to the dim light of the stars and their reflection off the river. Looking around, he realized how conspicuous he was, a solitary figure beside this tiny building in the middle of a wide lawn. The first sign of dawn was in the gray sky above the dark line of the hills. Lights would be coming on, houses coming to life.

He had to leave but didn't know how to say goodbye.

"Maybe I'll come back and we can talk again. One out-of-luck guy to another . . ." He let that sentence fade into the chatter of the Run. "But every once in a while, something good happens. You might bet against it, then it happens anyway." Bill didn't believe that last part, it certainly didn't apply to him. But what kind of guy would he be, to leave this man without a word of hope?

He walked back uphill, leaning forward against the incline, straining against the grade, and went through Mrs. Mac's gate and climbed the narrow wood stairs to his little room and slept soundly and woke up to the noon sun on the sill and the smell of a late shift breakfast on Mrs. Mac's stove, the bacon and eggs he was famished for.

**

The first part of a shift is full of details. Every miner keeps a mental checklist of all-important tasks, whether

276

timbering, blasting, or loading. All have to be done with care, but in Bill's mind timbering was most important because no work is safe without a safe roof. No set of timbers is ever sawed one-hundred percent true, so shims need to be driven into the gap between roof beam and upright timber. But if the timber is too short, no quantity of shims will make it safe.

"No, that'll never do," Gerald said, as he pushed the timber into a vertical position and felt at the gap. He tossed it into the cart along with the other short timbers. "They'll have to send us replacements. Not much to do until we get a load back," he said, and sat down to wait.

There were a hundred and one tasks they could've kept themselves busy with, but Bill didn't want to push Gerald this early in the shift. No doubt he'd have to do it later. He sat down beside him. A mine can be a chaos of sound, bellowing voices, iron on iron of cart wheels on rails, and blasting, which always sounded like it was going off right at your ear. Blasting hadn't bothered Bill when he'd worked in the mines out west, because they were better organized. Here, miners might be blasting in an entry nearby or directly overhead.

Bill respected the fact that his partner, although he might appear lazy, was a very capable and knowledgeable miner. He liked the fact that he was underground with someone whose safety instinct prevailed over his hurry-up-and-get'er-done instinct.

If Gerald would have known Yiddish, he might have said, "Proper equipment or I'm not doing *bupkus*."

Which suggested a thought that made Bill chuckle. What if all these coal miners had been born Jewish? What if Jews, instead of settling on the Lower East Side, had come to West Virginia? Would the backwoods people in the surrounding areas eat knishes and teach their children Yiddish?

Bill suppressed his laughter, as he sat in the mud, the roof of their entry no more than two feet above his nose. It was like working in the crawlspace under a house. Then a question occurred to him. "You ever know anyone who had the misfortune to serve time in that little jail by the river?"

"My fool of a brother-in-law's there right now. If you think I'm a big, stupid guy, you should rest your eyes on Percy. Funny thing is, he looks like me, like we could be blood brothers. But he's even uglier and a whole lot stupider, hard as that may be to imagine."

Even in a small town where everyone seemed to be related, this coincidence was unnerving. Especially so, because it made Bill feel like he was beginning to lose control. He didn't want to shed what little was left of his false identity. It was useful insofar as it kept these curious people from probing. He weighed the new information and wondered if it was a bad omen. Was he beginning to believe in omens? People who've lost control over their lives and given up on reasonable solutions put great stock in superstitious things. Into an empty life comes foolishness, and it has great meaning.

Into Bill's life.

**

In the weeks that followed, he went back to the jail on his way home from work, always past midnight. He'd convinced himself that he was actually safer in continuing his visits. Gerald would learn about his fugitive status, but he trusted Gerald. Besides, if there was damage, it had already been done. And by continuing he was more likely to win Percy's trust, and his silence.

Then, one night, Percy spoke. "Maybe you work with my brother in law, Gerald Whitaker . . ."

"He's...he's my...my...partner," Bill stammered. Realizing an explanation was needed, he continued, "I trust him with my life. But he doesn't know that Bill isn't my real name, and I'd rather you didn't tell him until I've had a chance to."

"Maybe he knows more than you think." Percy spoke slowly, picking his words. "But don't worry, your secret's safe with me."

Those were the last words Bill would get from Percy, but they were enough. He went back again and again to the brick building. On his first few visits, he'd spoken softly, afraid someone might overhear. And even that whisper had seemed thunderous. But after a few nights, the repetition of what he was doing wore away the caution.

Caution serves as a bulwark against danger, an earthen dam. But it's no match for the floodwaters that enter our lives.

"Have you ever had a little girl that you could take to ballgames, a five-year old who trusted you, who wanted to walk around town and learn about life from you?" He paused for the answer that wouldn't come. Then continued, telling his new friend about having lunch with Ruthie at Schrafts. Bill spent several nights describing the ballgames they attended. He assumed a prisoner would want to hear some news about baseball, even though he'd be a fan of the Pittsburgh Pirates not a team in Brooklyn.

"I'd put my hand on her head and she'd look up at me with a big smile and take my hand in hers. That's the toughest part for me now. Thinking of that smile and how she trusted me and thought I'd always be there . . ."

On those cool April nights Bill told the inmate things he'd never told anyone but Hannah. He may have been entertaining this man with his stories, which helped him and tortured him, both. It had come as a relief, more so than he would have thought, to finally tell someone about the joy he'd known and how he'd been stripped of it. He wanted to relive those late-night talks with Hannah, but without the pain the memories stirred. On their first night together, as they lay in bed, she'd stared back at him, her eyes bright in the darkness. Her smile was a mix of skepticism and affection and seemed to be telling him, "You haven't told me everything, and I need to hear it all." Over the next days and nights he'd unburdened himself. He told her about seeing the coffins of so many men he'd known and, what was worse, the faces of their loved ones as they stood in the lines at the many viewings that had taken place all over Butte. Then he told her about holding Frank's body at dawn and how his brother's skin was already colder than the night air.

As he walked uphill from the river, heading back to Mrs. Mac's, something gnawed at him. When he'd tried to explain his parole to the inmate, his account didn't ring true. "It was the cruelest part of my sentence," he'd said, as if everyone knew what those words meant. Then he remembered Arnoldson's charge of $180 for the four bales. Such an inflated price for feed or straw was a telling thing. And then one of the questions he'd been resisting over the years pushed its way through. Were such payments connected to the network Virgil had alluded to? What was the implication of the story about Centralia? If his parole boss had somehow played a role in that murder, what about Frank's murder? But there was no solid information about such a connection, and Bill liked solid information over guesswork.

He undressed and got in bed and couldn't sleep, recalling the day he'd first met Arnoldson. He'd just been ushered into the warden's office. Warden Middleton was deep in conversation with this giant of a man. Normally, the warden would have proposed a name for parole pursuant to instructions from the parole board. Overcrowding meant that some good-behavior prisoners were being released. All that was common knowledge. But Bill wasn't the only good-behavior prisoner, and he had no influential friends to push for him. So why had the warden or the parole board selected him? Or had someone else made the selection, like Arnoldson?

18.

The next Sunday, April 23, he woke to a pounding rain. The room in Mrs. Mac's had a good view across the river to the hillside beyond. But the window didn't have much appeal on a rainy day. As if he needed another reason to be down in the dumps, today was when they'd always celebrated Ma's birthday. Like the birthdays of many older people, no one was sure of the date. Her mother had told her it was April 22, then revised it to April 23. By mutual agreement of Frank and Bill it was the 23rd. This gave them an extra day to find a present. Sometimes they forgot entirely, although they seldom missed sending her money each month. Today she would've been 55. Except for the sadness he'd forced on her, she'd be alive today.

He looked out at the puddles and the brown mud showing through slick green weeds and realized that if she was alive right now, he'd be walking to the post office to mail her something, if he hadn't already. That thought was agonizing. It filled his body with a painful restlessness.

"I think I'll go out," he told Mrs. Mac after breakfast, as the rain thundered down on casement and glass. He'd come downstairs with Gerald's coat and his only hat.

"Are you daft, Bill? You can't go out in that hat. I've kept some of Mr. McGraw's hats for days like this. Don't worry," she added, after she returned from the closet with

283

her arms full. "You won't be the first young man to wear it. It's protected many a young lad's head. So, any bad luck from wearing a dead man's hat wore off long ago."

It wasn't bad luck he was thinking about—he didn't have such a high opinion of his own luck—it was her kindness that gave him pause. And the hat was a fine one for the rain, a Stetson, broad-brimmed and oil-skinned. He pushed it down and felt the hatband dig into his scalp, stiff but secure. He hadn't worn a Stetson since leaving Montana. Mrs. Mac beamed at him. But she wasn't done and next insisted that he shed his jacket in favor of the slicker that went with the hat. Having already accepted one item, he wasn't able to refuse its mate.

She said that Jimmy Collins, another lodger, had worn it just last week.

He trudged uphill, and even before the top of Carmichael Street, the cuffs of his jeans were soaked. He was thankful not to be in Gerald's jacket, or his legs would've been soaked as well. It was a lousy day. Tea-brown runoff coursed downhill, overwhelming the gutters. Clouds the color of wet cement were thick with more rain. He hadn't thought ahead to where he'd go, but there was really only one place on such a gin-drinking day: Serbtown.

The hand-lettered sign was in a language not much more understandable to him than Yiddish or Chinese. The characters, however, were closer to English characters and looked like *Rockao*. For that reason, it was called Rocky's by the non-Serbs who drank there. It was a not-too-well-concealed prohibition club. Once, Gerald had brought him here, so he hoped Tony— who was actually Italian not Serbian—would remember his face.

"You look like a drowned rat—what'll you have?"

"I'll take some gin, Tony."

"You know damn well I only serve beer and whisky."

Only two other patrons were there, one from his shift— he recognized the man, whose name was Bertie, but had never spoken with him; and Sonny, who worked cleaning up at the tipple.

"But I do have a whisky that tastes like gin. You can try it for free, but after that you pay."

"What about me," Sonny hollered. "Don't I get a sample? I'm partial to the taste of gin."

"You've been drinking this whisky more than a few years, now, and never told me once it tasted of gin."

He finished his free sample and gave Tony three quarters to pay for a round, including the other two, then sat down at their table. Sonny was leaning back in his chair and Bertie was slumped over his drink. They knew Bill, at least by face, and he hoped this would make them less curious for the life story some men request when they've been drinking.

But after a couple of rounds— "I was born in Poland," Sonny said, for no apparent reason.

"I know that's where you was hatched, but where'd you fall out of the nest?" Bertie responded.

Sonny regarded this as a rude question and turned to Bill. "They brought me over when I was a babe, and I've lived in this valley ever since. Pa worked the coke ovens and died before he was forty."

"That stuff eats your lungs out faster than coal dust. I'm not sure I'd take a job on the ovens, even if they asked me. What about you guys?" Bill was trying to shift the discussion off of life stories.

"I picked slate as a kid, so I doubt there's much left of my lungs," Bertie responded. "Beginning when I was eleven, glued to them coal belts when I should've been playing baseball. In the Monongh Mine, if you can believe it. Pop hated that mine and moved us up here, just before the explosion."

In 1909 the Monongh Mine had been the scene of a cave in and fire that took the lives of nearly 400 men. Monongh was a little south of Rices Landing, near Fairmont, WV.

"My family's been around these coal fields going back a couple of generations. Before that"—Bertie paused to finish his drink— "before that. County Cork, if you can put good faith in the family legends."

The two men waited for Bill to chime in with his own story, a drunken gape on their faces. Bill busied himself gesturing for another round. After it was delivered to their table, he raised his glass and drank it off in one gulp.

"Gents, I have to run." He'd already bought them two rounds and didn't owe them an autobiography.

"Gonna' go Tom-cattin' to Crucible?" Sonny asked as Bill disappeared out the door.

The bright light from outside hit him hard. The rain had cleared, and the sun was dazzling, rays reflected off puddles, refracted in the rainwater dripping from gutters and leaves.

Half-dazed, he walked up the hill to Route 88. Now, he was warm and overdressed, not quite steady on his feet, lightheaded and laughing to himself that he'd already spilled out his story to a prisoner, who may have told Gerald. Why not tell a few more guys at Rocky's? Why not just put a sign on his back that said "fugitive"? He'd stepped into a new self, *another* new self, and it made him dizzy, like when he'd first awakened to the fact that he was on the run, in a truck headed out of Montana. Only this time he seemed to be peeling off layers, taking off disguises, instead of putting them on. And for one simple reason: he didn't care anymore. He felt free as a balloon in the wind. But it was the uncomfortable kind of freedom, just blowing, with nothing to moor him.

He caught his breath at the top of the hill and stared down all the way to the river. It wasn't yet late afternoon, but shadows had gathered around the copse at Pumpkin Run. From this high up he couldn't see the jail, which he wasn't going to visit in daylight. He walked up the pike, through the heart of town. None of the stores were open and no one was about. He took off the raincoat and folded it over his arm. He would've abandoned it by the road if it was his. He walked past The Rice Hotel, which looked dustier than ever, even after the rain, like a cloud would explode from it if you slammed the front door. He stood on the tracks and looked toward the empty station. Beyond that, the tracks disappeared into a screen of trees. Sunlight glistened off iron rails; gray ballast stones mounded up under ties that were stained dark brown from the rain. Time was passing slowly, whether he stood still like a dazed dog, or put his legs in gear. If anybody from work saw him just standing there, gaping about, they'd let Gerald know that his partner wasn't right in the head. He moved on, hopping over the tracks. Not until contemplating suicide in Penn Station had he ever thought much about how deadly they might be. But this was an afternoon for self-pity not suicide. He scrambled up on the platform and slumped down on a bench, out of breath. Mining coal for just a few months and his lungs had already gone to hell. This was a town of coughing fits, of men greeting each other, starting up a conversation, and turning away while their lungs made a racket.

The station was empty. Only one train ran on Sunday, and it had left hours ago. The platform brought back memories of his arrival, stepping off the train without any idea that he was in Greene County, the place Virgil had invented for him. He put the slicker next to him on the bench and felt a little breeze stirring after the rain, the air blowing through his shirt, flowing over his chest, around his neck, across the sweat on his face. Normally, such idle moments frightened him. He picked up the slicker and began absentmindedly to rummage through the pockets. His hands felt lint deposits in the flannel lining. To his surprise, something was folded up, like a roll of bills. That caused him a little excitement, but of course he'd turn it over to Mrs. Mac, who'd give it to the last person who used the slicker, Jimmy Collins, she'd said.

But it was just a sheaf of papers folded up. Would Jimmy have written anything on them? No, they were blank, but creased inside them was an envelope. He held it, trying not to get it smudged in his hands, which always had a little coal ground into them no matter how often he washed. The dust was always there, around his nails, ground into the print of his thumbs. He turned the envelope over and saw, in the corner, a one-penny stamp. It struck him as funny, to find an envelope with postage already applied, forgotten by someone. Jimmy had probably meant to walk up here to the station and mail it to someone who lived miles away. Not to Ireland, on a one-penny stamp, but maybe Pittsburgh or Philadelphia. Or even New York. Jimmy might've been sitting on this very bench, trying to compose a letter before stuffing it back in the pocket.

Bill wasn't surprised at what he found next, a short writing pencil. He took out his knife and ran the blade over the point, lightly, to whittle it without breaking the soft lead. It was almost sharp when it broke off, making him think that the lead was cracked inside the wood. If that was the case, it wouldn't do much good to try to sharpen it. But he had nothing better to do and started over, whittling more carefully this time, stroking the blade over the lead, shaving it, trying to coax it to a fine writing point.

Good enough. But he had no one to write to and could only remember one address. Arnoldson might be keeping tabs on mail going there. But that wasn't the main reason he wouldn't send a letter to that address. It wouldn't do Hannah and Ruthie any good. It was better for them not to know where he was. He wasn't a part of their lives anymore. He'd once trusted Ruthie with a secret, and for all he knew she'd kept it. But trusting people can be a way of exposing them to danger.

By now the warmth he'd felt earlier from the whiskey had worn off. It was late afternoon. A shadow fell across the neat block letters he'd printed on the envelope—

122 East Fourth Street, Apt 2C
New York (Manhattan)
New York

Then, he put "from" and Mrs. Mac's address on the flap.

Why would he have written Hannah's address on a letter he had no intention of mailing? It wouldn't help her to know where he was. She and Ruthie had already lived through enough heartache on his account. He needed to let them forget about him. He'd tear it up and pay Jimmy back for the paper and stamp. But in the meantime, he savored the address and unfolded a sheet of paper to begin a letter he had no intention of sending—

Love, I'm living at Mrs. Mac's boarding house—

He thought of all the things he wanted to tell her— how he was actually living in Greene County, if she could believe it; how terrible he felt on a beautiful day he couldn't share with her; how dangerous the mines were and what a good partner lazy Gerald was. And the jail, you wouldn't believe what a remarkable little jail they have here. As the words poured through his mind, he felt like he was sitting in bed with her, after making love. He hadn't felt so close since leaving New York. Close to the heartbreak as well.

The mail slot was right there in the wall of the station master's office. Inside was a canvas bag stamped US MAIL. But he got up and folded the slicker in the crook of his arm and walked off the platform, feeling like he'd done good, just by resisting the temptation to mail the letter. And more desolate than ever.

**

Before handing the coat to her he stuffed his hand in the pocket and rummaged around for the soiled envelope, but the hand came up empty. He searched the other pocket and looked on the floor in case he'd dropped it when he'd shut the front door, but it wasn't there either.

"Thanks, Mrs. Mac, but I have to run out again."

She protested that Sunday dinner was on the table, but he was already outside, retracing his steps. The air was like crystal after the rain. He ran up Carmichael Street, feet splashing in puddles, and down the tracks, searching in the ballast cinders and along the muddy siding as he went. The station was ahead of him, the colonnaded roof silhouetted against the early evening sky. The shiny boards of the platform were already in shadows. He searched the platform and bench, but the envelope wasn't there.

**

"You look like a cat in a roomful of rocking chairs," Gerald greeted him.

"Yesterday, I had a couple of drinks at Rocky's, and they hit me pretty hard."

"I never drink on a rainy day for precisely that reason," Gerald responded. "Gives me a hangover every time. Too much water. Makes the brain soggy."

291

As they got into the shift, Bill tried to put things in perspective. He'd gotten careless, but the letter wouldn't be a problem. It would get blown down the tracks or swept into the trash by the station janitor. Or someone else would throw it away. Maybe they'd try to pry off the stamp. What he had to do now was put things in focus, regain some of the caution he'd tossed away.

Meanwhile, Gerald's eyes were dancing over the new section they were working in, estimating the work ahead, trying to figure out how they could get out of it. He was lazy, yes, but in a deep and careful way. By now, Bill knew what Gerald was thinking. But did Gerald have any idea what Bill was thinking? He was sharp, but unless Percy had betrayed a confidence—or Gerald was as perceptive as Virgil, which Bill doubted—he wouldn't have guessed the extent of Bill's secrecy.

They took lunch in the haulage way. In these mines, men had no place but where they worked to eat, rest, or relieve themselves. Which meant a snack and a cup of water from the bucket was all he generally had the stomach for, no matter how much Mrs. Mac packed for him. But Gerald had a good appetite and often enjoyed Bill's leftovers.

"I don't care if we never set another charge," he said, as he sat beside Bill. "I can sit on my ass until hell freezes over. Or at least until quitting time. Or at least until I have to get up and take a piss. That'll probably come first."

Bill leaned back against the wall of the tunnel. A tram car was directly in front of them. It was full of slate they'd picked up from a roof fall where they hadn't yet timbered. This entry would require a lot of work to make it safe. He wondered how they survived down there, and was again struck by how lucky he was to have such a safety-minded partner. Then he blurted out a question. "Any idea when they're going to let your brother-in-law out of jail?"

"Percy? Bless that big ape, he's been out a few weeks. But he'll be back in soon enough. That boy ain't got the sense of a bucket of hair."

That news came as a shock. He'd gotten used to the idea that he'd been talking to Percy. "Do they leave it vacant for the next time Percy does something stupid?" Bill asked, trying to hide his concern.

But the answer was more worrying. "That little cottage stays busy. Snake Aberdeen's in it now. But he won't be there for long, either. He's slick. They call him Snake for a reason."

"A back-stabber?"

"Definitely not. Most folks don't let him get close enough to stab them in the back. He's a violent man but cunning. I've known a few miners who stayed underground in this hellhole rather than venture out with Snake on the loose. You'll be okay so long as you don't get caught in the crossfire between him and his enemies. He doesn't kill bystanders, at least not on purpose."

Bill was at a loss for words,

"You've got quite a curiosity about that little room. I hope you're not thinking about making a reservation."

When had his confessor changed? How much had he told this man, Snake Aberdeen, this killer? He sat in the tunnel, elbows on knees, trying to look calm as he worked out what he'd said and when. He'd spent the last several nights, maybe a week, telling the inmate, apparently Snake, about his happy life on the Lower East Side. He hadn't given out names or addresses, and it seemed unlikely that this Snake Aberdeen would go all the way to New York to hunt down new victims. But it made him uneasy to know that he'd described Ruthie and Hannah to a killer. He tried to imagine how this story would strike an inmate trapped in a cramped cell. It was probably entertaining, maybe even laughable, to hear a broken-hearted sap pour his heart out night after night. But it shook Bill up to know that now a second inmate had entered the picture, and a killer. He'd been describing his loved ones to a killer.

That, plus the letter.

"You're sweating, Bill." Gerald was kneeling over him now, peering into his eyes. "Just sit still while I get the blasting ready. You only slow me down anyway."

"The hell!" Bill hollered and leaped up, glad to get his mind off the latest turn of events.

**

After work he found himself again walking that familiar path, across the lawn toward the brick building. Based on what he now knew, he shouldn't be doing this, not if he was in his right mind. He'd picked the wrong man to confess to. But on that night, who else was available?

"Was it cowardly of me to run like that," he asked, trying to peer through the opaque window. "Surely, it would've been worse for me to fight it out. I'd have made a scramble of their lives as well as mine. Even if I'd beaten Arnoldson,

I'd still lose. And if I'd killed him, which is what he deserves, I'd get the death penalty."

Bill was seeking affirmation, but as always, the man inside held his tongue. What light could Snake have shed on the moral dilemma that plagued Bill? As a killer, he wasn't a man to turn to for ethical guidance.

"Maybe you've traveled, like me," Bill began again, always careful not to address the inmate as Snake in case that nickname was a delicate issue. "Maybe you've been to Pittsburgh and know what a big city is like. I'd lived in Butte, but that was a Wild West town, nothing like New York. Have you ever heard of the Lower East Side? That's where I lived." He said this with pride and proceeded to tell Snake what it was like.

"I know about Jews." The voice was unexpected, the words uttered in a hoarse whisper. The tone was more knowing than Percy's, with something else, maybe a trace of sarcasm. Was that tone because Snake felt he was being talked down to? Or that he knew about and didn't like Jews? Hard to tell through the layers of brick and glass that separated them.

It gave Bill pause. He'd forgotten about this prejudice, which so many held. Would this man he was speaking to be like one of those "Black Hundreds" monsters Virgil had told him about? He would have liked to see whether the face was twisted in hatred before he continued. But what difference would that make? In fact, it would be all the more reason to talk about those he loved. Even more important to defend them if Snake didn't like Jews.

"Everyone in New York learns a little Yiddish, which is the language Jewish people speak. They have a lot of colorful words. When you're frightened you say '*Oy gavalt.*' In fact, that's what Bill felt like saying in earnest, as he stood there, in the dawn chill, saying such things to a hardened killer. But he thought of Virgil's love for Yiddish culture. Maybe he couldn't make Snake understand that richness but shouldn't he try? "If a man is proud and bold, people say he has *chutzpah*. A loser is a *nebbish*. Those are things that everyone in New York says, whether they're Jewish or not."

Did this make any sense to Snake, a man who'd probably never met a Jew outside of the owner of Blum's Merchandise in Carmichael? He probably took no interest in Mr. Blum, other than as a possible target for a burglary. One thing for sure, he'd never known Jews as poor as he was, on an equal footing with him. Had he drawn the conclusion that all Jews were different, an alien people, money lenders and such? What would it have been like to hear a man outside his window, in a little river town, telling him about a whole city full of Jews?

More than once Bill had prefaced a statement with the words, "You might not believe this." Snake might not. Just as Bill himself found it hard to believe that he'd led such a rough, failed life. And maybe in that survival there was something to admire. A stupid life, crowned by the stupidity of this rambling confession to a man named Snake.

**

"I don't blame you for being curious about Snake," Gerald told him the next day, as they took a break waiting for powder to be sent down. "I'm a good fella to ask since I know him as well as anybody. And I have no grudge against him, which not everybody in this little valley can say.

"Anyway," he continued, "me and Snake go way back. We grew up together and went into the mines together. We worked our first shift at the Dilworth mine a little more than ten years ago. You see how slow and careful I am now? That's partly to make up for how wild and foolish I was back then. Snake was smarter than me. He knew enough not to go underground when he was drunk, which was a lesson I hadn't yet learned. Snake saved me more than once."

Gerald seemed about to retreat into a thoughtful silence. Then he shook his head and continued. "I'm not going to tell any tales on myself, but I once passed out right after setting a charge."

Bill had come to know Gerald as a man whose pretense of making light of everything was easy to see through. He was extremely serious about life and limb, both his own and those belonging to other miners. And pain. He was not about to bruise his knuckles or sprain his back to put more coal in the furnaces up in Pittsburgh. Gerald's face was unlined, which gave him an innocent, almost foolish appearance. Maybe as he aged, his face would come to reflect his caring nature with more accuracy.

"So why do people hate him so much?"

"Not everyone does," Gerald was quick to point out. "Mostly, they're afraid of him. Unlike me, Snake was smart enough to see that there was no future in the mines, none except dirt and death. Prohibition is what gave him his chance. He stole guns and outfitted a gang that began to market good quality moonshine. He defended his business against the Sicilian family that controlled Pittsburgh. Most people around here supported Snake because he was a local boy. But after a few killings, some local people turned against him.

"The Stefanos let people have a taste of Canadian whiskey, like the kind they sell at Rocky's. They were making inroads into Snake's turf so he retaliated. You probably didn't know a war had been taking place in this peaceful valley, and still is. In the long run Snake can't win. He'll never be able to match the wealth or firepower. But in the short run, Snake's a hard man to beat. The Stefanos would like to get their hands on him, but they can't. They can buy a judge and hope for a conviction, but Snake has a few allies here and there, enough to hang a jury or hold off a gang of thugs, with shotgun and Winchester.

"To make a long story short, that little jail isn't going to hold Snake forever. In fact, I'm surprised he's been locked up this long. And when he gets out, don't get caught in the crossfire."

**

It was May 10, Mother's Day. The florist shop wouldn't have anything fresh this time of year, but they'd have something on ice. The demand for flowers in a mining town never lets up. A roof fall or explosion. The florist and the funeral home do business.

Bill had never had the chance to take Ruthie to the florist on Mothers' Day and help her pick out a bouquet. He thought of the smile that would have appeared on

Hannah's face as her daughter held the flowers up to her. A smile, then tears of happiness, in a woman who seldom cried. Bill had been robbed of this experience. Imagining it made him feel all the worse. But he did have someone to get flowers for.

He paused on the cement walk, about to pull on the handle of the florist's door, when he had a feeling that something was wrong. The street had been empty a moment ago, so why did he feel that someone or the shadow of someone was behind him? He wheeled about and looked up and down Main Street but couldn't see anything, only a blur in the air, real or imagined, as if someone had ducked behind the Sears and Roebuck building, vanishing behind the rainspout at the corner of the building, a faint crunch of gravel where the boots dug in.

He shook off this feeling and entered the store. "Not much smell, but it's the thought that counts," the florist's boy admitted. The bouquet sat on the counter, red petals emerging from a mouth of crinkly foil.

"You want them delivered, Mr. Waite?"

"No thanks," he told the boy. "I'll deliver them myself."

"If I know Mrs. Mac, this bouquet will make her day." Bill hadn't told him, but not hard to guess, in this town, who a rootless miner would buy flowers for. And Mrs. Mac was the only mother he had left. He held them to his nose. The petals were still wet and cold from the ice. Then he abruptly handed them back, for he thought he heard something move out on the street.

"Hold on to these for a minute, son."

He bolted out the door and turned left, dodged between the florists and Sears and ran to the alley in back. From somewhere he heard the clang of a trash-can lid hitting macadam. It echoed like a church bell through the quiet afternoon. But whoever had jostled it had already fled from sight. Maybe it was a stray cat or raccoon.

**

The roses he'd bought the day before were a bright touch in Mrs. Mac's front window. They contrasted with his dark mood today.

"Are you okay, Mr. Waite?" Mrs. Mac was observing him over the top of her spectacles. She wasn't a nosy person, but her eyes didn't miss much.

In fact, he wasn't okay. The dizziness he'd first experienced after drinking at Rocky's had returned several times now without any alcohol involved. He'd started to feel lost and forgetful, though fortunately not when he was underground. He no longer knew how or why he was making his decisions. It wasn't rational to continue his jailhouse visits. Yet he'd begun heading there from work almost every night. Sooner or later, someone was going to see him talking to himself, for that's the way it would appear. Work provided some escape from these episodes of forgetfulness. But, in truth, he was losing his connection to Rices Landing, blundering down an unknown path.

"If you're not feeling well, you should rest. Take the afternoon off and I'll cook you a plate of fried chicken livers and parsley-potatoes to get your strength up."

"No thank you, Mrs. Mac, that wouldn't be fair to Gerald. We're pretty near the end of this entry, and he needs me at his back."

"Nonsense. I know Gerald, and he wouldn't want you to work when you're sick."

He'd never heard her challenge anyone. It was a side of her he hadn't seen, and he liked it. But he wasn't going to follow her advice. He couldn't imagine being idle with a mind so full of worries.

He grabbed the lunch bucket that she'd prepared and ran out, glancing down at several letters just inside the front door. He was on the manlift when the writing on the top envelope came into focus. Unless it was his imagination, the handwriting was familiar. It was addressed to "The lodger at 14 McRae Avenue, Rices Landing, Pennsylvania." He could only hope no one else at Mrs. Mac's would open this letter.

After work, he came straight home without visiting the jail. No one had opened it.

19.

His traveling grip was at his feet, on the platform. His eyes darted nervously to the ticket he'd just purchased: *Pennsylvania Railroad, ONE PASSAGE, Rices Landing to New York City. Good for two days including date of sale.*

He'd set something in motion that Sunday, after a few drinks at Rocky's and a lightheaded walk. The letter to New York was an accident. But once a letter finds its way into the US mail you can't call it back, even if you want to.

The return letter from Hannah contained three words: "We need you." He'd read those words over and over. As he did so, he heard her speaking in the soft but insistent voice she'd used that night when she'd told him, "It's about time you start calling Ruthie your daughter. I know she wants to think of you as her father." It was as simple as that. She was telling him what he should do.

So that's what he should do.

Yet he was still afraid of the consequences. As long as Arnoldson was in pursuit, weren't she and Ruthie better off without him? He'd weighed this issue for a full week while Hannah's return letter sat on the sill in his bedroom. He read it over and over, intoxicated with joy, fearful of taking the next step. He might have procrastinated still longer, but an overtime shift was schedule for Sunday. He'd be on the train before Gerald or anyone else knew he was gone. While Mrs. Mac was on the second floor cleaning the rooms, he'd put the letter and a few other items in his grip and snuck out.

Two dozen people milled around him on the platform, a big crowd for Rices Landing. Where were they going? Headed east to visit children in Uniontown, parents in Hazelton? He didn't recognize anyone. But this was a small town, so someone in the crowd surely recognized him. They knew who he was and wondered where he was going. Gerald and Mrs. Mac would find out soon enough that he was leaving Rices Landing on the eastbound train. A brave person would have said goodbye—he barely had the courage to buy a ticket. Mining coal isn't a courageous thing, not like saying goodbye.

People speak cautiously to each other while waiting for a train. They whisper, guarding the privacy of the moment. To say too much before a journey opens the way for bad luck. The platform was full of soft voices, a hushed and expectant stillness. Facing the platform, a forest of trees in full foliage ranged up the hill. A few timbered-out patches showed through the dense cover, like sore spots in a dog's fur. The jungle climbed from river and town to a silhouette against the sky, which today was a pure blue. An all-night drizzle had rinsed the air clean of coke-oven soot and smog.

The little crowd in the station waited patiently in the picture-book stillness. Hundreds of feet of earth insulated these innocent people from the life and death struggle taking place below them, the din and drama of the mines, a chaos where miners battled roof falls, shielded their faces from the storm of rocks and shards stirred up by blasting, lived in drifts and tunnels, in a nonstop struggle to stay alert or die. But hazards are everywhere. Who doesn't know that? Even above ground in the sweet, still air.

Two fifty-seven. Three minutes to go. Right now, the daylight men were nearing the end of their Sunday shift, rejoicing that they still had all the fingers and toes they'd begun the shift with. Gerald was waking from his last nap of the afternoon, in a bad mood because he wouldn't have Sunday off; and Mrs. Mac, who liked to worry for all her boys, was making sandwiches for Bill's lunch. She had his bucket out, would pour drinking water into the bottom and fit in a tray for the sandwiches. No one gave a thought to how the parts in a miner's bucket fit together. Tin squeezed into tin, airtight.

The crowd at the station was made up of small family groups, arrayed like tiny actors waiting for the curtain to go up. This platform was their stage. They were cool and tranquil on the outside, a turmoil of fear and expectation within. They had started fidgeting. One man flashed a confident grin as he hoisted a little boy in his arms. What excitement or worry was this man hiding from his little boy?

What Bill knew, knew for a fact, was that no one on this platform would know the total rapture he was about to experience when he paused before Apartment 2C. He'd hold his breath for an eternity, then gently put knuckles to wood. And the happiness of watching Hannah caught in a flood of emotion and fighting to compose herself. She'd wipe her eyes and turn to Ruthie, who'd be waiting just inside the door. "Should we let this fellow in?"

But was she aware, when she welcomed Bill, of what else she was letting in the door? He had tried to calculate this unknown, as if it was part of a mathematical equation. But there was no neat formula that would solve the brute threat they were sure to face.

He felt his heart beating and wondered if everyone else in the crowd could hear it. But they were filled with their own excitement. It's not a small thing, the approach of a locomotive. At a train station, there are no petty concerns. What would soon be changing in their lives was not as big as what would be changing in his. No one else on this platform had taken such a risk. He was about to emerge from hiding. He was the one who'd announced himself, drawing those who stalked him back into the spiral of his life. He squared his shoulders. All is risk. Get used to it. Go out in the morning. Run through the rain. Work. Do what you have to do. But know that it's risk. If you're lucky enough to survive the risks you take, you'll look back, years from now, and the knowledge of what you did long ago will scare you to death.

Maybe he *was* a target, on this very platform, but such a small one. One small life so many miles from where the authorities might think to look. He used that word, "authorities," quite certain that they were not so concerned with his whereabouts.

But Arnoldson was.

When he thought of the man, an image came into his mind. He was at Arnoldson's church. There was a small crowd, like this one at the station. Arnoldson's shoulders loomed above everyone else, even when he was seated for the sermon. The church had lovely pine rafters, varnished and sunlit. The preacher had a flat voice that almost put Bill to sleep. After the sermon, as they'd trooped past the preacher, Arnoldson had introduced them. "This is the hired hand. He's from the prison. He seems to be working out."

The preacher had cringed, like Warden Middleton. In fact, all the churchgoers made way for Arnoldson. A circle of fear surrounded him. At one point four or five men had gathered about him, almost as if they were his troops, waiting for orders. A shiver ran through Bill's body. It told him that the fight he'd always dreaded might be moving a step closer.

Relax, he told himself. He'd outrun Arnoldson twice. Maybe the confrontation he feared was inevitable, though surely not on this platform. And probably not on his arrival in Pennsylvania Station. Hopefully not in the Lower East Side either, at least not right away. He needed to get settled in, to reknit his ties. Virgil was his friend and ally. If anyone could guide him through the hazards, it was Virgil.

A less faithful friend than Virgil would simply turn to him and ask, "If you're so worried, then why did you come back?"

The little crowd seemed to sense the approach of the train even before it was announced by the distant clacking of the rails. Heads turned toward the bend where the tracks emerged from the trees. People peered around trying to read in each other's faces the meaning of this thing that was approaching. The power of a locomotive goes way beyond steel and steam. It changes lives. The way it can mend or tear apart. Finally, the engine crept from the forest, a small black cylinder, a toy coming towards them. Then it was on top of them, a huge glistening thing of coal and iron hissing and spitting steam.

The engine braked and the steel side rods locked in their hubs. The wheels screeched and slid with a cutting ferocity, and the crowd took a step back. Bill seized his bag and fell back with them. He tried to mask the excitement that was flooding through him. A station employee in cap and starched blue shirt arranged stepstools for the passenger car. Above them, a conductor peered out, played with his moustache for a moment, then gripped the handrails and prepared to leap down to assist passengers as they stepped from the car.

"Let'em out folks," the station worker bellowed from below. "No need to push."

The crowd fell back a little. They wanted to obey but were too excited by this great iron machinery, this destiny panting before them. Bill was entranced by the spectacle. Then he looked up to the daylight between the cars. He could see the conductor, who was toying with the passengers, holding them back a little longer than was needed. Bright sunshine outlined his erect bearing and caught an angle of his face where a smile played, the relaxed expression of a man in authority. Then something happened to the conductor. His grip on the handrails was broken and his body was pushed aside as a much larger figure appeared.

Bill saw the figure, a shadow looming over the platform. He wanted to live in the excitement of the crowd for another moment, as if safety might survive for as long as denial stood strong. As if acknowledgment was the real danger. That brief mood collapsed as the figure leaped down on the platform, knocking the station attendant aside. The crowd sensed something about this man, a lurking power they wanted nothing to do with. People melted away, leaving Bill at the center of Arnoldson's gaze. He looked even larger than Bill had remembered him, great hands extending from jacket cuffs. Another man was with him, powerful and squat.

Arnoldson's eyes locked on to Bill's and a smile spread across his face. Had he ever smiled in Bill's presence? Certainly not like this, a wide crescent, an open trap. This smile was more frightening than a face clouded with anger.

Bill retreated a few steps, searching for a place to make a stand. But it was the squat man who launched the pursuit, scuttling across the platform, arms spread wide, narrowing the distance between them to about ten feet. Then paused, took a fighter's crouch, and shuffled forward. He was probably about Bill's age, but with a worn face and mushroomed nose. The man's eyes held a gleam. He was an experienced fighter, eager for the battle.

As Bill noticed a set of handcuffs dangling from the thug's belt, he lost track of his location on the platform. With another step he felt something strike the back of his leg, the very bench where he'd absentmindedly jotted his note to Hannah. His attention momentarily diverted, he made an easy target for the squat thug, who lunged, knocking him off balance. As he fell backward, he saw the roof beams and the hanging light. Then he was down on the bench with the squat man on top, his bad breath in Bill's face.

Bill thrust up his arms, aiming to wrap his hands around the thick neck, get him in a chokehold, and wring out the life. But the squat man's fists shot out, swatting Bill's effort aside. The two men jabbed at each other but Bill was still pinned beneath the other man. Neither had enough space to land a punch with full power. The thug laughed, breathing warm, sour breath into Bill's face.

He'd been bowled over by the shock of the assault. He was still pinned, wrenching his body about, needing to make it impossible for the thug to apply the handcuffs, squirming for a chance to break free. He almost retched from the weight of this monster with sour breath. He'd had such high hopes a moment before. Now, he was in the fight of his life, and losing. Then he felt the compact frame of his assailant draw back for a blow and instantly recognized an opening. As the monster rose over him, lifting himself up, Bill used this newfound leverage to thrust up his right knee. The blow may not have been as hard as he would've liked, but it was perfectly placed. His attacker rolled away clutching his groin.

Bill leaped to his feet, free, at least for the moment. He looked around the station. Departing passengers had already scurried on to the train; arrivals had either melted away or retreated to a safe distance to watch the spectacle. What did they think of the struggle that had been unfolding? Maybe that it was another battle in the ongoing liquor war, Snake's gang versus the Stefano's.

Bill gathered himself, confident now that he could beat this bully. He was stronger and had him writhing in pain on the platform. A well-aimed kick would end it, still with a hope of catching the train. But before he could end that fight, he was seized around the torso, arms pinned to his sides. He was being held in a hug so strong he couldn't turn to face his captor. But he knew who he was.

He could feel Arnoldson's breath in his ear. "You didn't think I'd let you escape, did you?" The question was punctuated by a squeeze across the lungs that took Bill's breath away. "You didn't think I was going to let you make a mockery of the Montana justice system?" Bill gasped again as the embrace tightened. "Montana justice took care of your brother . . ." Arnoldson was now dragging Bill across the platform toward the tracks. "Your brother couldn't escape from me. Five of us held that skinny red agitator. He kicked and bit, but couldn't break free. Good riddance to a troublemaker."

Bill felt a wave of nausea as the truth was being driven home. This man had also murdered Frank. He was the central organizer of Montana 'justice.' Bill desperately shook his own strong shoulders, but without effect. The man he hated more than any other held him fast.

He was aware of the pulsing of the engine, powerful but restrained as it idled beside them. He tried not to listen to Arnoldson, whose mouth was next to his ear. "You might want to know how Frank's face looked as we held him and slipped the noose over his neck. I'll have plenty of time to tell you about the panic that replaced that smart-aleck expression. He watched us loop the other end over the

311

trestle. You wouldn't believe how terrified that *tough* agitator became." Arnoldson spit out this last in mocking tones.

"Then he fell through the air, kicking. Your brother, legs beating the air like a gutted hog. I thought of telling you back at the farm. But no, you were a good parolee—I had hopes for you. You would have become famous as the reformed brother of Frank Little."

Bill thought back, again, to the four bales in the statement, a smudged piece of paper resting on the kitchen table. He'd missed that clue; he'd missed all the clues—and now the vigilante network was claiming another victim.

"I've never let one escape. We're headed home, young man. You'll be my guest on the westbound train, which I'd estimate is due in about twenty minutes. We can chat all the way back to Montana."

The squat thug now peered into Bill's face, handcuffs hanging from an index finger.

"Snap them on while I hold his hands," Arnoldson said, shifting his grip to secure the wrists. Bill doubted that he could break free but had to try. This might be his last chance. He was about to swing an elbow toward Arnoldson's face but never had the chance, for Arnoldson gave Bill's other wrist a vicious twist. A sharp jolt of pain ran from wrist to shoulder. The giant hand tightened its hold. Bill stopped fighting as despair sapped what strength he had left.

Now the train, Bill's train to New York, was beginning to inch forward along the tracks. The engine yanked at its load, the iron connecting knuckles stretched out for a moment then clanged tight. Arnoldson had tightened his grip even further. "Less painful to hold still," he said, with mock consideration.

Bill tried to muster some courage in the face of his miserable prospects. But brutality had won the day. Wasn't that the way of the world? Bill thought back over the generosity and tenderness he'd received and how this one wretched man had destroyed the caring of so many: those truckers and their code of the road; Virgil, guiding him into a new life on the Lower East Side; Hannah and Ruthie providing a love beyond any he'd ever hoped for; and even Gerald, that lazy, kind man.

At least Bill was leading Arnoldson west, away from his loved ones. He could hold his head high. It might not count for much in this world, where terror defeats kindness at every turn, but he was a better man than his captor, now poised to slip handcuffs over his wrists.

He'd experienced kindness, small and large. He'd survived underground conflagrations and river blowouts; climbed down a ladder, story after story, risking his life to save people surely already dead; and he'd clambered into the muck under the Hudson in search of a drowning Irish boy. And he'd taken a little girl to ball games and distracted her from the fear of losing her momma. But most of all, he'd truly and passionately loved Hannah, and he could taste her lips on his right now. Arnoldson for all his power could not lay claim to a single experience like these.

He was a better man, but one whose future was life in prison. Or worse. If Arnoldson decided that another hanging was more to his liking, he could easily engineer it. Arnoldson continued to taunt him, the voice growling an octave below the sound of the train, which was now shuddering forward. "You're bigger than your brother but not as tough . . ."

He might have wanted to add more, but at that moment a furious movement was taking place. Bill couldn't see what was happening but felt the tight grip on his wrist give way. He spun around just as an eerie cutting sound pierced the air. His eyes searched the platform but couldn't find a trace of Arnoldson, only the squat thug, eyes wide. The station attendant stood there. His mouth opened for a scream without a sound emerging from it.

At last the attendant did scream, desperate syllables that somehow the engineer was able to interpret. The side bars quickly locked in their hubs. The wheels ceased to turn and began to slide on the rails. The conductor leapt down on the platform. He strode over to the tracks, knitting his face, peering down at the blood-stained iron. Although it had moved less than fifty feet, the train had gone far enough to change the look of Bill's world.

"Too bad about that fellow," Bill heard someone and noticed a wiry man standing near the tracks. The man stepped forward and seized Bill's hand with surprising strength. "Must've lost his balance and fallen. Looked almost like a dive." He finally released Bill's hand and fixed him with a knowing grin. "No friend of yours, I guess."

Arnoldson's thug had disappeared. The wiry man continued to smile up at Bill, as if they were old acquaintances. "I saw the whole thing," he told the conductor. "He slid right under the wheels. Must've been drunk."

"We see it all the time," the conductor replied, trying to regain his composure. "Hope the passengers didn't get a good view."

The wiry man turned back to Bill, and there was something frightening about his smile, the nose broken and hooked, and the eyes coal-black. Whoever he was, he knew how to get results from what physical strength he possessed. Quick and final results.

And Bill's bag was still on the platform, where he'd dropped it.

"From what you told me, I thought that son of a bitch would be tough," the man said, as Bill struggled to think of when he might have told this stranger anything at all. "But like a lot of bullies, he wasn't so tough.

"You'd better grab your bag. Lucky for you that big goon fell or he might've made you miss your train. And I know how much you need to get back to New York."

"Snake?" Bill whispered.

The wiry man flashed a crooked smile, slapped Bill on the back, and turned to leave the station. As he loped across the platform, his boots clicked on the boards.

"Thanks, thanks for . . ." Bill tried to call after Snake, who was already out of range, climbing up the hillside toward Route 88.

Bill mounted the stairs to the train, still shaking. He expected that everyone would turn to stare as he walked down the aisle, but no one seemed to pay the least attention. Maybe the scene on the tracks had taken place out of view. Or maybe the other passengers thought it was best to withdraw into their own thoughts. They had important journeys ahead of them, and destinations of great meaning. They had enough violence in their own lives and didn't need to be searching for more. This was a railroad car full of heartache and joy. The drama of many small lives is never small. Maybe Bill's life wasn't the largest part of it. He nodded to an old man and sat beside him. He scanned the hillside for a last glimpse of Snake, but he'd already disappeared.

The train picked up speed, heading east through the valley, through forests slanting up to a blue sky. Greene County was a breathtakingly beautiful place on clear days like this one. But Bill was going home.

Acknowledgments

Thanks to the magazines *december* (issue 27.2) and *Kestrel* (issue 39) for first printing chapters from *A Place to Hide*

The main characters are fictional, but the historical events are recorded accurately. The protagonist's brother, Frank Little, was once a well-known labor martyr. A lively account of Frank Little and other figures from that time period can be found in James P. Cannon's *Notebook of an Agitator* (Pathfinder Press).

For more information on the construction of the Holland Tunnel, I consulted *Highway under the Hudson* by Robert W. Jackson (NYU Press). This book plus my own experience with industrial work helped me to imagine the conditions in the tunnel.

I lived in the Lower East Side when it was still a working-class area with Yiddish roots. *World of our Fathers* by Irving Howe (Galahad) is a ready source on Yiddish culture in 1920's New York.

I spent four years living in West Virginia 20 minutes from Rices Landing, and worked with many former coal miners who filled me in on coal mining and its discontents, low coal in particular. The mining disasters described here are covered in many books.

The novelists William Heath and Damian McNichol deserve much thanks for reading *A Place to Hide* and for their suggestions. Also, thanks to the production team at Apprentice House for their diligent and faithful work.

Last but by no means least, great thanks to publicist Lily Bisson.

About the Author

David Salner worked all over the U.S. as iron ore miner, steelworker, machinist, bus driver, garment laborer, teacher, librarian. Author of four poetry collections, his work appears in Threepenny Review, Iowa Review, Ploughshares, North American Review. Salner received grants from the Puffin Foundation, Dr. Henry and Page Laughlin Fund, two from Maryland State Arts Council, Lascaux Prize for Poetry, Oboh Prize, and eight Pushcart nominations. He has an MFA from the Iowa Writers Workshop. On three occasions Garrison Keillor read Salner's work on NPR show Writer's Almanac. Salner lives in Delaware with his wife, Barbara Greenway.

Apprentice House Press
Loyola University Maryland

Apprentice House is the country's only campus-based, student-staffed book publishing company. Directed by professors and industry professionals, it is a nonprofit activity of the Communication Department at Loyola University Maryland.

Using state-of-the-art technology and an experiential learning model of education, Apprentice House publishes books in untraditional ways. This dual responsibility as publishers and educators creates an unprecedented collaborative environment among faculty and students, while teaching tomorrow's editors, designers, and marketers.

Outside of class, progress on book projects is carried forth by the AH Book Publishing Club, a co-curricular campus organization supported by Loyola University Maryland's Office of Student Activities.

Eclectic and provocative, Apprentice House titles intend to entertain as well as spark dialogue on a variety of topics. Financial contributions to sustain the press's work are welcomed. Contributions are tax deductible to the fullest extent allowed by the IRS.

To learn more about Apprentice House books or to obtain submission guidelines, please visit www.apprenticehouse.com.

Apprentice House
Communication Department
Loyola University Maryland
4501 N. Charles Street
Baltimore, MD 21210
Ph: 410-617-5265 • Fax: 410-617-2198
info@apprenticehouse.com•www.apprenticehouse.